D0998557

Workers and Peasants in the Modern Middle East

The working people, who constitute the majority in any society, can be and deserve to be subjects of history. Joel Beinin's state-of-the-art survey of subaltern history in the Middle East demonstrates lucidly and compellingly how their lives, experiences, and culture can inform our historical understanding. Beginning in the middle of the eighteenth century, the book charts the history of peasants, urban artisans, and modern working classes across the lands of the Ottoman Empire and its Muslim-majority successor-states, including the Balkans, Turkey, the Arab Middle East, and North Africa. Inspired by the approach of the Indian Subaltern Studies school, the book is the first to present a synthetic critical assessment of the scholarly work on the social history of this region for the last twenty years. It offers new insights into the political, economic, and social life of ordinary men and women and their apprehension of their own experiences. Students will find it rich in narrative detail, and accessible and authoritative in presentation.

JOEL BEININ is Professor of Middle East History at Stanford University. His publications include *The Dispersion of Egyptian Jewry: Culture, Politics, and the Formation of a Modern Diaspora* (1998) and *Was the Red Flag Flying There? Marxist Politics and the Arab–Israeli Conflict in Egypt and Israel, 1948–65* (1990).

The Contemporary Middle East 2

Series editor: Eugene L. Rogan

Books published in *The Contemporary Middle East* series address the major political, economic and social debates facing the region today. Each title comprises a survey of the available literature against the background of the author's own critical interpretation which is designed to challenge and encourage independent analysis. While the focus of the series is the Middle East and North Africa, books are presented as aspects of a rounded treatment, which cuts across disciplinary and geographic boundaries. They are intended to initiate debate in the classroom, and to foster understanding amongst professionals and policy makers.

1 Clement M. Henry and Robert Springborg, *Globalization and the Politics of Development in the Middle East*

Workers and Peasants in the Modern Middle East

Joel Beinin

Stanford University

CAMBRIDGE
UNIVERSITY PRESS

PUBLISHED BY THE PRESS SYNDICATE OF THE UNIVERSITY OF CAMBRIDGE
The Pitt Building, Trumpington Street, Cambridge, United Kingdom

CAMBRIDGE UNIVERSITY PRESS
The Edinburgh Building, Cambridge CB2 2RU, UK
40 West 20th Street, New York, NY 10011-4211, USA
10 Stamford Road, Oakleigh, VIC 3166, Australia
Ruiz de Alarcón 13, 28014 Madrid, Spain
Dock House, The Waterfront, Cape Town 8001, South Africa

http://www.cambridge.org

© Cambridge University Press 2001

First published 2001

Printed in the United Kingdom at the University Press, Cambridge

Typeface Plantin 10/12   *System* QuarkXPress™   [SE]

A catalogue record for this book is available from the British Library

Library of Congress Cataloguing in Publication data
Beinin, Joel, 1948–
Workers and peasants in the modern Middle East / Joel Beinin.
      p.   cm. – (The contemporary Middle East; 2)
Includes bibliographical references and index.
ISBN 0 521 62121 6 – ISBN 0 521 62903 9 (pbk.)
1. Working class – Middle East – History.   2. Artisans – Middle East – History.
3. Peasantry – Middle East – History.   I. Title.   II. Series.
HD8656.B44 2001
305.5'62'0956–dc21   00-068950

ISBN 0 521 62121 6 hardback
ISBN 0 521 62903 9 paperback

To the spirit of the Thälmann Battalion
and the Abraham Lincoln Brigade,
and those who carry it forward today

Contents

Tables

Acknowledgments

This book synthesizes and develops much of what I have offered in my graduate colloquium on Economic and Social History of the Modern Middle East for over a decade. The students I have had the privilege of teaching in that class occupy a very special place in my heart. I have enjoyed immensely learning from them and sharing their companionship and sense of purpose.

Eugene Rogan and Marigold Acland first proposed to me that I write this book and accompanied it through its completion. I am most grateful that they did. The process of writing has forced me to think more broadly and clarified many issues in my own mind.

In addition to them, Rob Blecher, Elliot Colla, Kenneth Cuno, Zachary Lockman, Karen Pfeifer, Marsha Pripstein Posusney, Nancy Reynolds, and Shira Robinson read parts or all of the text at various stages in its development. They offered many valuable comments and saved me from some careless errors. Had I been able to implement all their suggestions, this would undoubtedly have been a better book.

Papers that evolved into chapter 4 were delivered in the spring of 1999 at the International Workshop on Modernity in the Middle East: History and Discourse at Ben-Gurion University of the Negev; the Seminar on Empires and Cultures Annual Workshop at Stanford University; and the Conference on Nation and Cultural Perceptions of Identity at UCLA. Early versions of chapter 6 were presented at the 1998 annual meeting of the Middle East Studies Association and the Conference on New Approaches to the Study of Ottoman and Arab Societies at Boğaziçi University in 1999. An early version of small sections of chapters 5 and 6 was published as "The Working Class and Peasantry in the Middle East: From Economic Nationalism to Neoliberalism," *Middle East Report* no. 210 (Spring 1999):18–22.

A brief research trip to the Middle East in 1997 was supported by a Hewlett Faculty Research Grant. Much of the text was written during 1999–2000 while I was a fellow at the Stanford Humanities Center – an extraordinary institution for which I wish much continued good fortune and success.

This is the first book I have written without being in close contact with its subjects. Nonetheless, some of them have always been in my mind and heart. I can never repay the debt I owe to Fathi Kamil, Hasan ʿAbd al-Rahman, Muhammad ʿAli ʿAmir, Muhmmad Jad, Muhammad Mutawalli al-Shaʿrawi, Atiyya al-Sirafi, and Taha Saʿd ʿUthman – Egyptian workers whose insights and memories of their own lives launched me on my academic career and who affirmed through their struggles and their kindness to me the values we share.

As always, Miriam has supported me with her care and love.

Glossary

'aliya – wave of Zionist immigration to Palestine

amir or *hakim* – commander or prince, the hereditary ruler of Mount Lebanon

'ammiyya – commune, the name for peasant uprisings in nineteenth-century Mount Lebanon and Hawran

aradi al-filaha or *athar* – lands on which peasants had usufruct rights in Egypt

aradi al-usya – lands granted to the mamluks in Egypt

ayan (Tur.), *a'yan* (Ar.), also called *derebeys*, *aǧas*, or *mütegallibes* – provincial notables or warlords who enhanced their power at the expense of the central Ottoman state

bilad al-sham – greater Syria, including current-day Syria, Lebanon, Jordan, Palestine, and Israel

boyars – local notables who became absentee landlords in Wallachia and Moldavia

çift–hane system – the normative agrarian land-tenure system of the Ottoman Empire. Each peasant household (*hane*) had the right to perpetual tenancy on a farm (*çift*) large enough to sustain the family on state-administered land as long as taxes were paid and cultivation maintained

çiftlik – a farm, sometimes, but not always, a large, market-oriented estate

colon – a European settler in Algeria

dira – the collectively held tribal domain in North Arabia and lower Iraq

dunam/dunum – Palestine: 1 dunam = 0.23 acres; Iraq: 1 dunum = 0.618 acres

effendiyya – primarily an Egyptian term, the urban middle strata educated in a western style and adopting European dress

esnaf (Tur.), *tawa'if* (Ar.) – urban guilds of artisans, merchants, and service workers, rarely peasants

faddan – the standard Egyptian land measure, 1.03 acres

farda (Ar.), *ferde* (Tur.)– head tax imposed by the Egyptian regime during the occupation of greater Syria in the 1830s *gedik* – originally, the tools necessary for a craft; subsequently, the right to practice it

Hatt-ı Şerif – 1839 Gülhane Edict, marking the onset of the Tanzimat reforms

Histadrut – the General Federation of Hebrew Workers in (the Land of) Israel established in 1920

hospodars – wealthy Greek merchants who ruled Wallachia and Moldavia indirectly for the Ottoman state

ibʿadiyya – a tax-free grant of uncultivated lands in mid-nineteenth century Egypt

iltizam or *muqataʿa* – tax farming or the plot of land itself

imara – the hereditary principality of Mount Lebanon

iqtaʿ – the land-tenure and administrative system in Mount Lebanon, often misleadingly translated as feudalism

irad-ı cedid – the fiscal apparatus established to finance the *nizam-ı cedid* military unit

Islahat Fermanı – 1856 Reform Decree, the second of the major Tanzimat measures

ʿizba – an Egyptian estate where peasants were given a dwelling and land to grow subsistence crops in exchange for labor service on the landlord's cotton or other cash crops

Jabal Nablus – a district in the north of the central mountain chain of Palestine

Janissary Corps – a musket-bearing infantry unit of the Ottoman army

jiflik – Arabization of *çiftlik*, an estate given to members of the royal family in mid-nineteenth-century Egypt

kharajiyya – peasant lands defined by the 1854 Egyptian land law

malikâne – life-term tax farm

mamluk (Ar.), *memlûk* (Tur.) – an elite warrior-slave

mevat (Tur.), *mawat* (Ar.) – waste or uncultivated land

milk (Ar.), *mülk* (Tur.) – privately owned land

miri – state-administered land

mugharasa – a cultivation contract common in Mount Lebanon: an owner would engage a peasant to plant trees on his land and cultivate them in return for a portion of the land and the trees

mültezim (Tur.), *multazim* (Ar.) – holder of a tax farm

muqataʿa – a district in the land-tenure and administrative system of Mount Lebanon administered by a hereditary local notable, or *muqataʿaji*

mushaʿa – collective form of landholding in Syria and Palestine

musharaka – sharecropping

mutamassirun – permanently resident Greeks, Italians, Armenians, Syrian Christians, and Jews in Egypt *mutanawwirun* – in Syria, the term for the urban middle strata educated in a western style and adopting European dress

nizam-ı cedid – the European-style military unit established by Sultan Selim III (1789–1807)

Rumelia – the European parts of the Ottoman Empire

salam – a contract in which a merchant lends a peasant money and the peasant agrees to deliver a harvest to the merchant in return for a specified price or portion of the proceeds from the sale of the crop

sarifa – a hut made from palm branches (Iraq)

sened-i ittifak – 1808 Document of Agreement confirming the powers of the provincial notables

shariʿa (Ar.), şeriat (Tur.) – Islamic law

*Sipahi*s – Ottoman cavalry soldiers

sufi – a Muslim mystic. Mystical orders *(turuq)* were often mobilized for political and social purposes

Tanzimat – mid-nineteenth-century elite-initiated legal, administrative, and fiscal reforms of the Ottoman Empire

timar – a rural land holding used to support a *sipahi* and his retainers. Larger holdings were called *ziamet* or *hass*.

tujjar – long-distance merchants of Cairo

ʿuhda – a land grant to a military or civilian official in mid-nineteenth-century Egypt

ʿulamaʾ (Ar.), *ülema* (Tur.) – Muslim scholars

ʿushr (Ar.), *öşür* (Tur.) – Ottoman land tax calculated as a percentage of a crop, variable by region

ʿushuriyya – privileged estates (*ibʿadiyya, jiflik,* and *ʿuhda*) according to the 1854 Egyptian land law

vakıf (Tur.), *waqf* (Ar.) – a public or family endowment established in accord with Islamic law

Wafd – the leading nationalist party of interwar Egypt, named for the delegation formed to negotiate independence at the Versailles peace conference

Acronyms and abbreviations

ASP – Arab Socialist Party (Syria)

ASU – Arab Socialist Union (Egypt)

AWC – Arab Workers' Congress (Ittihad al-'Ummal al-'Arab, Palestine)

COLA – cost-of-living allowance

CPI – Communist Party of Iraq

CUP – Committee of Union and Progress (Ottoman Empire)

DİSK – Devrimi İşçi Sendikaları Konfederasyonu (Confederation of Revolutionary Trade Unions, Turkey)

DMNL – al-Haraka al-Dimuqratiyya lil-Tahrir al-Watani (Democratic Movement for National Liberation, Egypt)

DP – Democrat Party (Demokrat Partisi, Turkey)

EMNL – al-Haraka al-Misriyya lil-Tahrir al-Watani (Egyptian Movement for National Liberation)

FATULS – Ittihad al-Niqabat wa'l-Jam'iyyat al-'Arabiyya (Federation of Arab Trade Unions and Labor Societies, Palestine)

FLN – Front de Liberation Nationale (National Liberation Front, Algeria)

GFETU – General Federation of Egyptian Trade Unions (al-Ittihad al-'Amm li-Niqabat 'Ummal Misr)

JNF – Jewish National Fund

JP – Justice Party (Adelet Partisi, Turkey)

LP – Labor Party (Egypt)

MİSK – Milliyetçi, İşçi Sendikaları Konfedarasyonu (Confederation of Nationalist Workers' Unions, Turkey)

MTWU – Niqabat 'Ummal al-Sana'i' al-Yadawiyya (Manual Trades Workers' Union, Egypt)

NCWS – al-Lajna al-Wataniyya lil-'Ummal w'al-Talaba (National Committee of Workers and Students, Egypt)

NLL – 'Usbat al-Taharrur al-Watani (National Liberation League, Palestine)

PAWS – Jam'iyyat al-'Ummal al-'Arabiyya al-Filastiniyya (Palestine Arab Workers' Society)

PCGFETU – al-Lajna al-Tahdiriyya lil-Ittihad al-'Amm li-Niqabat 'Ummal

Misr (Preparatory Committee for a General Federation of Egyptian Trade Unions)

PCP – Palestine Communist Party

PSD – Parti Socialist Destourien (Destourian Socialist Party, Tunisia)

RPP – Republican People's Party (Cumhuriyet Halk Partisi, Turkey)

TLP – Türkiye İşçi Partisi (Turkish Labor Party)

Türk İş – Türkiye İşçi Sendikaları Konfederasyonu (Confederation of Turkish Trade Unions)

UAR – United Arab Republic

UGTA – Union Générale des Travailleurs Algériens (General Union of Algerian Workers)

UGTT – Union Générale Tunisienne du Travail (General Union of Tunisian Workers)

The Ottoman Empire, 1699–1914

Aral Sea

RUSSIA

Ural

Volga

Caspian Sea

Persian Gulf

KABARDIA 1774

ABKHAZIA 1829

KARS 1878

Azov 1774

Tigris

Mosul

Aleppo

Euphrates

Basra

Baghdad

Kuwait

Medina

Mecca

Red Sea

Black Sea

CRIMEA 1783

PODOLIA 1699, 1774

MOLDAVIA

BESSARABIA 1812

YEDISAN 1792

Dniester

Dnieper

N. WALLACHIA

N. SERBIA 1876

S. BULGARIA 1876

N. BULGARIA 1876

Istanbul

Bursa

Izmir

ANATOLIA

Ankara

Adana

CUKUROVA

Hama

Homs

Beirut

Damascus

Jerusalem

Jaffa

CYPRUS British colony 1878

Tal-Mahalla al-Kubra

VIDIN

Vidin

HUNGARY (1699, 1718)

BOSNIA 1878

MONTENEGRO 1878

SERBIA 1876

ALBANIA 1912

EPIRUS

DODECANESE 1912

Yanina

THESSALY 1881

GREECE 1830

CRETE 1912

Salonica

AUSTRIA

Danube

ITALY

SICILY

SARDINIA

CORSICA

FRANCE

SPAIN

PORTUGAL

Atlantic Ocean

Mediterranean Sea

CYRENAICA Taken by Italy from Ottoman Empire 1911; allied control 1943–1950; kingdom 1950

EGYPT Ottoman from 1517; British protectorate 1882–1922; kingdom 1922

Alexandria

Cairo

Nile

TRIPOLITANIA

TUNIS Taken by France from Ottoman Empire 1881; independent 1956

Tunis

Constantine

KABYLIA

Algiers

ALGERIA Taken by France from Ottoman Empire 1830; independent 1962

Oran

MOROCCO Filali dynasty from 1631; French protectorate 1912–1956

Legend

1878	Date of cession
	Independent of Ottoman Empire
1830	Date of independence from Ottoman Empire

The Ottoman Empire at its greatest extent

Ottoman territory 1912

Ceded by Ottoman Empire to Russia, with date

Ceded by Ottoman Empire to Austria, with date

Ceded by Ottoman Empire to Greece, with date

0 200 400 600 800 1000 1200 1400 1600 km

0 200 400 600 800 miles

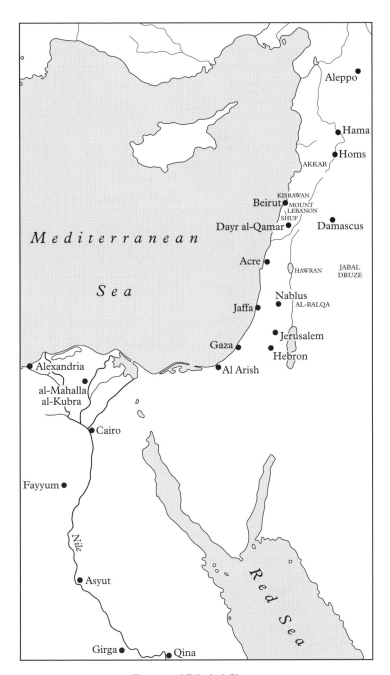

Egypt and Bilad al-Sham

The Middle East in the Twentieth Century

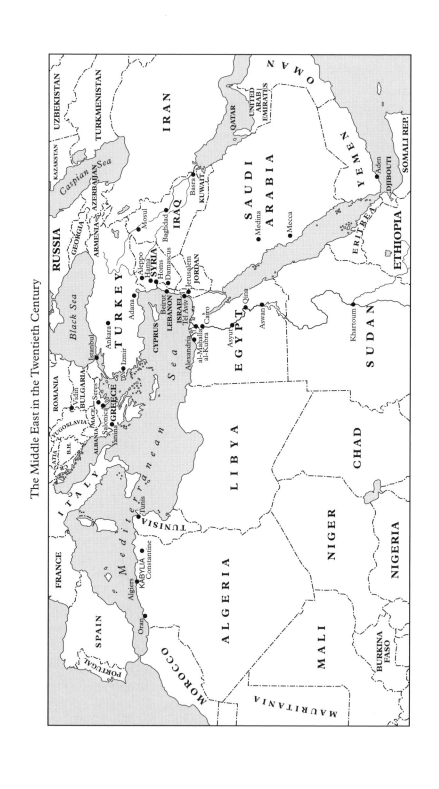

Introduction

The working people who constitute the majority of any society can and deserve to be historical subjects. Many aspects of their lives can not be represented by the methods typically deployed to write histories of the political activities and ideas of elites and lettered classes. Investigations into the experiences and consciousnesses of working people cannot retrieve their "true" voice and should not aspire to remake them into the universal subjects of history. But such investigations can tell us many important things about common people and their position in society. Rethinking historical understandings from these premises can demarcate the limits of the powers of states and other institutions of authority and discipline or the ideas of elites and their organic intellectuals. It can also reveal relations of hierarchy and power, processes by which they are established and maintained, and instabilities, tensions, and struggles within societies.

Until the late 1970s most histories of the Middle East took as their subjects either the religious, legal, philosophical, and literary texts of Islamic high culture or the political histories of states. Concentrating on such topics virtually ensured that peasants, urban artisans, small merchants, service workers, and slaves were peripheral to the main concerns of "history." The rare appearances of common people in historical writings were usually refracted through the vision of elites or intellectuals close to them, who had an interest in obscuring prevailing social hierarchies and discourses of power.

Historians of Europe and the Americas dissatisfied with these limitations developed a "new social history" that sought to give more prominence to experiences and cultures of working people. They adopted various methodological approaches: reinvigorated liberal, social democratic, or Marxian labor history, British cultural Marxism, French structuralist Marxism, populist nationalism, peasant studies, feminism, ethnic studies, etc. Just as it began to go out of fashion in European and American studies, new social history made its way to Middle East studies (Batatu 1978; Abrahamian 1982; Tucker 1985; Beinin & Lockman 1987; Baer 1964; Baer 1969b; Baer 1982; Porath 1966).[1]

1

Some new social historians assumed that class was a material reality that ultimately determined all else. Until challenged by feminists, proponents of ethnic studies, and others, they typically focused on white working men in the public sphere and devoted inadequate attention to race, gender, ethnicity, religion, generational difference, and sexual orientation – categories often identified as "cultural" (Scott 1988). Writing primarily about public struggles such as strikes or political campaigns tended to obscure the activities of daily life in neighborhoods and families, accommodation to structures of power, and weapons of the weak: everyday forms of resistance that avoid direct confrontation and overt collective defiance such as "foot dragging, dissimulation, desertion, false compliance, pilfering, feigned ignorance, slander, arson, sabotage" (Scott 1985: xvi). Many new social historians hoped that examining neglected documentary evidence or reading previously known evidence against the grain would allow them to retrieve the experiences of workers, peasants, African slaves, women, ethnic minorities, etc., speak for them, and restore them to the historical record. This often resulted in an act of ventriloquism. Subordinate subjects were presented as saying what sympathetic historians thought they would or should say.

This book seeks to synthesize some of the achievements of the new social history and its legatees in Middle East studies and simultaneously to mitigate some of the limitations of these approaches by adopting the following propositions. Ideas and materialities do not constitute an absolute dichotomy. They are mutually interpenetrable and interdependent. The spheres of culture, politics, and economics are historically constructed and intertwined, but become relatively autonomous forces once the ideas and social relations they configure win broad acceptance. Classes, nations, modes of production, religious communities, gender identities, and other such categories are formed by an amalgam of historical processes, social relations, and discourses. They are not objective entities independent of consciousness. They acquire social force as people understand their experiences through them and engage in debates over their "true" meaning. The actual beliefs and practices of individuals who identify with or are identified as members of any historically constituted group are unpredictable, though certain combinations are observable historical patterns. Neither the working class nor any other social group has a historical mission. I agree with Salman Rushdie that "description is itself a political act" and "redescribing a world is the necessary first step towards changing it" (Rushdie 1991: 13, 14). It is possible, though not in any final and definitive way, to describe a world. We need not be limited to analyzing texts or representations of a world.

Workers, peasants, subalterns, classes

This book presents a synthetic narrative covering a broad geographical and chronological range. Can there be a unified history of workers and peasants whose lives were configured largely within highly diverse localities, even if they were not nearly as isolated and self-sufficient as traditional conceptions commonly assert? According to Antonio Gramsci, "the history of subaltern social groups is necessarily fragmented and episodic." Gramsci offers a long list of topics that are formally external to the subaltern strata, but which must be examined to approach an understanding of subaltern experience and consciousness (Gramsci 1971: 54–55). Several sections of this book adopt this method.

The term "subaltern" suggests that the subordinate social position of artisans, workers, peasants, and other social groups – slaves, tribal nomads, heterodox religious minorities, women – cannot be explained solely by class relationships. I use it when seeking to emphasize other aspects of social domination or the shared subordinate status of peasants, artisans, and workers with others. Appropriating Gramsci's terminology, the Indian Subaltern Studies school proposes that histories of these groups cannot be written either from the point of view of European imperial powers or entirely in terms of the nationalist movements that eventually arose in opposition to imperialism and established independent states in the image of western Europe. Subalterns are typically only incidentally and indirectly the subjects of archival records or cultural productions of the lettered classes. This makes their experiences and consciousnesses very difficult – some would argue impossible – to retrieve (Spivak 1988).

This book owes a great conceptual debt to the ideas of the Subaltern Studies school and those who have engaged with them. Can those interested in other parts of the world learn something from a history of the Middle East informed by these ideas?[2] Several distinctive features of the Middle East are of comparative interest. The economic, political, and cultural ties of the Middle East with Europe are more substantial and more long standing than is the case for any other part of the world. The central Ottoman Empire was never subjected to colonial rule. It maintained its nominal independence until its demise, albeit over a shrinking territorial base from the late seventeenth century on. Many developments commonly attributed to British colonial rule in India were brought to the Middle East by elites of the Ottoman central government or virtually independent provincial rulers. The settler colonial experiences of Algeria and Palestine are distinctive. Useful comparisons have been made between them and with the cases of South Africa and Ireland

(Lustick 1993; Younis 2000). Other comparisons that consider the particularities of the Middle East are also possible. In most of the Middle East, colonial rule arrived later and was briefer and weaker than in Latin America, India, and parts of Africa. Muslims preserved a literate, high cultural tradition that was both independent of European modernity and in historical tension with Christianity. This may have enhanced the capacity for cultural resistance to European imperialism in the Middle East. Movements of politico-religious revivalism that arose in many parts of the world in opposition to colonialism, imperialism, and the consequences of Euro-American modernity appeared in the Middle East (and some Muslim regions of Sudanic Africa) much earlier. Do these differences matter for the subaltern strata? Insofar as they are subordinated in comparable ways, they may not. However, it is worth investigating whether any relevant differences can be attributed to variations in regional histories.

The category of social class is imbedded in a certain way of understanding the history of Europe. It is common to write the history of the Middle East and all of Asia, Africa, and Latin America against a standard established by the categories and processes of European history. Many scholarly debates in Middle East history are concerned with when and how successfully one or another part of the region entered on the same historical trajectory as Europe and its white settler extensions. This approach virtually ensures that the Middle East will be judged deficient or inferior in comparison to Europe, and it obscures many complexities and local specificities of the region that do not fit the European model, which is often an idealized abstraction in any case. Nonetheless, it must be acknowledged that certain ideas and institutions – the nation-state, capitalism and its attendant social classes – which originated in Europe spread to other parts of the globe and became a part of their local histories.

I agree with Dipesh Chakrabarty that history as a category of knowledge is, like economics, inseparable from the coerced imposition of modernity on non-Europeans in the colonial era and from the power of colonial and post-colonial states (Chakrabarty 1992: 57). This is because history is most commonly written using the records of modern structures of domination, especially the nation-state. But precisely because the concept of history and the institutions associated with it have become globalized, those who were the subjects of Euro-American domination now seek to empower themselves by, among other things, developing a sense of their own historical identities. Histories of subaltern groups tend to undermine the discursive power of states, social hierarchies, and nationalist mystifications, and this book is offered in that spirit.

Where is the Middle East?

The mapping of politico-cultural zones is not an innocent process. It is a modern technique of power that asserts the boundaries of sovereignty and "civilization." In this book the Middle East, with some qualifications, refers to the territories of the Ottoman Empire and its successor states in which Islam is the dominant cultural tradition. This definition privileges a state and a religious tradition, though I do not essentialize either of them and fully acknowledge the ethno-linguistic and religious diversity of the region. Like any abstraction, this definition can be critiqued by local empirical details, and I offer it provisionally.

Many definitions of the Middle East include Morocco and Iran, which, though they never came under Ottoman rule, share much with the Ottoman Empire and its successor states. Desert areas of contemporary Algeria, Tunisia, Libya, and the Arabian Peninsula are on the margin of this definition because of the weak Ottoman presence there, and they are peripheral to this book because of the irregular character of agriculture and the paucity of any stable group that might be designated as artisans or workers. Sudan partially entered the Ottoman realm only in the nineteenth century. Israel is in the Middle East, but its ruling circles have sought to ensure that it is not an integral part of the region culturally or politically.

Focusing on regions that were once part of the Ottoman Empire somewhat artificially excludes regions – such as Iran and Morocco – that could quite reasonably be included. I do so partly to enhance the coherence of the narrative in this book and partly to emphasize that much of Europe was politically, economically, and culturally connected to the region for hundreds of years. That is to say that the boundary between Europe and its others is not nearly as sharp and impermeable as it is often thought to be.

The Ottoman Empire, the longest continuous dynastic state in human history, extended its rule from its Anatolian and Balkan heartland to much of the Arabic- and Berber-speaking regions from 1516–17 until World War I. Ottoman rule was not, as commonly portrayed by Arab nationalists, an era of political oppression and economic stagnation for Arabs, nor was it, as Islamists and Turkish nationalists assert, a golden age. Muslims of many ethno-linguistic identities – Arabs, Berbers, Turks, Kurds, Circassians, Abkhazians, Albanians, Bosnians, etc. – considered Ottoman rule legitimate in Islamic terms. Christians and Jews found secure and recognized places for themselves under the Ottoman umbrella, though certainly not as citizens with equal rights – categories which are equally anachronistic for both the Ottoman Empire and premodern Europe.

The territories comprising post-World War I Greece, Albania, Macedonia, Serbia, Bosnia, Kossovo, Romania, Bulgaria, and other parts of the Balkans were central components of the empire. These regions – Rumelia, in Ottoman parlance – share with Anatolia and some of the predominantly Arab areas the lack of a landed aristocracy, a peasantry relatively free from personal dependence and serfdom, and cities that were fully integrated into the structure of state power, unlike medieval western Europe (Todorova 1996: 60–61). Therefore, from the fourteenth to the nineteenth centuries, it is reasonable to consider topics such as the state of the peasantry, the landholding regimes, and urban guilds in the Balkans in conjunction with those questions in Anatolia and the predominantly Arab provinces of the empire. I do not do this as fully as possible because of intellectual limitations shaped by training in area studies. Despite their common Ottoman heritage and majority Muslim populations, it would be idiosyncratic, though not necessarily unfruitful, to consider Albania and Iraq part of the same politico-cultural zone in the twentieth century. The primary focus of attention in this book is Anatolia, greater Syria (*bilad al-sham*), the Nile valley, the Tigris–Euphrates valley, and the coasts of the Arabian Peninsula. Other regions are addressed when it is analytically useful.

Orientalism and its critics

Traditional Orientalist scholarship argues that the Ottoman Empire, after an exceptional period of fluorescence, began a period of protracted decline in the late sixteenth century (Lewis 1961). In the 1950s this conception was buttressed by the postulates of modernization theory, which divides history into two periods: "tradition" and "modernity"(Lerner 1958). Scholarship guided by these conceptions viewed the eighteenth century as a period of economic, political, and cultural stagnation in the Middle East (Gibb & Bowen 1950). According to Orientalism and modernization theory, Napoleon's invasion of Egypt in 1798 and its corollary, Egypt's occupation of greater Syria in the 1830s, marked a radical rupture and initiated the modern era by providing the impetus for the ideas of secularism, nationalism, and liberalism, the state system as we know it today, economic development, and scientific and technological progress (Safran 1961; Lewis 1961; Vatikiotis 1969 and subsequent editions; Polk 1963; Maoz 1968; Polk & Chambers 1968; Hourani 1962; Shamir 1984).

Since the late 1970s, the Orientalist conception of Ottoman "decline" and the dichotomy of "tradition" and "modernity" posited by modernization theory have been largely discredited. Scholars inspired by rejection of Orientalism and modernization theory have established that at no time was the Ottoman Empire or any of its component parts frozen in timeless tradition. On the contrary, the years between 1600 and 1800 "were the point of departure for the modern experience" (Barbir 1996: 101).

Political economy

Edward Said's denunciation of hostile and essentialist representations of the Muslim world in the West, though it is the most widely known and influential, is not the first or the most intellectually powerful critique of Orientalism and modernization theory (Said 1978). Some scholars working within the Orientalist tradition wrote economic and social histories that shed light on the experiences of ordinary people or demonstrated that the normative prescriptions of Islamic texts were very broadly interpreted and did not constrain daily life in ways commonly imagined (Rodinson 1978; Goitein 1967–93). Studies of political economy – liberal, empirical versions and several varieties of neo-Marxism – argued for a new periodization of the modern history of the region and focused attention on the economic relations between Europe and the Middle East and the connections between economic exploitation and political domination (Chevallier 1968; Chevallier 1971; Owen 1969; Owen 1972; Owen 1981a; Raymond 1973–74; Davis 1983).

One political economy school – world systems and dependency theory, developed by Immanuel Wallerstein, Samir Amin, and others – was very influential for a time. In opposition to the traditional Marxian focus on relations of production, this approach argued that through relations of circulation regions of the globe where capitalist production did not prevail became peripheral parts of the world capitalist system as early as the sixteenth century. Indeed, the development of industrial capitalism in Europe and North America depended on unequal trade with the noncapitalist world and forms of coerced labor such as slavery, indenture, or debt peonage. Several of Wallerstein's Turkish students brought a research agenda inspired by his theory to Middle East studies (Wallerstein 1979; Wallerstein & Kasaba 1983; Kasaba 1988; Islamoğlu & Keyder 1987; Keyder & Tabak 1991). World systems theory situates the Middle East in relation to the emergent European center of the world capitalist economy. The principal question posed in this conceptual framework is when the region or some part of it was incorporated into the capitalist world economy. While it directs attention away from the Ottoman state apparatus and Islamic high culture, world systems theory is ultimately Eurocentric and teleological. It reduces complex local histories to a single, albeit a very important, dimension: integration into the capitalist market. Focusing on long-term economic trends shaped by dynamics at the capitalist center and on the undeniable fact that western Europe did come to dominate the Middle East economically and then politically draws attention away from the diverse local processes and chronologies in particular regions. Though their conceptual framework was flawed and the explanations they proposed proved empirically unsustainable, those who adopted or developed Wallerstein's ideas posed a useful question. The debate over world systems theory and other political economy approaches stimulated research on the economic and social history of Ottoman provinces in the eighteenth and nineteenth centuries (McGowan 1981; Schölch 1982; Schölch 1993; Thieck 1992; Gerber 1987; Schilcher 1985; Schilcher 1991a; Marcus 1989; Khoury 1991; Cuno 1992; Khoury 1997; Doumani 1995; Khater 1996; Fattah 1997).

What is modernity?

As its intellectual proponents conceived it, Middle Eastern modernity is a derivative project seeking to remake the region and its people in the image of Europe by deploying science and technology to achieve economic development, enhanced military prowess, and cultural and moral revival. Modernity was to be inculcated by educational and political reforms: study of the European curriculum, revision of the Islamic curriculum, and selective introduction of responsible government, human rights, citizenship, and moderate women's emancipation – ideas and institutions cultivating individuals, mass politics, and nation-states. These reforms were organized by a belief in the idea of progress that assumed that the Middle East must follow the trajectory of European history, with some nonessential modifications to accommodate the local culture.

The elite and new middle-class promoters of Middle Eastern modernity sincerely desired to change their societies. Simultaneously, as the rulers and teachers of their peoples, they acquired and maintained an array of privileges by deploying modernity as a political strategy. Recalcitrant, "traditional," primarily lower-class sectors of the population were often coerced into adopting "modern" practices, exemplified by the conscription of peasants for factory work and the army in nineteenth-century Egypt and restrictions on women wearing the veil in republican Turkey and its outright ban in Pahlavi Iran. Such coercion is inseparable from the developmental or liberatory content of expanding education, emancipation of women, increased income from wage labor, etc. Because new ideas and institutions can not remake the world *ex nihilo*, Middle Eastern modernity, like modernity everywhere, is an untidy phenomenon incorporating attitudes and practices that its local and Euro-American promoters label "traditional" or "backward." Modernity is constituted by an ensemble of ideas, built physical structures, institutions, social relations, and public and private practices. It is simultaneously a discursive strategy deployed by elites and middle classes to reshape their societies and create new social hierarchies and a field of social struggle. The experience of modernity is inseparable from the contest over its meaning.

When does the modern era in the Middle East begin?

As is the case with mapping regions, periodization is both a necessary and a provisional element of historical understanding. No single moment or event changes everything of significance for all the topics addressed here in equal measure. The chronological scope of this book and the periodizations of the chapters are offered as approximations and arguments that draw attention to conjunctures which are often rather different from those that are commonly emphasized in narrating the political histories of states and their elites or the development of high culture and its prominent figures.

Rejecting the proposition that the experiences of Europe and its white settler extensions constitute universal terms of modernity requires us to locate at least some of the constituent elements of Middle Eastern modernity in the region and in the dynamic interaction between Europe and the Middle East. In the mid-eighteenth century the internal structure of the Ottoman state and society and Ottoman–European relations were reconfigured. These changes should not be understood as leading inevitably to the breakup of the Ottoman Empire. However, from this period on, the spread of capitalist relations of production, circulation, and consumption, the formation of new social classes and hierarchies, and the reformation of understandings of political community and self did produce changes that can be associated with the demise of the Ottoman Empire and the formation of the contemporary Middle Eastern state system. Substantiating this proposition requires investigation into: (1) the Ottoman state and central government; (2) regional particularities; (3) the relations of production, circulation, and consumption; (4) the changing character of elites and social hierarchies; (5) the daily lives and culture of peasants and artisans; and (6) the production and circulation of ideas and other cultural forms. Some of this work has been done, though vast areas of relative ignorance remain. Here I will only outline the major events and processes that justify this periodization.

The main features of the Ottoman Middle East in the mid-eighteenth century are: the diminished power of the central government; the rise of provincial notables and warlords; accelerating trade with Europe and localized economic growth; the first sustained period of self-conscious adoption of European styles and techniques by elites; and the rise of Islamic movements challenging the legitimacy of the state. Towards the end of the century the loss of Ottoman capacity to challenge Europe militarily and the declining power of the central government over the provinces led successive sultans and their bureaucratic elites to institute military and administrative reforms modeled on their understanding of European practices.

After the failure of the second Ottoman siege of Vienna in 1683 and the associated efforts of the Köprülü grand viziers to revive the centralized system established by Sultan Süleyman the Lawgiver (1520–66), the Ottomans experienced even more decisive military defeats by the Hapsburg Empire resulting in the loss of Hungary (1699) and parts of Serbia and Wallachia (1718). Consequently, some Ottoman elites began to look towards Europe as a source of techniques and technologies that might restore the power of the central state apparatus. During the Tulip Period (1718–30) the central government attempted to restore its power through innovations such as the first Turkish printing press and the appointment of the first European military advisor to the Ottoman army. The recentralization efforts of the Tulip Period were blocked by the 1730 Patrona Halil revolt.

Consequently, around the middle of the eighteenth century provincial notables (*ayan*, Tur.; *a'yan*, Ar., also called *derebey*s, ağas, or *mütegallibe*s) were able to consolidate power and undermine the authority of the central Ottoman state. Some notable families – the Kara Osmanoğlus of western Anatolia (1691–1813); the Jalilis of Mosul (1726–1834); the 'Azms of Damascus and Hama (1725–57, 1771–83); the Shihabs of Mount Lebanon (1697–1841) – had established themselves in the late seventeenth or early eighteenth century. The number and power of provincial notables increased after 1760 (Hourani 1968: 42–44). They formally acknowledged the sultan but established virtually independent rule over key regions. Loss of control over the provinces and confirmation of Ottoman military inferiority by defeat in the first of three wars with Russia (1768–74) led Sultan Selim III (1789–1807) to establish a new European-style military unit (*nizam-ı cedid*) and a new fiscal apparatus to finance it (*irad-ı cedid*) – the first systematic adoption of western European military and administrative techniques. Selim III was deposed by notables and others who opposed his efforts to restore the authority of the central government. His successor confirmed the rights of the provincial notables in the 1808 Document of Agreement (*sened-i ittifak*) – the acme of the decentralization process (İnalcık 1991: 24).

Some provincial regimes were based on coalitions built by skillful individuals or households of elite warrior-slaves (*memlûk*, Tur.; *mamluk*, Ar.). Zahir al-ʿUmar (1745–75) began his career as a tax farmer (*mültezim*, Tur.; *multazim*, Ar.) in northern Palestine and then established his capital in Acre. His successor, Cezzar Ahmed Pasha (1775–1804), extended his power from Damascus to Acre. In Baghdad, the governorship was held by a dynasty of Georgian mamluks (1748–1831) whose power peaked with the rule of Süleyman Pasha (1780–1802). Egypt was the most important quasi-independent provincial regime. The neo-mamluk Qazdaglis – ʿAli Bey al-Kabir (1760–72) and Muhammad Bey Abu al-Dhahab (1772–75) – attempted to assert their autonomy from the Ottoman central government in ways that were consummated by Mehmed ʿAli Pasha (1805–48). By far the most successful of the autonomous provincial governors, Mehmed ʿAli came to power during the anarchic period created by the demise of the Qazdaglis and Napoleon's invasion. The first Wahhabi state in the Arabian Peninsula (1745–1818) was both an autonomous provincial regime and an Islamic movement critical of Ottoman laxity. Provincial notables and warlords were also prevalent in the Balkans in the late eighteenth and early nineteenth centuries. The best known are Ismaʿil Pasha of Seres in Macedonia, Osman Pazvantoğlu of Vidin, and ʿAli Pasha of Yanina in Albania/Greece.

The diminished power of the central Ottoman state is not equivalent to the decline of the empire. Provincial regimes with a local social base often provided greater security and economic prosperity. Several eighteenth-century provincial governors – Zahir al-ʿUmar, the Shihabs, and ʿAli Bey al-Kabir – exported agricultural products directly to Europe and retained the taxes on this trade locally. Izmir, Acre, and other port cities flourished in the eighteenth century. Important differences among Ottoman regions, historical developments before trade with Europe became substantial, and local determinants of social and economic change cannot be addressed in this capsule summary.

Some of those who reject Orientalism and modernization theory assert that there was a potential for an independent Middle Eastern modernity by arguing that economic and cultural impulses towards the development of an indigenous Middle Eastern capitalism and modernist Islam can be discerned in the mid-eighteenth century (Gran 1978; Voll 1982; Levtzion & Voll 1987). Recent research by meticulous scholars refutes this notion. The eighteenth century now appears to be a period of both continuities with earlier periods and locally varied, incremental changes. Thus, Kenneth Cuno finds "no evidence in the countryside of a development – that is to say, a gathering momentum – towards capitalism in . . . eighteenth century" Egypt, though cash-crop farming, markets, and money were familiar to peasants in the eighteenth century and as early as the Ptolemaic period (Cuno 1992: 4; Cuno 1988a:114–15). In the realm of cultural production, Ahmad Dallal argues that

> The problems that informed eighteenth-century reform ideas bore no resemblance whatsoever to those that inspired and drove later reformers. Thus, Europe is notably absent from the thought of all the major thinkers of the eighteenth century. Even when some of these thinkers were aware of the infringements on Muslim lands, they did not appreciate the extent of the threat presented by these infringements, nor did such events influence their thought: Europe was completely absent.
>
> The intellectual "outside" of the eighteenth century was not European but Islamic, and it was not threatening but redeeming. For most eighteenth century thinkers, the Islamic past was still a continuous reality . . . For the thinkers of late nineteenth and early twentieth centuries . . . this past had to be rediscovered and reconstructed. (Dallal 2000:9–10)

The end of the period I am designating as the beginnings of the modern Middle East and the transition to a new period are configured by the destruction of the Janissary Corps in 1826, the 1838 Anglo-Ottoman Trade Convention, which imposed free trade on the Ottoman Empire, the 1839 Gülhane Edict (*Hatt-ı Şerif*) which initiated political and administrative reforms known as the Tanzimat, and the 1841 Treaty of London, which both radically limited the regional power of Mehmed ʿAli and installed his family as hereditary rulers of Egypt. The new period is marked by diminished provincial autonomy (except for Egypt), sustained efforts of sultans and bureaucrats to enhance the power of the central government, economic subordination to Europe leading in several cases to political subordination and military conquest, and a politico-cultural debate over the reform and revival of Islam and the appropriate place of European ideas and culture.

Peasants and agrarian production

Peasants are not an undifferentiated mass. One useful distinction is between horticulture and open-field cultivation, primarily of grains. In greater Syria and some other regions this corresponds to the difference between privately owned (*milk*, Ar.; *mülk*, Tur.) and state-administered (*miri*) land. Syrian horticulturalists (dubbed peasant-gardeners by Hanna Batatu) lived on the outskirts of cities, provided their food supply, had close ties with urban life and mores, and were more immediately affected by trade with Europe. Peasants who farmed open fields in the Euphrates valley or the Hawran plain were more mobile. Some were sedentarized or semi-sedentarized bedouin. Many other distinctions among peasants can be made: pacific or martial, orthodox or heterodox, and clanless or clan-linked (Batatu 1999: 10–37).

Agricultural production in the Ottoman Empire was normatively conceptualized as the *çift–hane* system.[3] Each peasant household (*hane*) held a theoretical right to perpetual tenancy on state-administered land as long as cultivation was maintained (İnalcık 1991: 18). The size of the archetypical peasant farm (*çift*) – originally defined as the land one man and a team of oxen could plow in a day – was to be adequate to sustain a family. In return for the right of usufruct, peasants paid a regionally variable percentage of the crop as a land tax (*öşür*, Tur.; *'ushr*, Ar.). Other forms of land tenure included collective holding (*musha'a* in Syria and Palestine, *dira* in the northern Arabian Peninsula and lower Iraq), freehold – usual for vineyards and orchards but otherwise uncommon – and family or public endowments (*vakıf*, Tur.; *waqf*, Ar.). Uncultivated or waste land (*mevat*, Tur.; *mawat*, Ar.) was sometimes granted as freehold to individuals in or close to the ruling elite.

In the classical era, the *çift–hane* system was allied to the *timar* system. Cavalry soldiers (*sipahi*s) were granted revokable rights to a share of the revenue from a rural area (*timar, ziamet* or *hass* for larger holdings). The income from this military land grant supported the cavalryman, his retainers, and their military equipment. In return, a *sipahi* had to answer a sultan's call to arms.[4] From the late sixteenth century on, military strategy relied more heavily on musket-carrying infantrymen, the Janissary Corps. To raise cash to pay the enlarged Janissary Corps, tax farming (*iltizam, muqata'a*) was introduced. *Timar*s and tax farms coexisted for many years in some localities. A prospective tax farmer competed in an annual auction for the right to collect the land tax of a rural region or sometimes an urban tax. Tax farms were renewed at the pleasure of the sultan and were not, in principle, hereditary. In 1695 a new category of life-term tax farm (*malikâne*) was established. *Malikâne* holders managed their lands as they saw fit, and their heirs had preferential rights to renew the lease. This was one of the institutions that enabled local notables to consolidate power while remaining integrated in the Ottoman system.

In the late sixteenth century large farms known as *çiftlik*s were established. As proponents of world systems theory identify these farms as the site of export-oriented commercial agriculture that integrated Ottoman regions into the European-centered world capitalist system, it is important to clarify this term. *Çiftlik* does not have a fixed meaning: the size of the farm, the timing and mode of its creation, and its relations of production varied. Some *çiftlik*s were created in the seventeenth and eighteenth centuries by notables who received grants of wasteland beyond the boundaries of traditional, state-administered land, often in Balkan regions close to routes of communication and markets such as Thessaly, Epirus, Macedonia, Thrace, the Maritsa valley, Danubian Bulgaria, the Kossovo–Metohija basin, the coastal plains of Albania, and parts of Bosnia (İnalcık 1991: 25). The mid-eighteenth century seems to be a period of accelerated formation of large farms, when some life-term tax farms were turned into *çiftliks*.

How should this agrarian system be classified? Even the cursory description offered here indicates a dynamic process of change over time.

Clearly, it is not a static, "traditional" mode of production, as anthropological studies using equilibrium models derived from functionalist theory and Orientalist premises propose (Eickelman 1998: 55–65). Some ethnographers have gone to great lengths to deny the existence of any historical dynamic and social change in peasant villages before the arrival of western modernity. A particularly egregious example is Richard Critchfield's life history of an upper Egyptian peasant youth, Shahhat, which is full of sterotypically negative characterizations of "the peasant personality" (Critchfield 1978). Timothy Mitchell demonstrates that Critchfield heavily plagiarizes Henry Ayrout's widely read study of twentieth-century Egyptian peasant life and other works written well before the period Critchfield professes to be writing about (Mitchell 1990a; Ayrout 1963). While Critchfield did spend time in an upper Egyptian village, Ayrout conducted no direct investigation of rural life. He grew up in Cairo but left Egypt at the age of eighteen and wrote his book as a dissertation in Paris ten years later. His information was apparently based on correspondence with former schoolmates whose families owned large agricultural estates (Mitchell forthcoming). Thus, there is a well-established western discourse imputing changeless tradition and other negative characteristics to peasants without serious investigation of rural histories.

If rural life was not timeless, why was there no transition to capitalism, as in western Europe? Some seek to answer this question by defining the Ottoman agrarian system more precisely.[5] Both Orientalists, who note important empirical differences from the European model, and some Marxists, who emphasize state administration of the land and collection of taxes, not rent, from peasants and therefore prefer the terms tributory or Asiatic mode of production, criticize the loose use of the term "feudalism" to describe Ottoman agrarian relations. Chris Wickham adopts the classical Marxian view that the key factor determining a mode of production is the form of surplus extraction. Western feudalism is defined by rent collection, not by its political–juridical aspects – fiefs, vassalage, military service, private justice, serfdom, and labor service. Asian tributary modes of production are defined by tax collection. Thus, according to

Wickham, the Ottoman system was not feudal (Wickham 1985). Halil Berktay replies that most Ottoman peasants were legally tenants of the state. Though the claim on their surplus was called a tax, it was functionally indistinguishable from rent. Hence, the Ottoman agrarian system was feudal. "The Western transition to 'private' feudalism . . . is the exception . . . the various Oriental transitions to 'state' feudalism . . . are the rule" (Berktay 1987: 317).

French structuralist Marxism inspired anthropologists and others who reject static functionalism and kindred theoretical approaches that inadequately attend to rural social structure and social conflict to construct precise definitions of modes of production and to specify how different modes are articulated with each other. Proponents of the articulation of modes of production school often seek to locate a zone of peasant life not subsumed by the expansion of capitalist relations of production and circulation (Glavanis & Glavanis 1990). This approach is problematic because well before the twentieth century many peasant villages were not isolated from markets, cities, and broader cultural currents. Today, hardly a village in the Middle East has not been touched by capitalism, the nation-state, and the mass media, though the attendant changes in village life do not necessarily conform to the expectations of modernization theory. Village studies that avoid formalist, theoretically abstract idealization of peasants (positively or negatively), account for links of peasants with the world beyond, and give due consideration to social structure and social conflict provide important local micro-social studies which are essential to a historical understanding of subalterns.[6]

Debates over modes of production would be unintelligible to peasants, who may have experienced no difference between tax and rent. Both were collected by the same methods. But Ottoman peasants who farmed state-administered land had more rights than European feudal tenants because they could not be evicted so long as they maintained cultivation and paid taxes. Talal Asad suggests a useful approach that avoids the formalism of debates over modes of production:

The history of noncapitalist societies can not be understood by isolating one a priori principle . . . the important thing always is to try and identify that combination of elements (environmental, demographic, social, cultural, etcetera) in the past of a given population that will serve to explain a particular outcome . . .

There is no key to the secret of noncapitalist societies . . . Only in capitalist societies, based as they are on production for profit, on the drive for unceasing growth, on the penetration of money-values into various spheres of life, and on the continuous transformation of productive forces, is there something approaching "a key" to its [sic] understanding . . .

The concept of "the capitalist mode of production" is a way – the most powerful way – of writing a particular history of relations, institutions, processes, that have hegemonised (but by no means homogenised) the world. There is not and cannot be any conceptual parallel to it in the form of "precapitalist modes of production" (Asad 1987: 603–04).

This insight leads me to suggest that the Ottoman agrarian regime was neither an Asiatic nor a feudal mode of production. The state administered the largest share of the land. A tendency towards feudalization developed in certain regions in the mid-eighteenth century, as provincial notables tried to wrest control of the land and the peasants from the central government. But that tendency was blocked and reversed as the central government regained power in the nineteenth century. This formulation preserves the specificity of local practices and avoids defining the Ottoman experience in relation to the trajectory of Europe.

Artisans, guilds, and workers

The history of pre-industrial artisans, craft workers, and service providers is a part of the subject of this book. They do not comprise a single social class but include relatively prosperous masters who employed other workers, skilled journeymen, wage laborers, and those with no fixed place of work.

Until the 1830s, manufacturing in the Middle East consisted almost entirely of small, labor-intensive, artisanal enterprises using hand, animal, or water power. But there is no clear break between the pre-industrial and industrial periods. Throughout the nineteenth and twentieth centuries, artisanal and industrial production simultaneously competed and coexisted. Although artisanal work was often disparaged as "premodern," or "traditional," it was sometimes required to sustain industrialized production. Artisans often filled niches left open by large-scale industry or undertook aspects of the production process unsuitable for factory production in Middle Eastern conditions (El-Messiri 1980; Koptiuch 1994; Vatter 1994).

Before the introduction of mechanized industry and well afterwards, most of the urban working population – not only artisans of every sort, but also merchants, service providers, and professionals – were organized into guilds (*esnaf* Tur.; *tawa'if*, Ar.). Because guilds are a well-known medieval and early modern European institution, most studies of Middle Eastern guilds are either explicitly or implicitly comparative, almost always to the detriment of Middle Eastern guilds. Several scholars of early modern and modern guilds concur that a guild is "a group of town people engaged in the same occupation and headed by a *shaykh*" (guild master) (Baer 1964: 18; endorsed by Raymond 1973–74: 507; and with reservations by Ghazaleh 1999: 37; Rafeq 1991: 495 emphasizes the element of guild autonomy). This definition does not account for the diversity of guild forms, social practices, and relations with the state. It also excludes the guilds of horticulturalists who provisioned Damascus and Aleppo from the seventeenth to the nineteenth centuries and peasants on the outskirts of Homs, Hama, and Antioch may also have been organized in guilds (Batatu 1999: 98).

Ottoman guilds may have grown out of popular religious or social solidarity associations that became consolidated as craft associations between the fifteenth and seventeenth centuries, depending on the locality. In the seventeenth century, there were 260,000 artisans in Istanbul organized into 1,109 guilds and 119,000 members of 262 guilds in Cairo. In the mid-eighteenth century, there were 157 guilds in Aleppo and a similar number in Damascus. The French savants enumerated 193 guilds in Cairo (excluding suburbs) in 1801. In the 1870s, there were 198 guilds in Cairo with 63,487 members, 116 guilds in Salonica, and 287 guilds in Istanbul (Faroqhi 1994: 590–91; Raymond 1973–74: 204–05; Marcus 1989: 159; Baer 1964: 24; Ghazaleh 1999: 30; Quataert 1994a: 894; Rafeq 1991: 498).

There is considerable debate about what guilds actually did and how they functioned. The basic assumption of the guild system was that every producer had the right to a certain share of the market. Guilds often acted to restrain unfair competition, regulate entry to professions, and establish standards of quality. They could also be responsible for administrative tasks such as collecting taxes (though not in Istanbul), fixing prices and wages, supplying labor and services, supplying and distributing goods, and arbitration of disputes among members. Guilds offered mutual assistance, though the character of such aid could vary widely from redistribution of income to loaning money. Guilds also provided a social framework for members.

The norms and regulations of specific guilds and localities changed over time. The powers of a guild master were not fixed and depended on the craft and the power and interest and capacity of state authorities to regulate the guild. No single model is adequate to define the functioning of guilds throughout the Ottoman period. The available research deals only with eighteenth- and nineteenth-century Cairo. Even for Cairo, the vast documentary record has been only partially examined and does not support comprehensive generalizations.

Despite their associations with Islamic popular cultural practices and the affiliation of some guilds with *sufi* orders, until the nineteenth century Christians and Jews usually belonged to the same guild as their Muslim colleagues, with the obvious exceptions of kosher butchers and the like (Raymond 1973–74: 522–26; Marcus 1989: 159; Quataert 1994a: 893).

Women often worked in their families' shops and sometimes worked for wages, especially as spinners or in other branches of textile manufacturing. But they usually were not permitted to be guild members.

Guilds were quite specialized. In seventeenth-century Istanbul there were sixty-four guilds for makers of different musical instruments and twenty guilds for cooks and sellers of different foods. In the eighteenth century, one guild specialized in weaving ribbons for the fire brigade (Baer 1982: 152). Makers of each style of footwear, headgear, or garment had their own guild.

Orientalist scholarship has commonly viewed guild monopolies as causing the stagnation of production techniques – the social history counterpart of claims about Islamic intellectual decline. In addition, the inflexibility of the guild system is among the reasons adduced for the collapse of Middle Eastern crafts in the face of the influx of European manufactured goods. Bernard Lewis's association of guilds with "the unchanging character of the forms of production in the Islamic lands from the twelfth to the nineteenth centuries" is surely overstated (Lewis 1937: 36). In his monumental study of artisans and merchants in Ottoman Cairo, André Raymond argues that the reluctance of Cairo's powerful long-distance merchants (*tujjar*) to invest their profits in production was the primary cause of technical stagnation in eighteenth-century Egypt. Nonetheless, he also seems to endorse Lewis's negative view of guilds (Raymond 1973–74: 225, 585).

Guilds were neither islands of civil society in an ocean of Oriental despotism nor merely administrative units that served the state by collecting taxes and supervising the urban population. Under certain circumstance they exercised a high level of autonomous regulation over their crafts and their members. Guilds were linked to the state through the confirmation of masters in office by a state-appointed judge. This allowed considerable room for maneuver between the practices of election, imposition by governmental authority, and hereditary accession. Ottoman authorities tended to control certain strategic guilds more tightly than others. In nineteenth-century Cairo, guild masters collected taxes for the state, but their loyalties and obligations to their members influenced their behavior and outlook (Ghazaleh 1999: 35–53). Their location between the state and craftspeople may have allowed guild masters to develop a conception of the "national interest." Participating in guild life provided members some training in democratic practices that became a component of nationalist politics (Cole 1993: 167–74).

Abandoning a search for defects in Ottoman guilds compared to those of Europe enables us to see the ambiguous cultural and institutional legacy of the guild system in the formation of a modern working class.

Guilds sometimes formed the basis of resistance to the penetration of manufactures and labor processes imported from Europe. Sometimes they could not withstand the competition and collapsed altogether. Sometimes artisans successfully maneuvered to remain in the market by finding specialized niches or performing ancillary functions for mechanized industry. Sometimes the introduction of mechanized industry and transport was accompanied by new organizations called guilds but which functioned very differently from earlier guilds. As elsewhere, the transition from the culture, institutions, and production processes of artisans to those of a modern working class was complex and uneven.

The traditional model emphasizing abrupt technological innovation and urban factories is as inadequate to explain industrial development in the Middle East as it is for Europe. Labor-intensive production in rural areas, often by women, and improved or coercively sped-up manual techniques rather than technological innovation were responsible for a large share of increased output in Britain from 1760 to 1830. In the Middle East, as in Europe, the transition to large-scale mechanized production was prolonged; older and newer production methods coexisted for some time, especially in the textile industry (Quataert 1991a; Quataert 1994b: 14–15; Quataert 1994a).

Trajectory of the book

Working people, with all the variations in their local experiences, are a major force in the modern history of the Middle East. Late eighteenth- and nineteenth-century rulers understood the need to mobilize them for state-building projects. Subsequently, the salience of working people as producers, consumers, and citizens increased, as modern forms of production and circulation, political association, and culture – capitalism, the nation-state, political parties, trade unions, peasant associations, women's unions, novels, newspapers, cinema, and television – proliferated. While this has not necessarily entailed expansion of democratic political rights, "the masses" have become the indispensable subjects of political regimes seeking legitimacy. Mass production, mass politics, and mass culture have enlisted the participation of the subaltern strata. In the process, they have undergone continual social and discursive reformation.

Peasants comprised the overwhelming majority of the working people of the Middle East until the 1960s. Since then, their demographic and economic weight has rapidly declined due to migration to cities and to other countries and the growth of capitalist manufacturing, transportation, petroleum extraction, and services. In Egypt, historically the agrarian society par excellence, a shrinking minority of the economically active population now engages in agriculture. Throughout the region, peasant family farms, which were rarely totally unconnected to markets, have increasingly been displaced by commercial agriculture, while the proportion of agriculture in national economies has declined. In some cases the expanded role of markets and cash has increased the economic dependency of rural women; in others the migration of men and enhanced access of women to cash has increased their social autonomy.

The relative decline of agriculture increased the social weight of urban wage workers and expanded the use of wage labor in both the countryside and cities. There has been a substantial interpenetration of cities and villages (El-Karanshawy 1998). Women increased their participation in the wage-labor force in both industrial and service occupations, but at a lower rate than in East Asia and Latin America (Moghadam 1993). While urban wage labor gave women somewhat more control over their lives, they were often subjected to oppressive patriarchal forms of discipline at work (White 1994). Turkey and Egypt underwent the most extensive industrialization in the region. However, by the late twentieth century this had not brought about the same the kinds of qualitative or quantitative social transformations popularly associated with the Euro-American industrial revolution.

Books like Frederick Engels' *The Condition of the Working Class in England in 1844*, Charles Dickens' *Hard Times*, and E. P. Thompson's *The Making of the English Working Class* teach us that the advent of industrialization in England is not a tale of unmitigated progress. Hardly any such texts exist to tell us about the experience of factory work in the Middle East in the nineteenth or early twentieth centuries.[7] Industrialization in the Middle East, like other topics of comparative interest, should not be judged by the standard of an idealized European model. At the same time, we cannot lose sight of the fact that capitalism, the nation-state, and their attendant cultural forms did become hegemonic, while collective action and daily behaviors of working people affected the course of their development. Workers and peasants constrained – and in certain conjunctures enhanced – the power of state builders, entrepreneurs, and elite intellectuals as production processes, consumption patterns, political and social institutions, associational patterns, gender relations, public and private practices, experiences, and consciousnesses were transformed.

1 The world capitalist market, provincial regimes, and local producers, 1750–1839

The large-scale economic and political processes that characterize the period of this chapter are the rise of autonomous provincial regimes, the expansion of agricultural production, and the intensification of links between several parts of the Ottoman Empire and the world capitalist market. Although this was a time of political weakness for the Ottoman central government, it was not an era of unmitigated political and economic decline, as traditional Orientalist studies of the eighteenth century maintain (Gibb & Bowen 1950). The political stability and enhanced physical security established by powerful local notables and provincial governors contributed to increased agricultural production. Parts of the empire favorably situated to benefit from trade with Europe including Macedonia and Thrace, lower Egypt, Izmir and its hinterlands, and Acre and the Galilee experienced economic growth and prosperity. However, there was no qualitative departure from the relations of production and circulation of earlier periods.

A long wave of European economic growth began in the 1740s and lasted, with ups and downs, until the end of the Napoleonic Wars in 1815, followed by an economic contraction lasting until the early 1840s. The central development of this mid-eighteenth- to early nineteenth-century economic expansion is the Industrial Revolution. European economic growth generated increased demand for agricultural products from the Middle East. During the subsequent contraction, prices of European manufactured goods dropped more sharply than prices of Middle Eastern agricultural goods. Low-priced European manufactures, especially finished textiles, began to appear in Middle Eastern markets in significant quantities. But the terms of trade for Middle Eastern agricultural products remained favorable. Consequently, in the Middle East the century from 1750 to 1850 was marked by rising prices of agricultural products and increasing exports to Europe (Tabak 1991: 138).

Periodization of long-term economic trends can only be approximate, and general tendencies must be modified by local histories and conditions. Cairo and western Anatolia are the only Middle Eastern regions where pre-twentieth-century local periodizations of economic expansion and contraction have been attempted. In Cairo, after frequent crises due to currency debasement, high prices, and food shortages from 1690 to 1736, there was a return to prosperity and high, but stable, wheat prices from 1736 to 1780. This period was ended by the demise of the mamluk regime, the French invasion of 1798, and the rise of Mehmed ʿAli Pasha (1805–48) (Raymond 1973–74: 81–106). After Mehmed ʿAli stabilized his rule, Egyptian economic expansion resumed, primarily due to investment in military industries and the export of newly developed long-staple cotton and other agricultural products. However, the Pasha established a command economy, regulating production and marketing closely by his orders. Efficiency and equity were not his highest priorities. Hence, there were many crises, and growth could not be sustained.

There was a major commercial boom in western Anatolia in the second half of the eighteenth and early nineteenth centuries. Izmir became the most important port for European trade with the Levant, which was dominated by France before the Napoleonic Wars (Frangakis-Syrett 1991: 97). From the 1750s commercial crops – cotton and other fibers, maize, tobacco, grapes, and livestock – were added to previously established contraband exports of wheat and other grains from Izmir, Salonica, and Macedonia to Europe (Kasaba 1988: 19). Cotton cultivation tripled in Macedonia and western Anatolia from 1720 to 1800. Most of the crop was exported, primarily to France and the Austro-Hungarian Empire.

The periodization I propose has some similarities with world systems theory conceptions that view the period from 1750 to 1839 (or 1815) as marking the incorporation of the Ottoman Empire into the capitalist world economy (Wallerstein & Kasaba 1983; Kasaba 1988). World systems theory also argues that Ottoman local notables responded to growing demand for agricultural products from Europe in the mid-eighteenth century by establishing large, commercialized estates (çiftliks) on which they sought to establish private property rights and impose harsher forms of labor control over peasants. Although something of this sort happened in parts of the sub-Danubian Balkans, it was not a general phenomenon throughout the Ottoman territories (Islamoğlu- Inan 1987: 12; Keyder 1991: 2). Even in the Balkans, many çiftliks were small (McGowan 1981). Local notables in western Anatolia, such as the Kara Osmanoğlus, did not have the capacity to oversee peasant labor and introduce large-scale capitalist production methods (Kasaba 1991: 115).

The character of eighteenth-century commerce between Aleppo and Europe, primarily France, also does not conform to the predictions of world systems theory. Aleppo's international trade increased markedly, but intraregional trade was more substantial and stimulated Aleppo's commercial relations with its agricultural hinterland and cities as distant as Mosul, Diyarbekir, and Basra. In the early eighteenth century, Aleppo's trade with Europe conformed to the typical colonial pattern predicted by world systems theory: exporting agricultural and pastoral raw materials and importing finished goods. But at the end of the century, Aleppo sold more finished goods to France than it imported (Marcus 1989: 146–50). Similarly, in Jabal Nablus in Palestine the active regional trade in soap and textiles involving Cairo and Damascus was not disrupted by the activities of European merchants in the coastal cities of Jaffa and Acre (Doumani 1995). These cases confirm that "the social classes and institutions of the Ottoman provinces were not simply remolded as a consequence of trade with Europe . . . They are not a dependent variable, as a reading of Wallerstein's theory might lead one to suppose" (Cuno 1992: 11).

In most of Anatolia and the Fertile Crescent large, privately owned estates producing cash crops for export to Europe were exceptional, though some were formed when market conditions were favorable. However, market relations in agriculture were a common feature of many regions. In the Bursa region and elsewhere in Anatolia, small commercial farms supplying local urban markets coexisted with peasant family farms (Gerber 1987: 30, 39). In lower Egypt, as early as the sixteenth and seventeenth centuries cash crops such as sugarcane, rice, and flax were cultivated. Processed sugar and linen as well as foodstuffs were exported to other parts of Ottoman Empire. Total agricultural output was far larger than subsistence (Hanna 1998: 85). There was a stratum of wealthy peasants in eighteenth-century lower Egypt (if not earlier), and villages around Mansura produced cash crops for markets including rice, sesame, and wheat (Cuno 1984). Sectors of the agrarian economy of the hinterlands of Mosul were integrated into a market economy before the Ottoman conquest (Khoury 1997: 27). Basra merchants advanced credit to owners of palm trees and shipped dates throughout the Persian Gulf/Indian Ocean regional market in the late eighteenth and early nineteenth centuries (Fattah 1997: 85–86). Similar credit practices were common in the olive oil agro-industry of Jabal Nablus (Doumani 1995). There was a market in usufruct rights for agricultural land in lower Egypt, Mosul, Jabal Nablus, and the hinterlands of Bursa at least as early as the middle of the eighteenth century and probably much earlier (Cuno 1992; Khoury 1997; Doumani 1995: 8; Gerber 1987: 23).

Linkages between the Ottoman Empire and the world capitalist market intensified during a period of rising agricultural prices and increasing production. This tended to benefit primary agricultural producers and enhance the viability of peasant family farms (Tabak 1991: 135–37). Agricultural commodities for export and local markets were generated primarily from the surplus of small peasant production, rather than centrally managed, large-scale, privately owned commercial farms. In the eighteenth and early nineteenth centuries most peasants retained control of their production process and usufruct rights. "Fiscal domination of the peasantry and not the organization of large estates to serve the export trade . . . was the primary rural source of power and fortune" (McGowan 1981: 171–72; see also Veinstein 1976; McGowan 1994: 672; Doumani 1995: 161). Hence, there was no wholesale restructuring of agricultural production and agrarian social relations in response to demand from Europe. In contrast to Europe, the Ottoman social formation embodied "a logic in which privatized large property was marginal . . . Commodity production by small-owning peasantry represents an alternative mode of integration into the market" (Keyder 1991: 2, 3).[1]

Detailed examinations of local relations of production and circulation and the cultural systems in which they were embedded reveal differences so substantial as to call into question the viability of the category of "the Ottoman peasant." Lower Egypt, Mount Lebanon, and Jabal Nablus represent very different agrarian regimes, yet the three cases converge in refuting the predictions of both the Orientalist paradigm of eighteenth-century economic decline and world systems theory. Well before the French invasion of Egypt and the Egyptian occupation of greater Syria, peasants in these regions produced commercial crops for regional markets and export to Europe, especially France. Commercial agriculture was not an innovation brought about by increased contact with European markets or the entrepreneurial activity of large landowners, although these factors stimulated and influenced its development. Peasants in regions more remote from transportation were less engaged in commercial agriculture. But there were no structural or ideological barriers to commercial agriculture in the mid-eighteenth or early nineteenth centuries.

Egypt: the peasants and the pasha

By the mid-seventeenth century Egyptian mamluk households had established considerable fiscal and political autonomy from Istanbul, collecting the land tax as tax farmers and spending much of it locally. Peasants had usufruct rights on their own plots (*aradi al-filaha* or *athar*) and paid their takes to the tax farmer. They also worked on the lands of the mamluks (*aradi al- usya*) sometimes for wages, sometimes as sharecroppers, sometimes as unpaid corvée laborers. The tax-farming system imposed many burdens on the peasants, not the least of which was the tendency of the mamluks to increase taxes to expand their military power and establish a competitive advantage over rival mamluk houses.

There is no evidence of a decline in the status of peasants, increased coercion of labor, or formation of large estates in the seventeenth and eighteenth centuries.[2] Peasants retained control of production and marketing on the lands on which they held usufruct rights, which they commonly bequeathed, sold, rented, and pawned (Cuno 1984: 314–15; Cuno 1992: 10–11, 66, 82–83). While *shari'a* law recognizes a distinction between ownership and the right of usufruct, peasants commonly disregarded it with impunity. In lower Egypt, where the area of annual Nile inundation and the cultivated land overlapped in a stable and predictable pattern, peasant plots were demarcated and families were individually responsible for the land tax. From what we know of Cairo prices, it seems likely that the prices of agricultural commodities in lower Egyptian villages rose in the eighteenth century. This would imply an increase in the income of peasant producers and the value of their usufruct rights, which may have been partly offset by increased taxation.

From 1780 to 1805, political instability, disruption of trade with France, and natural disasters resulted in recurring economic crises (Raymond 1973–74: 100–04). The mamluk chief, Murad Bey (1779–98), imposed a monopoly on customs collection and purchased and resold a large portion of the wheat crop to raise revenues for the military. When the French invaded, they seized many tax farms and declared them state-owned lands (Owen 1969: 15–16). In the same period Sultan Selim III (1789–1807) tried to finance his military reforms by restricting military land grants and tax farms in the face of strong opposition from provincial notables (Rivlin 1961: 37; Shaw 1971: 132).

These practices were more systematically and effectively implemented by Mehmed 'Ali Pasha after he became the Ottoman governor of Egypt in 1805. The status of peasants began to improve considerably after he consolidated his power and restored political stability by eliminating the warring mamluk factions in the infamous 1811 massacre at the Cairo citadel. The irrigation system was repaired and expanded, and idle land was brought under cultivation. From 1814 on, Mehmed 'Ali abolished tax farming and instituted a regime of direct collection of taxes from peasants by salaried government employees, monopolization of domestic and foreign trade, and compulsory delivery of harvests to state-operated depots at prices below the market rate.

The introduction of long-staple cotton in 1821 is associated with dramatic changes in the lives of peasants, though the effects of this innovation were not fully realized until the second half of the nineteenth century.

Cotton cultivation requires large inputs of water, fertilizer, and labor and is best undertaken on large plots. Cotton plants remain in the ground from February to September and must be watered heavily in the summer, when the natural level of the Nile is low. To increase the supply of summer water, the government recruited peasant workers by corvée to construct canals, barrages, water wheels *(saqiyyas)*, and water-lifting apparatuses *(shadufs)*. By the early 1830s cotton and other summer crops (rice, indigo, sugar) were cultivated on 600,000 *faddans* compared to 250,000 in 1798.

Detailed rules governing cultivation, harvesting, and marketing of cotton and other crops as well as more stringent tax-collection practices were codified in the 1829 Regulation of Peasant Agriculture *(La'ihat zira'at al-fallah)*, though peasants did not simply dutifully obey the Pasha's directives (Richards 1987: 216; Cuno 1992). The monopoly system imposed low prices on peasant crops, and the state attempted to regulate every aspect of production and marketing. Peasants had always performed corvée labor to repair irrigation canals in their villages and the like. But in the 1820s the number of corvée laborers increased to some 467,000 annually; many were compelled to work for two months a year or more far from their villages for nominal or no pay (Owen 1969: 48). Mehmed 'Ali raised taxes to support his large and modernized army and its expedition to Morea in support of the Ottoman sultan's failed effort to thwart the Greek independence movement (1824–28). Peasants were conscripted into the army for the first time. These massive intrusions of the state into the lives of peasant families reversed the improvements in their economic and social well-being.

Peasants responded through a combination of resistance and resort to the "weapons of the weak" (Scott 1985). The Pasha's Albanian cavalry massacred upper Egyptian peasants who rebelled following the government's seizure of their entire grain crop for the first time in 1812. In 1816 the army compelled recalcitrant peasants to grow government-specified crops. There were five peasant revolts during 1820–26 against increased taxation and the introduction of conscription, including three large uprisings in the upper Egyptian province of Qina. As many as 40,000 people participated in a two-month-long uprising in 1821 led by one Ahmad. Two years later an even larger revolt was led by another Ahmad, who sought to overthrow Mehmed 'Ali and appealed to Muslim salvationist sentiment by calling himself the *mahdi* (Baer 1969b: 96–98; Baer 1982: 77, 254; Richards 1987: 218–19; Cuno 1992: 125; Fahmy 1997: 95).

Commercial crops grown in Qina were marketed in Cairo, Istanbul, and Europe, especially *durra* (the local variety of wheat) and sugarcane. Qina was also a commercial hub linking upper Egypt with Sudan and the

Red Sea–Arabian Ocean commercial network; and it was a manufacturing center for textiles, pottery, and charcoal. Handicraft textile production in Qina province, including the export of some items beyond Egypt, prospered during the Napoleonic Wars and was seriously damaged by the influx of European textiles to Egypt after 1810. The profitability of grain exports diminished around 1820 due to competition from Russian wheat. The rise of sugarcane as the principal cash crop and the conversion of lands from food crops to sugarcane caused local food shortages. Thus, economic decline following a prosperous period may have motivated the revolts in Qina. In contrast to all others who have studied them, Fred Lawson argues that the Qina revolts should not be understood as peasant revolts against taxation and conscription, but "revolts by village artisans and pieceworkers against the supervisors and merchants in whose hands the control of the local sugar, wheat, and cloth industries rested" (Lawson 1981: 145). This is a functionalist argument unsupported by direct evidence about the social composition of the revolts: those most affected by economic decline should initiate a rebellion. Artisans may very well have collaborated with peasants in rebelling against the expanding power of Mehmed 'Ali's state under the banner of Islam. But the general consensus that Qina was a center of peasant resistance to conscription and taxation by Mehmed 'Ali seems well founded.

Peasants opposed the demands of the Pasha's regime in ways other than open revolt. Desertion from the army was common. Peasant conscripts mutinied in 1827 and 1832. When resistance to conscription was ineffective, peasants fled their villages or maimed themselves. Cutting off index fingers, removing teeth, and putting rat poison in an eye to blind one's self were common techniques of mutilation (Fahmy 1997: 99–103, 256–63).

The combination of peasant resistance/avoidance, hence a shortage of labor and declining revenue, the opposition of European powers to the exclusion of their merchants from the interior of the country, the power of the British navy, the administrative and technical weaknesses of the Pasha's regime, and the global capitalist crisis of 1836–37 forced Mehmed 'Ali to abandon the monopoly system and devise a new decentralized rural administration. These developments are the local markers of the end of the period treated in this chapter.

Lebanon: peasants and the emergence of communal politics

The Ottoman central government did not concern itself with the internal social structure and local customs of Mount Lebanon. It regarded Mount

Lebanon as state-administered land and the local notables as tax farmers. The northern part of the mountain was subject to the pasha of Tripoli; the southern part to the pasha of Sidon (whose actual seat was Acre after 1750). Christian historians have usually argued that Mount Lebanon was a single unit with a self-conscious identity and an autonomous and locally legitimized political regime and that the land was private property (Holt & Lewis 1962; Salibi 1988: 108–29). This view is becoming increasingly discredited.

The system of social hierarchy and decentralized political leadership in Mount Lebanon is commonly characterized as a feudal exception within the Ottoman Empire. This terminology tends to minimize the Ottoman context and accentuate the association of Lebanon and Latin Christian Europe. In the heyday of modernization theory this affiliation was commonly adduced as an explanation of Lebanon's "successful" adaptation to modernity – an interpretation that has lost credibility since the second post-independence civil war of 1975–91.[3] To avoid this misleading association, I use the local terms for the system, *iqta'*, its districts, *muqata'at*, and its notables, *muqata'ajis*.

The mountain was divided into *muqata'at* where hereditary Druze and Maronite *muqata'ajis* were responsible for collection of taxes and the administration of justice. Whereas most Ottoman tax farmers lived in cities, Lebanese *muqata'ajis* lived in their rural districts and held large plots of land (*'uhdas*) in their own names. Though not juridically tied to the land, peasants were required to perform labor service and buy marriage licenses and baptismal oil from their *muqata'ajis* and to offer them holiday gifts. From 1711 to 1841 the Shihabs were the leading *muqata'aji* family. The Maronite *muqata'ajis* concurred that Mount Lebanon was a hereditary principality (*imara*) and that a member of the Shihab family was the legitimate paramount ruler (*amir or hakim*); the Druze *muqata'ajis* accepted the Shihabs as tax farmers and did not seek to set up an alternative regime.

Maronites were originally concentrated in Kisrawan and northern Mount Lebanon and the Druze in the Shuf and southern districts. From the late seventeenth century, Maronite peasants began to migrate southward, where they became subject to Druze *muqata'ajis*, the most powerful of whom were the Junblats. The Maronite population increased more rapidly than the Druze and constituted the majority in Mount Lebanon by the nineteenth century. Reforms in the administration of the church initiated by the Council of Luwayza in 1736 led to expanding the network of church schools, and Maronite peasants began to be educated. Consequently, Maronites became the dominant force in the administration of Mount Lebanon. One expression of the increasing power of the

Maronites in the late eighteenth century was the secret conversion of a branch of the Shihab family, including the amirs Yusuf (1770–88) and Bashir II (1788–1840), to the Maronite faith.

The principal agricultural product of Mount Lebanon was raw silk produced from cocoons spun by worms who fed on the leaves of mulberry trees. Since the time of Fakhr al-Din Ma'n II (1593–1633) the amirs encouraged silk production in the religiously mixed Junblati *muqata'a* of the Shuf and in the Maronite district of Kisrawan, controlled by the Khazin family. Cultivation of mulberry trees and the export of raw silk from Sidon and later Beirut, primarily to France, was dominated by Maronites. The Junblats encouraged Maronite peasants to settle on their lands and even donated lands to Maronite monasteries to promote production of silk (Salibi 1988: 104–05). Until the late 1830s itinerant, seasonal peasant-laborers reeled raw silk into thread by hand (Polk 1963: 172).

Some peasants in Mount Lebanon owned small plots of land. But as they were usually too small to sustain a family, sharecropping (*musharaka*) arrangements with monasteries or aristocratic families who held most of the land were common. In the eighteenth century peasant holdings expanded, primarily through the use of cultivation contracts (*mugharasa*): agreements stipulating that a landowner supply the land, tools, and materials for a peasant to terrace and plant trees and tend them for three to twelve years, depending on the type of tree. During this period the peasant planted suitable food crops between the trees. When the trees were fully mature, a quarter to half of the land, or sometimes only the trees, became the property of the peasant (Firro 1990: 158; Dubar & Nasr 1976: 29; Chevallier 1971: 138–39). Mulberry, fig, almond, and olive trees as well as grape vines were planted under this system. *Muqata'aji*s maintained their rights to peasant labor and other forms of economic and social dominance if they expanded the area of cultivation in this way or sold parcels of land to peasants when they needed cash.

The reinvigoration of the Maronite church following the Council of Luwayza contributed to expanding agricultural production. The Lebanese Order of Monks, primarily comprising men from peasant backgrounds, began to enlarge their originally meager holdings through cultivation contracts, efficient organization of their collective labor, and pooling their savings and donations from the faithful. They acquired new properties from the *muqata'aji*s, who were pleased by the monks' productive activities and the educational and other services they provided. By the mid-nineteenth century the Lebanese Order owned fifty monasteries with large plots of land (Harik 1968: 112–14).

Most peasants were poor and socially and economically subordinated to the *muqata'ajis*. During the early years of Bashir II's rule, the governor of Sidon (Acre), Cezzar Ahmed Pasha (1775–1804), pressed the amir for increased tribute payments. To meet these demands, Bashir II increased the levies on the *muqata'ajis* and the peasants, confiscated the lands of rival *muqata'ajis*, and removed some of them altogether, consolidating their former holdings under his personal control. Ahmed Pasha's successor, 'Abd Allah Pasha (1818–32), also demanded higher tribute, forcing Bashir II to attempt to collect additional taxes to pay the pasha. Due to these repeated demands for extra-legal taxes, peasants lost much of their lands. By the first half of the nineteenth century about 10 percent – a high proportion by local standards – of the peasantry owned no land at all and supported themselves by sharecropping or as agricultural day laborers (Dubar & Nasr 1976: 28).

These conditions formed the context for peasant uprisings (*'ammiyyas*, or movements of the common people) in 1820 and 1821. The revolts were directed against both Amir Bashir II and his most important ally, Bashir Junblat. The Maronite bishop, Yusuf Istfan (1759–1823), played a leading role in the first revolt. He organized the peasants into village communes and had them choose a representative (*wakil*) to lead and represent each village. The Druze *muqata'ajis* blocked the collection of additional levies from Druze peasants or paid them themselves. The taxes were collected only from the Maronite peasants of Maronite *muqata'ajis* in the northern districts, who Bashir II thought lacked a leadership capable of opposing him. Therefore, although some Druze peasants and one *muqata'aji* family participated in the revolts, they primarily involved Maronite peasants in districts with Maronite *muqata'ajis*. This gave the movements a sectarian character, which was enhanced by the active participation of Maronite clergymen (Harik 1968: 208–22; Khalaf 1987: 33–35).

The 1820 and 1821 revolts challenged the *muqata'aji* monopoly on political leadership and expressed both peasant class and Maronite communal consciousness, which were sometimes mutually contradictory. The Maronite Khazin and Abillama' *muqata'ajis* opposed the revolts, but peasants in their districts participated nonetheless. The pact between the people of Bash'ala and their representative made during the second revolt is a rare expression of peasants' political voice and their capacity to articulate some surprisingly new ideas.

We the undersigned, all the natives of Bash'ala . . . have freely accepted and entrusted ourselves and our expenses to our cousin, Tannus al-Shidyaq Nasr, and whatever is required of us . . . with respect to the *'ammiyya*. His word will be final with us in all [matters] of expenses and losses . . . [W]e shall obey him in the recruitment of men . . .

This is what has been agreed upon between us and him, and he shall act according to his conscience, not favoring anyone over the other . . . Whatever he arranges as the tax, we shall accept; and if he relents in pursuing our interests, we shall hold him accountable. (Harik 1968: 213–14)

This radical departure from the previously prevailing political culture of Mount Lebanon led Ilya Harik to view the revolts as the first Lebanese expressions of the modern ideas of nationalism, the public interest, and individual rights. Harik acknowledges that some Maronite peasants understood their revolt to be directed against the privileges of the Druze *muqataʿaji*s (Harik 1968: 220–21). This communal aspect of the movements makes the dichotomy of "tradition" and "modernity" inadequate for the understanding of the 1820–21 uprisings. They were limited revolts against increased taxes, not revolutions against the social structure of Mount Lebanon. The deployment of ideas and institutions derived from the French republican tradition coexisted with communalism and sharpened tensions between Maronites and Druze (and Muslims). This undermined Lebanese national identity as much as it promoted it.

Bashir II fled Mount Lebanon in 1822 but resumed his demands for increased taxes when he returned in 1823. This led to a military clash with the Junblat family and its supporters in 1825 in which the Junblat partisans were decisively defeated and their lands distributed to supporters of Bashir II. Bashir Junblat was strangled to death by ʿAbd Allah Pasha at the request of Amir Bashir II, and his sons and other Druze notables went into exile. Bashir II's attacks on the *muqataʿaji*s and his repeated demands for additional revenues undermined the cohesion of the ruling class of Mount Lebanon and intensified conflict between Druze and Maronites that had been building since the mid-eighteenth century.

Bashir II's alliance with the 1831–40 Egyptian occupation further diminished his popularity. The Egyptians imposed a new head tax (*farda*), and despite its generally favorable attitude towards non-Muslims, the need for revenue to finance the army led it to insist on collecting the poll tax (*jizya*) from Christians and Jews, which Christians in Mount Lebanon had not previously been required to pay. In May 1840 Ibrahim Pasha ordered the Druze and Christians of Dayr al-Qamar to surrender their arms, widely understood as a precursor to conscription. Christians, Druze, sunnis and shiʿa met at Intilyas on June 8, 1840, drew up a covenant expressing their grievances, and resolved "to fight to restore their independence or die"(Khalaf 1987: 37). The revolt and the withdrawal of Ibrahim Pasha after Ottoman troops landed in Beirut with European naval support in September 1840 allowed the sons of Bashir Junblat and other Druze notables to return to Mount Lebanon and forced Bashir II into exile. To recover lands they had lost and over which they claimed ownership, the Druze *muqata'ajis* rallied Druze peasants to their banner, provoking widespread sectarian conflict that allowed the Ottoman central government to end the rule of the Shihab family in 1841.

Mount Nablus: peasants and merchants

Jabal Nablus, a predominantly Muslim region in northern Palestine, had some similarities with Mount Lebanon and Qina province in upper Egypt. It was a district of the province of Sidon whose regional economy and inland mountainous location fostered a high degree of political autonomy. In the lowlands of Palestine and Syria, an indeterminate portion of peasant lands were held as communal holdings that were redivided annually (*musha'a*). In the hills, communal holdings were less common; neither olive groves nor vineyards, which were widespread in Jabal Nablus, were communally held (Schölch 1986: 142). Commercial agriculture, a cash economy, social differentiation among the peasantry, commoditization of land, and links to markets beyond Palestine predated the Egyptian occupation (1831–40), the Ottoman Tanzimat, and Jewish colonization. Court cases in the eighteenth and nineteenth centuries indicate that, as in lower Egypt, peasants of Jabal Nablus disposed of their usufruct rights on state-administered lands as though the land was their private property (Doumani 1995: 8, 157–59).

Local merchants constituted the economic and social links among peasant producers of agricultural commodities, artisans, and local notable families. The expansion of commercial agriculture, the primary source of wealth in Jabal Nablus from the second half of the seventeenth to the twentieth century, allowed merchants based in the town of Nablus to establish their control over its agricultural hinterland (Doumani 1995: 20). The most important agricultural product of the region was olive oil, the raw material for the high-quality soap manufactured in factories in the town of Nablus and renowned from Damascus to Egypt. Peasants cultivated olive trees and other agricultural products and sold their harvest to city-based merchants. Until the 1830s most of the soap factories belonged to the notable families of the district – the Tuqans, Nimrs, Qasims, 'Abd al-Hadis, etc. From then on, merchants began to enter the lucrative soap manufacturing business.

Merchants and peasants were bound together by patron–client relations in which merchants clearly held the upper hand. These relations were the social vehicle for marketization of the economy.[4] Nabulsi merchants bought and stored goods for peasants, provided them with credit and references, and served as their hosts when peasants came to town. The commercial relationship was part of an elaborate fabric of economy, culture, and moral values.

One of the principal mechanisms that allowed the merchants to domi-nate peasants was the *salam* contract: a merchant lent a peasant money and the peasant agreed to deliver a harvest to the merchant in return for a specified price or portion of the proceeds from the sale of the crop. This arrangement left peasants in perpetual debt. Until the 1860s merchants did not usually expropriate lands of indebted peasants. Debt assured a merchant access to a peasant's crops, while the need to maintain a peasant's capacity to produce meant there was always room to renegotiate the relationship (Doumani 1995: 55–56, 140–42, 161).

Jabal Nablus was occupied by Egyptian forces led by Ibrahim Pasha in 1832. The local notables welcomed Ibrahim, and the ʿAbd al-Hadi family established its influence by becoming his principal local allies. Before the Egyptian invasion, Qasim al-Ahmad, a sub-district chief of the Nablus hinterlands and head of the Qasim family, had risen to prominence, bought a soap factory, and moved into the city. Ibrahim Pasha appointed him district officer (*mutasallim*) of Nablus but in 1834 replaced him with Sulayman ʿAbd al-Hadi. In response, Qasim al-Ahmad organized not-ables from Nablus, Jerusalem, and Hebron, who informed the Egyptians in May 1834 that they were unable to disarm and conscript the peasants and collect the head tax. Al-Ahmad then led the peasants of Jabal Nablus in a revolt against Egyptian rule. The uprising spread to Hebron, Jerusalem, and other mountain districts in what is known today as the West Bank. In July, the Egyptian army crushed the revolt, burning sixteen villages to the ground on the way to retaking Nablus. Qasim al-Ahmad lost his soap factory; 10,000 peasants were deported to Egypt; and the population was disarmed (Doumani 1995: 46, 208; Kimmerling & Migdal 1993: 7–11; Hoexter 1984: 192–93).

As in Mount Lebanon, sectarian factors played a role in the opposition to the Egyptians. Egyptian rule generally improved the status of Christians and Jews throughout greater Syria by measures such as includ-ing them in the local councils established in towns of more than two thou-sand inhabitants. Muslims and Druze felt their status was threatened, and this was expressed in sectarian conflict. During the 1834 revolt one zealous Muslim tried to mobilize the people of Nablus to join the revolt by denouncing Ibrahim Pasha as an infidel from the minaret of a mosque (Shamir 1984: 230). Peasants from the surrounding area invaded Jerusalem, attacked the Christian and Jewish populations, looted prop-erty, and raped women (Rustum 1938: 60).

Peasants and state formation in the Ottoman provinces

Peasants were hardly quiescent or isolated from politics. They resisted efforts of aspiring state builders to impose new taxes, to conscript their sons, and to tell them what to plant and to whom and at what prices to sell their harvests. The Lebanese revolts of 1820–21, the Palestinian revolt of 1834, and the Qina revolts of the 1820s indicate that peasants were not totally isolated from other sectors of society. The peasants of Mount Lebanon used new organizational techniques and ideologies as well as their existing relationships with the Maronite clergy to mobilize for rebellion. The economic and social integration of Jabal Nablus seems typical of smaller provincial towns where peasants, bedouin, and town-dwellers collaborated in producing and circulating commodities with relatively less regulation by guilds or the state. Such networks were probably mobilized in the 1834 rebellion. Similar links among peasant agriculture, rural artisanal production, and regional commercial networks in Qina were probably mobilized in the revolts of the 1820s.

The concentration of revolts in provincial towns and rural districts in the 1820s and 1830s may be due to the recent intensification of their contact with the state and their greater capacity to resist the encroachments of the early nineteenth-century state builders: Mehmed ʿAli, Ibrahim Pasha, and Bashir II. Revolts of ʿAlawi peasants in the Nusayriyya mountains in 1834 and 1835 and Druze peasants in Hawran in 1837–38 against the Egyptian occupation were part of the same pattern. The resistance of ʿAmir ʿAbd al-Qadir to the French occupation of Algeria (1830–47) was both a continuation of previous rural and tribal resistance to the extension of Ottoman state authority and a transition to a new phase of engagement with a European occupier more typical of the later nineteenth century (Burke 1991: 28).

The presence of an occupation army, whether Egyptian or French, introduces the question of incipient nationalism. Some have characterized ʿAbd al-Qadir's resistance to France, the Lebanese revolts of 1820–21, and the 1834 Palestinian revolt against the Egyptian occupation as the first steps towards self-conscious nationhood (Ruedy 1992; Harik 1968; Kimmerling & Migdal 1993). This is as improbable as the view that peasants were politically passive. The use of ideas and institutions derived from the Enlightenment and the French Revolution by Maronite peasants of Mount Lebanon to justify and organize their revolts is distinctive, yet far from an assertion of Lebanese nationhood. The Palestinian revolt of 1834 was concentrated in the hill country and did not involve the major urban centers of Jaffa or Acre. ʿAbd al-Qadir's resistance to the French occupation of Algeria relied heavily on his leadership of the Qadiriyya sufi order and was only effective in what is today western Algeria; resistance to the French in eastern Algeria was led by al-Hajj Ahmad.

Artisanal production in major cities

Textiles and apparel constituted the leading sector of production in almost all early modern Ottoman towns and cities; the other main manufacturing sectors were food, leather, and construction. Typically a male artisan owned his own shop and tools, bought raw materials, and produced and sold commodities on demand using his own labor, that of family members, and a small number of journeymen or apprentices. Capital investment was generally low. Exceptions to this pattern of small-scale production included the Cairo manufacturers of licorice, beer, starch, wax candles, and sugar, leather tanners, casters, dyers, carpet weavers, and bottle makers, who employed an average of 12.5 persons per workshop. These activities engaged only 14.5 percent of the workforce (Raymond 1973–74: 223). Wealthy Aleppine merchants sometimes organized production of commodities, especially textiles, by supplying working capital, cloth, and other materials, coordinating the different elements of the manufacturing process, and marketing the finished products (Marcus 1989: 164–65, 168). This was not common in Cairo despite the great wealth of its long-distance merchants, perhaps because they could make bigger profits by purveying luxury products (Raymond 1973–74: 213–14, 225).

Guild monopolies, like other practices and structures, emerged through specific historical circumstances and processes and were not a fixed characteristic of the guild system. In the seventeenth century entry into crafts and membership in guilds were loosely regulated. Around 1750 Istanbul guilds cooperated with the state to establish a certification process for those who wanted to practice a craft or open a retail shop. A similar process seems to have occurred earlier in Cairo, perhaps at the end of the seventeenth century. By the end of the eighteenth century a certificate (*gedik* – the term originally applied only to the tools necessary for a craft, not the right to practice it) was required to engage in most urban occupations in Istanbul and other Ottoman cities (Raymond 1973–74: 271, 549–50; Akarli 1985–86: 223; Marcus 1989: 178–79; Rafeq 1991: 503; Faroqhi 1994: 588–89; Quataert 1994a: 895). Around 1805, perhaps motivated by the opening of many new weaving workshops to produce cloth for the market void created by the withdrawal of French textiles from the Middle East during the Napoleonic Wars, the Ottoman government and textile guilds in cities in Anatolia and Syria agreed to establish a central location in each town for polishing cloth where the state would tax and stamp it. Only cloth bearing this stamp could be sold legally until this system was abandoned in 1878 (Quataert 1994b: 7; Quataert 1994a: 895; Vatter 1995: 41–42).

The proliferation of *gediks* and the tighter regulation of textile production are examples of a general trend towards increased state control of guilds from the mid-eighteenth century on, most clearly evident in Egypt under Mehmed 'Ali Pasha. In 1800 the French occupation force in Cairo created the post of director of crafts (*mudir al-hiraf*) – a government employee who supervised the guilds but was not organically connected to them (Raymond 1973–74: 558). Expanding on this French initiative, Mehmed 'Ali's regime was more actively interventionist than had previously been the norm in the internal regulations of the guilds. In 1829 the Pasha issued a decree regulating prices and commercial practices (*La'ihat al-ihtisab*). Like the Ottoman sultan, he used the guilds to recruit labor for state construction projects. As state intervention increased, the power of the guild masters over their members grew, and they assumed more administrative functions. Wealth began to be more concentrated among certain guild members, not always the master, from the mid-eighteenth century on, and guilds offered less mutual assistance to their members (Ghazaleh 1999). There are no detailed studies of guilds in cities other than Cairo for the late eighteenth and early nineteenth centuries, so developments there can only suggest a possible general pattern.

Guilds never exercised absolute control over the quality of commodities or techniques of production. The guild structure was sufficiently flexible to accommodate new crafts and production processes (Raymond 1973–74: 225, 584–85); nor did guilds block expansion of production in the face of competition from European manufactured goods. There may have been some decline in the manufacturing output of males organized in guilds in the nineteenth century. But manufacturing activity by women concentrated in rural areas and urban areas outside the framework of the guilds flourished. Weaving of cotton and mohair cloth, wool spinning, silk reeling, shoemaking, and carpet making expanded in Salonica and the Macedonian countryside, western Anatolia, north central Anatolia, southeast Anatolia, and northern Syria (Quataert 1991a; Quataert 1994b).

Nablus: soap making in a regional town

The Nablus soap-making industry offers a sharp contrast to the guild-based production systems in major cities such as Istanbul, Cairo, Damascus, and Aleppo. In the late 1820s leading local notable families began to increase their investments in the soap industry, raising capital through forming partnerships with merchants who, despite their increased their wealth and power, still sought the political protection such business alliances might provide. The soap industry continued to prosper and expand throughout the nineteenth century, with spurts of growth in the late 1830s to early 1840s and the 1860s. Unlike mercantile practice in Cairo, soap merchants provided the major share of capital investment to finance soap production, and their activities resulted in the vertical integration of the industry.

Soap making was a capital-intensive but not labor-intensive process. Peasants produced the raw material – olive oil. Bedouin supplied barilla plant ashes, which were mixed with the olive oil and cooked to make soap. They also comprised the seasonal unskilled laborers – ash pounders, oven stokers, etc. Only a small group of skilled and semi-skilled workers – fewer than fifteen per factory – were required for the production process. The soap-factory owners were organized in a guild, but not the unskilled or the craft workers. Teams of soap makers organized and led by a skilled and experienced boss (ra'is) circulated among the factories according to the workload. Factory owners did not control their labor directly, but rather through the intermediary of the boss, who managed both the workers and the production process. Workers were paid in cash and kind after each batch of soap was cooked. Soap-making jobs tended to be monopolized in families, and patronage relations were deployed to resolve disputes among the workers and between workers and factory owners (Doumani 1995: 188–201).

Three conclusions emerge from this vignette of artisanal production in a regional town. First, many important commodities, including some with a high commercial value, were produced outside the major urban centers and the framework of the guild system. Second, certain kinds of artisanal production prospered throughout the nineteenth century despite the influx of European manufactured goods from the 1820s on. Finally, the Nablus soap-making process illustrates the concrete social connections among peasants, bedouin, urban workers, and merchants that both integrated society and formed potential points of friction between sectors with different interests.

Guilds and urban politics

By the eighteenth century guilds had become an important institution of urban political life. They were often mobilized during moments of urban popular insurrection. The guilds of Istanbul artisans and shopkeepers were active in the 1730 Patrona Halil revolt that ended the centralizing efforts of the Tulip Era (Olson 1974). The Cairo guilds of butchers, fruit sellers, vegetable sellers, and grain carriers participated in the series of popular protests that erupted at the end of the eighteenth and beginning of the nineteenth centuries. Ahmad Salim al-Jazzar and Hajjaj al-Khudari, masters of the butchers' and the vegetable sellers' guilds respectively, were among the organizers of urban protest during the anarchy of the late mamluk era, the French invasion of 1798, and against the new governor installed by the sultan after the expulsion of the French in 1801. Al-Khudari and Ibn Shama – al-Jazzar's successor as master of the butchers' guild – along with some of the Muslim scholars (*ulama*) and the dean of the descendants of the Prophet (*naqib al-ashraf*), 'Umar Makram, led the Cairo uprising of May 12, 1805 that deposed the incumbent and proclaimed Mehmed 'Ali governor of Egypt. The sultan accepted this *fait accompli* the following month (Raymond 1975; Marsot 1984: 44–50). The participation of the guilds and the *'ulama'*, and the Islamic justification of the 1805 Cairo uprising are typical of early modern urban social movements (Burke 1986).

The guilds' capacity to lead urban protest led Sultan Mahmud II (1808–39) to secure their agreement when he decided to abolish the Janissary Corps in 1826. Many guild members had become Janissaries in order to avoid taxation, thus impeding the Ottoman state's ability to control the guilds and weakening the fighting capacity of the army (Bodman 1963: 65, 143; Marcus 1989: 58; McGowan 1994: 701–2, 705, 706–7). Mahmud II compensated the Istanbul guilds for their members' loss of income as Janissaries by giving master artisans and shopkeepers full control over their shops through deeds of usufruct (*gedik senedi*) and strengthening guild monopolies over their trades. In return, the guilds accepted the liquidation of the Janissary Corps (Akarli 1998: 33).

Urban social structure and income distribution

Some data about wages and the distribution of wealth in the eighteenth and early nineteenth centuries are available for Cairo and Damascus. Fragmentary information from Aleppo is consistent with that evidence. There are no quantitative data on the size of handicraft workshops, output, or wages in Anatolia until the last third of the nineteenth century (Kurmuş 1981: 85). Export–import merchants were the wealthiest and most powerful urban stratum, followed by retail merchants and artisans. Self-employed artisans earned more and had more prestige than wage workers.

In Aleppo, servants, doormen, and watchmen were the poorest wage workers and earned 1–3 piasters a month. Craft workers earned 4–6 piasters a month; assistants in retail shops, 8 piasters; and salesmen for import–export merchants, 17–20 piasters (Marcus 1989: 49, 162).

Artisans comprised over half the economically active population of seventeenth- and eighteenth-century Cairo, but their estates as recorded in the *shariʿa* court were only between 6.2 and 9.3 percent of the total value of estates recorded. Leather and food workers, except for the sugar refiners, were among the poorest artisans. Cairo artisans were economically subordinate to merchants. Their incomes declined from the late seventeenth to the late eighteenth centuries, while the incomes of merchants remained relatively stable (Raymond 1973–74: 231–32, 237).

Based on the value of estates registered in the Cairo and Damascus *shariʿa* courts, an index measuring inequality in the distribution of wealth has been calculated for several points in the seventeenth and eighteenth centuries. (The standard social science measurement is the Gini coefficient of inequality. On a scale of 0.0 to 1.0, 0 indicates equal distribution of wealth, while 1 means concentration of all wealth in the hands of a single individual. The higher the number, the greater the inequality.) Distribution of wealth was very unequal. The Gini coefficient for men in Damascus in 1700 was 0.75. Women had less wealth but were considerably more equal than men, with a Gini coefficient of 0.50 (Establet & Pascual 1994: 124). Between 1624 and 1798 Cairo's Gini coefficient fluctuated between 0.68 and 0.81 and averaged 0.76. Disparities of wealth increased during periods of crisis and declined somewhat in periods of prosperity (Raymond 1973–74: 375–76, tables 7 and 8 following 382).

In the early nineteenth century there was also a high degree of concentration of wealth in Cairo (Ghazaleh 1999: 76–86). Artisans in the leather sector remained the poorest, followed in ascending order by perfumers, construction crafts, services, textiles, food, retail, wood, masters of all guilds, metals, long-distance merchants, and tobacconists. The real value of the legacies of textile workers, the "average artisans *par excellence*," declined steadily from the late seventeenth century to 1849. Relative to other crafts, the legacies of textile artisans increased in the late eighteenth century and declined in the early nineteenth century because of the influx of European manufactured cloth and the monopoly policies of Mehmed ʿAli. Food workers' legacies also declined over time, but this cannot be attributed to competition from Europe. The wealth of metal workers increased steadily in both relative and absolute terms, especially during the period 1799–1849, perhaps due to the demand for their labor in Egypt's new factories.

Towards industrialization?

Industrial manufacturing was introduced to the Middle East as part of the drive to establish modern armies and extend the power of states.

Sultans Abdülhamid I (1774–89) and Selim III (1789–1807) brought European advisors to Istanbul to establish workshops to produce cannons, rifles, bombs, saltpeter, and gunpowder. The most technically advanced of these enterprises, the gunpowder works on the Sea of Marmara, used water power; the others used animal power (Shaw 1971: 10, 139–44). Selim III also initiated a woolen mill and a paper factory in the Istanbul area. Further industrial innovation was inhibited by the conservative forces that deposed him in 1807. Mahmud II waited until after he destroyed the Janissary corps in 1826 before establishing a spinning mill, a fez-making factory, a wool-weaving mill, a sawmill, and a copper sheet-rolling mill and converting the cannon foundry and musket works to steam power in the late 1830s. The state owned and managed these enterprises, and the army and the state were the principal consumers of their output (Clark 1974: 66). Guild artisans were recruited to work in them by paying them high wages and allowing them to continue to work in their own shops in their free time. Before being employed they took an examination to determine that they produced high-quality work (Shaw 1971: 140).

As in the arena of fiscal policy, Mehmed ʿAli adopted and extended these innovations with greater success than his nominal sovereigns. In 1815 he built a gunpowder factory on Roda Island in Cairo. Shortly thereafter he established a munitions foundry in the Cairo citadel, employing 400 men to produce high-quality cannons, swords, and muskets. The Pasha ordered new shipyards constructed at Cairo's port of Bulaq and Alexandria in 1829; the latter employed 4,000 workers who built twenty-two naval vessels (Owen 1981a: 71; Marsot 1984: 165). Other enterprises produced commodities with dual military–civilian uses: a soap factory, a fez factory, weaving mills for cotton, jute, linen, and silk, a textile bleaching and printing works, sugar refineries, rice mills, indigo works, tanneries, and a printing press. Cotton weaving was the leading sector of this effort. By the 1830s there were some thirty cotton mills employing 12,000–15,000 workers; at least three used steam power (Owen 1981a: 70).

Egyptian nationalist historians argue that there were a total of 180,000–260,000 workers in all Mehmed ʿAli's enterprises, some 4–5 percent of the population (Fahmy 1954: 84–85; Marsot 1984: 181). More cautiously, Roger Owen suggests that during the high point of operations in the 1830s there were only 30,000–40,000 workers (Owen 1981a: 72). Unlike in Selim III's Istanbul factories, many of the workers were peasants forcibly recruited from their villages. Their arms were tattooed with the names of their factories to enable them to be captured should they desert (Fahmy 1998: 162). Wages, generous to begin with, were just adequate for subsistence by 1832–33. Hours were long and discipline was harsh. In many cases workers sabotaged production, stole the products, and set the mills on fire (Owen 1969: 45).

No guilds operated in Mehmed ʿAli's factories, and it is unclear whether any of the workers were previously guild members. Except for textile weaving, most of the enterprises were new activities for which no guilds existed. But neither the textile guilds nor hand-loom weaving were eliminated by the Pasha's efforts to monopolize this sector.

In contrast to these state-led initiatives, European entrepreneurs established silk-reeling mills powered by water and then later steam in Bursa, Izmir, Edirne, and Salonica. The first such mills were set up in Bursa in 1838 and Salonica in 1839. The workers – typically unmarried non-Muslim girls from peasant or poor urban families – were engaged seasonally to produce silk thread for export to Europe. The factories were managed by European men who recruited French women reelers to teach the locals and serve as forewomen. By 1845 Salonica had nearly 2,000 silk-mill workers out of a population of 70,000 (Quataert 1991a; Quataert 1994b: 116–32). There were no guilds in the mechanized silk-reeling industry, even though silk spinning and weaving were well-established Ottoman enterprises.

The silk spinning and weaving industry in Mount Lebanon was similar to that of Anatolia and Rumelia. The first French-owned hand-reeling mill was established in Kraye in 1810, followed by several others in the 1830s. Around 1840, the first mechanized silk-reeling mill was established by Antoine-Fortuné Portalis in the village of Btater (Labaki 1983: 434; Khater 1996: 326).

Debate over the significance of these efforts is centered on Egypt, the site of the most extensive early-nineteenth-century manufacturing initiatives. Historians with a nationalist or third-worldist outlook portray this development as an "industrial revolution" (Fahmy 1954; Marsot 1984).[5] Others note that Mehmed ʿAli's factories were powered primarily by animals, by the workers themselves, and by a total of no more than seven or eight steam engines. By contrast, there were at least 10,000 steam engines and 2,000 power looms in England in 1822. Egypt had no class of bourgeois entrepreneurs, no "free" working class, and no free market. Most of the Egyptian factories as well as the state-owned enterprises in Anatolia failed by the late 1840s and 1850s, leaving an uncertain legacy when industrial development resumed in the 1860s. The nationalist tradition attributes this collapse to British intervention and the imposition of free trade through the 1838 Anglo-Ottoman Commercial Convention. Certainly, British naval power was a relevant factor. Others point out that Egypt had a small local market and no sources of fuel.

Mehmed 'Ali's factories relied heavily on foreign managerial and technical expertise. The administrative capacity of the Egyptian state, though substantially greater than in the eighteenth century, was still limited (Owen 1981a: 72, 308 fn. 85).

This debate is partly about whether Egypt, based on its own indigenous cultural, political, and economic resources, would have followed the modern European trajectory of development, in which the central institutions are the capitalist market and the nation-state. Paradoxically, nationalist historians agree with their mainly European and American interlocutors that this is the appropriate measure of progress, development, and modernity. If we do not suppose that there is only one path to the modern world, then these early industrial efforts can be assessed in different terms. Autocratic state builders – Sultan Mahmud II, Amir Bashir II, and Mehmed 'Ali Pasha – seeking to compete with each other and with Europe, did see European technology and industry as a model to be emulated. But they could not replicate the trajectory of textile-based industrial development pioneered by England. Extensive coal deposits and a global empire provided fuel, capital, raw materials, and markets for English industrial development and military preeminence. Egypt had no coal, and its regional empire was weak and short lived. Its textiles were unable to compete with England's goods in the global market, and it had no independent capacity to develop the iron and steel industries that led the second stage of England's industrial revolution and extended its industrial and military lead over potential competitors. These circumstances do not describe the deficiencies of Egypt compared to England but the conditions of global capitalist development in the early and mid-nineteenth century.

The recruitment and mobilization of peasants and urban artisans was essential for the late-eighteenth- and early-nineteenth-century state building, military expansion, and economic development projects of Sultan Mahmud II, Amir Bashir II, and Mehmed 'Ali Pasha. These rulers were neither democrats nor nationalists and often used coercive measures to achieve their goals. Coercion continued and in some respects increased during the subsequent, more self-conscious period of elite-led "reform" – the Tanzimat era. It is not surprising that subalterns resisted or evaded demands aimed at securing the interests of ruling elites. This should not lead us to idealize life and work before this period. Life was difficult, and incomes were barely adequate for most working people. Pre-capitalist production processes continued to flourish in the late eighteenth and early nineteenth centuries, and some sectors underwent considerable growth without any connection to the expansion of trade with Europe. Towards the end of the period, new techniques and products – primarily mechanized silk reeling in Anatolia, Salonica, and Mount Lebanon and the cultivation of long-staple cotton in Egypt – were introduced which had a very substantial long-term impact on the reformation of economies, societies, gender relations, and political regimes.

2 Ottoman reform and European imperialism, 1839–1907

The mid-nineteenth-century legal, administrative, and fiscal reforms known as the Tanzimat are widely considered the beginning of the modern period, inspired by the ideas of secularism and progress promoted by the French revolution (Lewis 1961; Davison 1963; Berkes 1964; Shaw & Shaw 1976–77). The salient politico-legal markers of the Tanzimat era are the 1839 Gülhane Edict (*Hatt-ı Şerif*), the 1856 Reform Decree (*Islahat Fermanı*), and the 1876 constitution, which was abrogated in 1878 by Sultan Abdülhamid II (1876–1909). The Tanzimat decrees abolished tax farming, introduced military conscription, and promised legal equality for all the sultan's subjects regardless of their religious community. They also marked the adoption of a European-influenced discourse of "reform" that justified practices elites hoped would strengthen the Ottoman state.

The Tanzimat decrees discursively authorized the central categories of a modern political economy: "citizens," the constituent elements of nation-states; and "the economy" as an abstract entity distinct from the state and subject to its own rules. The Gülhane Edict's promise of "perfect security to all the populations of our Empire in their lives, their honor, and their properties" resonates with phrases of John Locke and Thomas Jefferson, though its origin as a royal decree is in tension with the spirit of the words (Hurewitz 1975: I, 270–71). The 1856 Reform Decree deems the sultan's subjects to be "united to each other by the cordial ties of patriotism," and proclaims freedom of religion and equality of Muslims and non-Muslims in admission to governmental schools, treatment before the courts, military service, and taxation. It also orders that "everything that can impede commerce or agriculture shall be abolished. To accomplish these objects means shall be sought to profit by the science, the art, and the funds of Europe" (Hurewitz 1975: I, 315, 318). These edicts became foundational documents legitimizing the subsequent elaboration of the categories of "the economy" and "citizens."

Despite these discursive ruptures, the Tanzimat era is also an extension of earlier elite efforts to recentralize and enhance the capacities of the

Ottoman state. Fiscal and military reforms were introduced in the Tulip Period (1718–30) and again in the 1790s. These initiatives were successfully opposed by a coalition of regional notables, conservative scholars of religion (*ülema*), the Janissary Corps, and the Bektaşi *sufi* order. Sultan Mahmud II's abolition of the Janissary Corps in 1826 removed the most formidable institutional barrier to modernizing the army and liberalizing the economy. He also introduced a census and revoked all remaining rural military holdings (*timars*) in 1831, enabling more efficient tax collection.

The Tanzimat was also shaped by military and diplomatic demands of the moment. The Ottomans needed British support for ousting the Egyptian army from greater Syria and in the negotiations for the Treaty of Paris following the Crimean War. In exchange for their support for the territorial integrity of the Ottoman Empire from 1840 to 1878, British diplomats demanded public commitments to uphold the legal equality of Christians and Jews. The same European pressures that contributed to the 1839 Gülhane Edict also introduced a regime of free trade and intensified economic linkages between Europe and the Middle East.

The 1838 Anglo-Ottoman Commercial Convention, whose terms were subsequently endorsed by other European powers, ended all local monopolies and protectionist trade practices, imposed a low uniform tariff of 5 percent on Ottoman imports, and established special courts to adjudicate commercial disputes involving Europeans. The 1840 and 1841 Treaties of London confirmed the expulsion of Mehmed ʿAli's army from greater Syria, extended free trade to Egypt, and limited the size of the Egyptian army to 18,000. These measures delivered the final blow to the Pasha's industrial program by reducing the size of the primary market for products of his new factories and disallowing the protectionist measures necessary to sustain import-substitution industrialization. Trade between Europe and the Middle East was facilitated by new communications links: steamship service to eastern Mediterranean ports from 1835; steamboat navigation on the Tigris River from 1859; and the opening of the Suez Canal in 1869.

Long-term economic trends from 1839 to 1907 encompass three phases. The first, which substantially overlaps with the Tanzimat era, is the mid-Victorian expansion of 1838–73, when demand for Middle Eastern agricultural products increased sharply. Cotton and silk were the most important Middle Eastern exports throughout the nineteenth century. Egyptian long-staple cotton, first exported in 1823, commanded a premium because of its suitability to mechanical looms and luxurious fiber (Owen 1969: 34). Cereals, valonia (for tanning leather), madder and yellow berries (for dyes), and opium were also leading commodities. In the late nineteenth and early twentieth centuries, raisins, figs, and tobacco became increasingly important. As European trade with the Ottoman Empire grew, Britain replaced France as the dominant European trade partner. Between 1835 and 1850 the declared value of British exports to the eastern Mediterranean more than doubled; manufactured cotton goods comprised as much as 75 percent of the total (Owen 1981a: 85). The Ottoman Empire became Britain's second-largest export market. European direct investment contributed to the expansion of cultivation and early manufacturing stages of silk, cotton, and sugar in Lebanon, Egypt, and Anatolia. In 1852 European banks began offering commercial loans to the Ottoman central government and the increasingly autonomous provinces of Egypt and Tunisia.

During the recessionary phase of 1873–96, known as the "Great Depression," prices of agricultural commodities – the principal Middle Eastern exports – declined, and rates of economic growth in several countries diminished. "Both the rapid decline in world wheat prices and the establishment of European control over Ottoman finances were products of the same conjuncture, the post-1873 Depression" (Pamuk 1984: 116–18). The end of the mid-Victorian boom was accompanied by state bankruptcies and imposition of European financial control over Tunisia through the International Financial Commission in 1869, Egypt through the Caisse de la Dette Publique in 1876, and the Ottoman central government through the Public Debt Commission in 1881. These debt-collecting institutions consolidated "the economy" as a modern category separate from politics and dominated by Europe.

Financial domination followed by political and military interventions signaled the era of the "new imperialism" – an extension of the accelerated circulation of European commodities, capital, and people during the mid-Victorian boom and an intensification of European economic, military, and political domination over large parts of Africa and Asia in the last quarter of the nineteenth century involving increasing numbers of working people who were relatively unaffected by earlier commercial and financial interactions.[1] The loss of economic and then political independence was in part the consequence of intensified financial and commercial relations that undermined the stability of the old order as the mid-Victorian boom collapsed. The most salient Middle Eastern manifestations of the advent of the new imperialism were the French occupation of Tunisia in 1881 and the British occupations of Cyprus in 1878 and Egypt in 1882. In addition, during 1878–82 the European powers supported the secession of Bosnia, Herzegovina, and Bulgaria from the Ottoman Empire, while Russia occupied Kars and Ardahan.

The third phase of this period is the resumption of economic expansion during 1896–1913, interrupted by the economic crisis of 1906–08: a

London-centered recession exacerbated by a collapse in the price of silver (the basis of the Ottoman currency) in relation to gold (the standard for British pounds). That crisis influenced the development of the Egyptian nationalist movement and the 1908 Young Turk revolution, the markers of the beginning of the next period.

Social transformations related to economic ties with Europe were limited in time and space and not necessarily the primary motive force of social and economic developments or changes in the lives of workers and peasants. Some inland regions, such as Mosul, felt the impact of the world capitalist market only faintly and indirectly (Shields 1991). In its diverse local economy, winter grains constituted more than half of all agricultural production, but rice, tobacco, sesame, cotton, and fruits and vegetables were also grown. No large estates producing crops for export developed. The leather-tanning and cotton-weaving crafts continued to prosper. Indian and British machine-spun yarns were sometimes imported, but as a supplement to local hand-spun yarn. Mosul leathers and cottons were sold throughout a 500-mile radius in regions located in contemporary Iraq, Iran, Turkey, and Syria. Trade with Europe was secondary to local and regional trade. In other inland regions such as Transjordan, the extension of railway lines facilitated the cultivation and export of commercial crops and the settlement of bedouin (Rogan 1999). However, social changes linked to the impact of the world market in Transjordan were less substantial and of less regional significance than those in the port cities of Salonica, Istanbul, Izmir, Beirut, Alexandria, Tunis, Algiers, and their hinterlands.

Sectarian conflict and economic competition in greater Syria

Free trade and the proclamation of the legal equality of all Ottoman subjects widened the economic gap between Muslims and non-Muslims. Non-Muslim minorities became more firmly entrenched as intermediaries between European capital and Muslim merchants, craftsmen, peasants, and large landowners, while Europeans intervened in Ottoman affairs under the pretext of "defending Christian rights." From 1840 on, the relatively tolerant pattern of intercommunal relations was disrupted with increasingly violent consequences, reaching a crescendo with the ethnic cleansing of Armenians and Greeks from Anatolia in 1915–23.

A common assumption of the contemporary reports of European diplomats, merchants, and missionaries, subsequently accepted by many Orientalist scholars and more recently by proponents of the "conflict of civilizations" thesis, is that Muslims were always innately hostile towards non-Muslims.[2] Accordingly, they argued that in the mid-nineteenth century this primordial hostility was aggravated by the Tanzimat edicts and new Christian practices such as ringing church bells and displaying crosses in public processions. Some Muslims did regard these practices as provocations, and in some cases they were so intended. But economic competition and the sense that ordinary Muslims fared badly as the Ottoman Empire was integrated into an economic order dominated by Christian Europe and its local allies were also factors in the sectarian violence of the second half of the nineteenth and early twentieth centuries.

Aleppo had a history of religious toleration and economic collaboration among its several religious communities (Masters 1990). In October 1850 a demonstration against conscription developed into a riot. A Muslim crowd comprised mainly of bedouins, Turkmens, and Kurds from the eastern part of the city attacked a Uniate Christian neighborhood outside the city walls, massacred Christians, burned churches, and looted property – the first instance of Muslim violence against non-Muslims in Aleppo in Ottoman times. The rioters also demanded abolition of the head tax (*farda*, Ar.; *ferde*, Tur.) first imposed by the Egyptians.

The import of these events is best explained in the context of the city's economic decline. The head tax was less equitable than previous forms of collective taxation by city quarter or guild and fell disproportionately on less well-to-do strata. With the abolition of the Janissary Corps, former Janissaries, many of whom were guild members, lost their tax exemptions and military pay. While textile guilds persisted and found markets for their products, many service guilds disappeared. The guilds of the eastern quarters, where the caravanning and animal-products trades were concentrated, were among those most negatively affected. Thus, there was a general recession in the city which especially harmed Muslim residents of the eastern quarters of Aleppo, the main force in the riot against the Uniate Christians. Their guilds were dissolving, and they perceived themselves to be unfairly taxed while Uniate Christian merchants protected by European diplomats were prospering. Unlike the previous norm of religiously mixed guilds, segregation was increasing. These circumstances suggest that economic grievances are very likely to have been a substantial motivation of the 1850 riot.

In Mount Lebanon communal tensions, already evident in the 1820s and 1840s, erupted into civil war in the spring of 1860. The arrival of Lebanese Christian refugees in Damascus enhanced communal tensions there. The result was a large-scale Muslim attack on the Christians of the inner city on July 9, 1860 in which some 2,000 were killed.[3]

Antagonism between the various religious communities in Damascus was greatly exacerbated by "the growing gap between the rich and the poor" and competition between Christian and Muslim hand-loom textile weavers (Fawaz 1994: 100). In 1859 there were 3,436 silk looms owned by Christians, nearly 3,000 of which were destroyed in the riot. By 1864 the looms were reestablished, but over 2,000 of the 3,156 looms were Muslim owned. One explanation for the greater prosperity of the Christian hand-loom weavers is that from the 1830s some weavers began to use imported English cotton yarns rather than local hand-spun thread. Lack of credit or access to foreign exchange may have limited Muslim weavers' access to imported yarn. Weavers in the Maydan quarter did not have such difficulty because merchants of the district sold grain to Europe and could supply them with foreign currency. There were no Christian weavers in the Maydan, and its Christian residents were not attacked (Schilcher 1985: 97).

Hand-loom weavers resented the introduction of mechanical looms, and Christian initiatives in this arena lent the issue a sectarian character. ʿAbd Allah Bulad, a Christian protégé of France, imported three jacquard looms to Damascus which were destroyed in the 1860 riots. The ten jacquard looms functioning in 1860 in Dayr al-Qamar – the stronghold of Maronite power and wealth in Lebanon – were reduced to one in 1863, probably also as a result of communal conflict (Rafeq 1983: 429; Maoz 1968: 232; and Owen 1981a: 169 also note economic motives for communal conflict in Lebanon).

Throughout greater Syria, Muslims had grievances against Christians connected to European political, economic, and missionary activity. In the cases above and other less prominent ones, such as the anti-Christian riot in Nablus in 1856, Muslim anger was directed at Christians, specific Christian sects, or Christian neighborhoods, but usually not at Jews. Muslim–Jewish relations, while not problem free, remained good (Maoz 1968: 205–09, 226–28, 238). The stability of Muslim–Jewish relations strengthens the argument that intensified Muslim–Christian (in Lebanon, Druze–Maronite) conflict was not caused by primordial Muslim antipathy toward non-Muslims or blind resentment over the improved status of non-Muslims stipulated in the Tanzimat edicts, but by grievances of small merchants, craftsmen, and transport and service workers who fared poorly as the Ottoman Empire was integrated into the world capitalist market.

Commercial agriculture, large estates, and peasant family farms

Liberal economists view nineteenth-century changes in the agrarian regime as a linear-progressive response to the challenge of an industrializing and expanding capitalist Europe in which communal forms of land tenure were replaced by private ownership and subsistence farming gave way to production for the market. The orthodox Marxist approach is structurally similar, though it is more attentive to the negative consequences for workers and peasants (Issawi 1982: 4; Issawi 1988: 9, 269–89; Smilianskaya 1966; Smilianskaya 1988). Both these interpretations are built on the faulty premises that Middle Eastern economies were stagnant in the eighteenth century and that production for markets was rare. Michael Gilsenan's study of the Akkar district of northern Lebanon suggests that the highly uneven development of capitalist agriculture created new forms of noneconomic subordination with many regional variations. However, for reasons given in chapter 1, I prefer the indigenous Lebanese terms – *iqtaʿ* system, tax farming (*iltizam*), and sharecropping – over Gilsenan's loose use of the category of feudalism.[4]

Feudality arises . . . not as integral to some supposed "traditional" Akkari society, but as a product of a particular political and economic articulation with the growing power of Europe and of the capitalist world system in the nineteenth and twentieth centuries . . . it is therefore a modern and in this form peripheral phenomenon made possible in its full development by factors transforming society in the area as a whole throughout this period. (Gilsenan 1984: 452)

Late-developing serfdom in Wallachia and Moldavia

Where export-oriented, large estates were established in the eighteenth century, they were expanded and advanced under the mid-nineteenth-century free-trade regime, and conditions of peasants deteriorated. The Romanian principalities of Wallachia and Moldavia, which were ruled indirectly by the Ottoman Empire through *hospodars* drawn from the Phanariot Greek mercantile oligarchy, exemplify this trajectory. In the eighteenth century the local notables (*boyars*) became absentee landlords and imposed a particularly harsh, late-developing serfdom on the peasants who leased their lands. In contrast to the traditional norm of three days annual labor service to the village headman, peasants now owed the *boyars* labor service of twenty-four to thirty-six days annually in Wallachia and over fifty days in Moldavia in addition to rent and taxes. By the late eighteenth century Romanian grain was being exported to Istanbul and foreign ports. The 1829 Treaty of Adrianople, which set the terms for Greek independence and the autonomy of Serbia and the Romanian principalities, also ended the Ottoman government's preemptive right to purchase Romanian grain. Production and exports increased dramatically. From 1830 to 1848 acreage of corn and wheat increased three to six times, as conditions of the peasants deteriorated. The

Organic Regulations adopted as stipulated by the Treaty of Adrianople recognized the *boyars* as legal owners of the land, not merely village headmen, and increased peasant labor service to between fifty-six and sixty days annually. The *boyar* leaders of the nationalist uprising of 1848 were afraid to mobilize peasants, and this was one of the reasons for its failure. After the principalities became unified and virtually independent in 1859, 4 percent of the landowners held over 50 percent of the land. This was in sharp contrast to other Balkan lands, where the legacy of direct Ottoman rule led to more equitable distribution of agricultural lands (Stavrianos 1958: 341–44, 349–55; Shaw & Shaw 1976–77: II, 135; Jelavich 1983: I, 267–74; Quataert 1994a: 866; Todorova 1996: 60–61).

The 1858 land laws

The linear-progressivist account of agrarian development argues that the Ottoman and Egyptian land laws of 1858 legalized private property in agricultural land and were critical to the development of export-oriented estates (Gerber 1987). The more immediate (and probably intended) effects of these laws were to reassert the ownership rights of the state over nominally state-administered lands (*miri*), which had been eroded by tax farming (*iltizam* and *malikâne*), facilitate tax collection, and reinforce patriarchal authority (Baer 1969b; Karpat 1968: 86; Cuno 1992: 189–97; Quataert 1994a: 856–61). Both laws required that cultivation rights be registered by title deed and placed land in the hands of those able to cultivate it and pay the tax. These measures did ultimately contribute to consolidating property rights, but with differential consequences. In Anatolia and parts of Rumelia, consistent with historic Ottoman policy, the law consolidated the predominance of peasant family farms. By disallowing collective forms of tenure (*musha'a* in greater Syria and *dira* in the northern Arabian Peninsula and lower Iraq) the same law facilitated large estate formation in the Fertile Crescent. The Egyptian law promoted large estates by disqualifying the claims of most peasants who lost lands during the rule of Mehmed 'Ali and recognizing the privileged estates established after the late 1830s as private property. During the expansionary phases of 1838–73 and 1896–1913, formation of new export-oriented estates was stimulated by European demand and firmer recognition of private property rights in land. But large estates and private property in agricultural land were not an automatic response to the European market or the consequence of legal fiat. They were also the outcome of local processes.

Cotton and the formation of large estates in Egypt and Çukurova

In Egypt, the breakdown of the monopoly system and the decline of agricultural exports during the global economic crisis of 1836–37 impelled
Mehmed ʿAli to raise revenue by granting lands to his family, military officers, and others in return for advance payment of taxes. By 1844–48 the
combination of lands granted to military and civilian officials (ʿuhdas),
tax-free grants of uncultivated lands (ibʿadiyya), and estates given to
members of the royal family (jifliks) comprised 53 percent of the surveyed
land of Egypt and two-thirds to three-quarters of the most fertile, best
irrigated cotton-growing lands of the Nile Delta (Cuno 1992: 163–64;
Richards 1987: 220–21; Owen 1981a: 73– 74; Owen 1969: 61). ʿAbbas
Pasha (1850–54) abolished the ʿuhdas, but many peasants lost their usufruct rights because they could not pay the land tax and fled their villages.
In 1854 the government differentiated peasant lands (kharajiyya) from
the privileged estates (ʿushuriyya). The 1858 land law recognized these
privileged estates as private property.

During the American Civil War of 1861–65 the northern blockade of
the Confederate states prevented their cotton from reaching British
markets. The resulting boom in the cultivation and export of Egyptian
cotton transformed it from one of several export crops to the overwhelmingly dominant factor in the economy and the decisive factor integrating
Egypt into the world capitalist market (Owen 1969: 81). Khedive Ismaʿil
(1863–79) contracted several new foreign loans during the cotton boom.
When American cotton returned to the market, cotton prices, exports,
and tax revenues declined, creating a state fiscal crisis. To repay the
foreign debt, Ismaʿil raised taxes; by 1868 peasants paid 70 percent more
land tax than in 1865 (Richards 1987: 233). The 1871 Exchange Law
(muqabala) gave holders of privileged estate lands (kharajiyya) who paid
six years' tax in advance a perpetual 50 percent tax reduction. Few peasants benefited from this law, which effectively further concentrated agricultural holdings. By the early 1900s about half the agricultural land of
lower Egypt was held in estates of 50 *faddans* or more, considered "large"
by Egyptian standards, and cotton was grown on 45 percent of the cultivated area. Only 20–25 percent of all agricultural land continued to be
exploited by peasant households, and they were concentrated in upper
Egypt, where perennial irrigation did not arrive until after the construction of the first Aswan Dam in 1902 (Owen 1981b: 523–25; Richards
1987: 229–30; Richards 1982: 58–69). Thus, from 1840 until the enactment of the 1912 law banning seizure of lands of those who held 5 *faddans*
or less for nonpayment of debts, cotton cultivation expanded while
Egyptian peasants lost their lands through seizure by Mehmed ʿAli, flight

to escape conscription, corvée, or taxation, and foreclosure for inability to pay taxes or debts.

Large landowners were well positioned to benefit from the cotton boom. In the 1850s they had begun to organize *'izba*s – estates where peasants were given a dwelling and a small plot of land to grow subsistence crops in exchange for labor service on the landlord's cotton or other cash crops. The subsistence plot was usually cultivated on a sharecropping basis, but sometimes the peasants paid rent. On some *'izba*s, resident peasants, known as *tamaliyya* workers, owed a certain number of days of labor service to the landlord; on others the landlord's estate was cultivated by sharecropping; in a few case peasants received wages. At harvest or irrigation canal-cleaning time, additional migrant daily wage laborers (*'ummal al-tarahil*) were employed. Their situation was, and remains, the worst among the peasants (Toth 1999). Most large holdings were operated by the *'izba* system; a minority were rented out to peasants or intermediaries for cash.

Judith Tucker argues that *'izba*s promoted a gendered division of labor. Women typically tended peasant family plots, receiving no wages or compensation in kind for their work. Men cultivated the landlord's crops for cash or shares. Thus, women's labor was relegated to the private sector and devalued, while men's social labor had a market value. Reviewing Tucker's evidence, Cuno concluded it is insufficient to prove that peasant women's status declined in nineteenth-century Egypt and that her argument is inappropriately based on a paradigm derived from studies of middle-class women in the West (Tucker 1985: 43; Cuno 1988b). No other studies have been done on nineteenth-century peasant women in Egypt or elsewhere, leaving questions about the effects of commercial agriculture on gender relations unresolved.

In Egypt, the *'izba* system is commonly considered a form of feudalism.[5] Many forms of extra-economic relations of coercion and deference persisted on *'izba*s. But extraction of surplus was based on private ownership of the means of production, production of commodities for a market, commodification of labor, rational calculation of profits, a tendency toward capital accumulation, and bureaucratically supervised large-scale enterprises. Therefore, *'izba*s can be considered a form of "backward colonial capitalism" (Abdel-Malek 1969: 112; Owen 1981b: 537; Richards 1982: 65).

One motive for establishing *'izba*s was the need to mobilize labor in conditions of scarcity (Alleaume 1999: 341–44). In Anatolia, however, labor scarcity allowed peasant families to retain control of most of the land. Therefore, two additional factors must be added: state policy and the technical requirements of cotton growing. In contrast to Ottoman state policy, from 1840 to 1952 the Egyptian state was biased towards large landowners and came to be dominated by them (al-Disuqi 1975). Cotton requires large inputs of water, fertilizer, and seasonal labor as well as the capacity to keep a crop in the ground for seven months without an income. These conditions favored large landowners with access to capital and credit over peasants.

The most important site of large estates in Anatolia, the Çukurova plain on the southeast coast, was also a cotton-growing region. Because it was populated mainly by nomadic *yörük* tribes until the mid-nineteenth century, much of the land was legally waste land (*mevat*). Cultivation began after the state established control over the territory and drained the delta in the early 1870s. The high quality of the land, proximity to the sea, and, towards the end of the century, a good rail link encouraged entrepreneurs to buy land from the Ottoman state and develop cotton plantations. The social cost of establishing private property rights was low because there were no previous claims on cultivation rights. Sultan Abdülhamid II established large royal estates here as well. To alleviate the labor shortage, seasonal migrants were imported. During the economic expansion of 1896–1913 the Çukurova plain became a highly commercialized region with the support of the German-owned Anatolian Railway Company. Its export-oriented cotton plantations imported German farm machinery and employed 50,000–100,000 migrant laborers in the harvest season who came from as far away as Mosul. Large cotton plantations were also established by Italian entrepreneurs in the plain of Antalya in the decade before World War I (Pamuk 1987: 103–4; Quataert 1981: 75; Quataert 1994a: 875; Gerber 1987: 86–87).

Coexistence of peasant family farms and large estates in Anatolia, Rumelia, greater Syria, and Iraq

Peasant family production and small to medium-sized holdings remained the predominant form of agricultural production in Anatolia and much of Rumelia, even in some areas where commercial agriculture became important (Pamuk 1987: 82–107; Quataert 1994a: 861–75). Due to favorable agronomic conditions and proximity to ports, agriculture in the provinces of Salonica, Monastir, Thrace, and the Izmir–Aydin region of western Anatolia was relatively more commercialized well before the mid-nineteenth century. The most important export crops were tobacco, raisins, figs, cotton, silk, and olive oil. In 1859 three-quarters of the land of Monastir province was owned by large landlords, and in 1863 a British consular report estimated that 40 percent of all farms in Salonica province were larger than 200 hectares (Pamuk 1987: 100; Issawi 1980: 203).

In Thrace and western Anatolia the land-tenure regime was completely different. The Ottoman recentralization drive of the 1820s and 1830s succeeded in confiscating large tracts of land controlled by local notables, abolishing corvée labor obligations on the peasants, and redistributing land to peasant households in small parcels. Some tax farmers retained large estates, but they were broken up into smaller parcels cultivated by peasant families under leasing or sharecropping arrangements. Mid-nineteenth-century British consuls reported that peasant farms of no more than 8 hectares – the amount a household of four to five and a pair of oxen could farm on its own with only occasional outside help in conditions of the time – comprised the great majority of holdings in the regions of Edirne, Istanbul, Izmir, Bursa, and Gallipoli. In 1909, the first year for which comprehensive data are available, 72 percent of all farms in western Anatolia were under 5 hectares. The average size of a plot in seven different districts ranged from 1.1 hectares (Istanbul) to 5.4 hectares (Karasi) (Issawi 1980: 203; Kasaba 1988: 61–63; Pamuk 1987: 100).

Peasants retained some bargaining power in many regions of Anatolia because of a persistent labor shortage (Kasaba 1988: 64; Pamuk 1987: 100). For example, European investors bought lands from a leading notable family in the Izmir region hoping to develop a plantation-style estate by utilizing the labor service of peasants. As the Europeans could not perform the patronage functions of a local notable, the peasants refused their labor. The investors were forced to resort to sharecropping (Quataert 1981: 75).

Sultan Abdülhamid II held extensive estates in greater Syria, including the northern valleys of Palestine, the Jordan Valley, and along the Hijaz Railway in Transjordan. The sultan's largest Syrian estates were south and east of Aleppo, where he owned some 445,000 hectares in 567 villages (Batatu 1999: 111). Despite these considerable royal holdings, there is no consensus on the extent of large estates in the diverse land-tenure regimes of greater Syria in the nineteenth century.

Quataert and Gerber regard the large private estates of the Homs–Hama region, such as those of Abdülhamid II, as exceptional. Evidence presented by Rafeq, the Slugletts, Schilcher, and Mundy indicates that they were common in many parts of the country, though not in the wheat-exporting district of Hawran (Quataert 1994a: 867–68; Gerber 1987: 83; Rafeq 1984; Farouk-Sluglett & Sluglett 1984; Schilcher 1991a; Mundy 1994). The plain of Akkar north of Mount Lebanon was entirely owned by large landlords (Gilsenan 1984; Gerber 1987: 84). According to one rough estimate, plots of 100 hectares or more comprised 60 percent of Syria's cultivated area in 1913; 25 percent was held by peasant farmers in plots of less than 10 hectares (Hannoyer 1980: 288). Many large holdings were rented out in small parcels to peasants for shares or cash, so the number of centrally managed estates is unclear. We may tentatively conclude that there was a tendency toward consolidation of land ownership in greater Syria from the eighteenth century on but, as in Jabal Nablus, sharecropping and fiscal domination of peasants were the principal mechanisms of surplus extraction until the late nineteenth century.

Sultan Abdülhamid II also established estates in lower Iraq. His holdings occupied nearly 30 percent of the cultivated area of Baghdad province (Quataert 1994a: 868). In Baghdad and Basra provinces, tribal shaykhs established ownership rights over large tracts of lands formerly held collectively.

The great diversity of land-tenure regimes surveyed here demonstrates that large estates and peasant family farms coexisted in the Ottoman Empire in the last two-thirds of the nineteenth and early twentieth centuries. Only with capital-intensive crops such as cotton and sugar is there a necessary connection between commercial agriculture and large estates. In Thrace, western Anatolia, Mount Lebanon, and Hawran export-oriented agriculture did not necessarily involve the formation of large estates and the expropriation of peasants or tribal populations. Localities where this did occur – Egypt, Çukurova, Antalya, lower Iraq, Homs–Hama and other regions of greater Syria, Algeria, and Tunisia (see below) – may have had a greater qualitative weight in determining the overall direction of the economy and society. Large landlords and landpoor peasants dominated the social agenda of twentieth-century Egypt, Syria, Iraq, Tunisia, and Algeria. While this is not the case in Turkey, both circumstances are due to developments of the late Ottoman period.

Expanding states and peasant resistance

Peasant cultivators avoided and resisted when they could states' efforts to tax, conscript, and count them as a result of the centralizing thrust of the Tanzimat and their loss of agricultural land and freedom to choose their crop mix where large estates were formed.

Peasants and French colonialism in North Africa

Land-tenure issues in North Africa are complicated by the presence of European settlers, especially in Algeria. Following the French invasion of Algeria in 1830 – an old-style mercantile–imperial expedition like the 1798 invasion of Egypt – settlers (*colons*) established farms on the fertile coastal plain. The French confiscated additional land during the military campaign against the anti-French resistance led by Amir ʿAbd al-Qadir and allocated them to *colons*. By 1851 some 428,000 hectares were distributed to 15,000 *colons* in plots averaging 28.5 hectares. After 1860, larger farms became the norm (Bennoune 1988: 43). The *colons* at first grew and exported wheat. From the 1880s on, settler viticulture replaced wheat as the leading agricultural sector, and wine became Algeria's principal export.

Peasant opposition to the formation of large estates in Algeria was concurrently resistance to settler colonialism. In 1871–72 Muhammad al-Hajj al-Muqrani rallied the peasants of the Berber region of Kabylia and the Rahmaniyya *sufi* order to rebel against increasing *colon* power. The defeat of the Muqrani revolt consolidated a colonial capitalist agricultural economy based on exporting wheat and wine. The primitive accumulation for this regime was accomplished by expropriating peasant agricultural lands. The defeated belligerents had to pay an indemnity and lost some 70 percent of their property. By 1880, 882,000 hectares throughout Algeria were transferred to the 195,000 *colons* living among nearly 2.5 million indigenes (Ruedy 1992: 79; Bennoune 1988: 42, 46–48). The eastern Algerian economy was ruined. Kabyle peasants became sharecroppers, laborers on *colon* farms, or migrants seeking work in France.

Europeans began purchasing agricultural lands in Tunisia in the 1860s. After the French occupation in 1881, French entrepreneurs purchased large plots of state land to plant olive trees. By 1892 French interests controlled 443,000 hectares, of which 416,000 belonged to sixteen owners (Abun-Nasr 1975: 266, 281, 344). The process of displacing peasant farmers was less violent in Tunisia than in Algeria. Purchase as opposed to confiscation was the norm, and there were far fewer settlers in Tunisia. The tribal revolt of 1864 was in part directed against the extended reach of the increasingly autonomous provincial government through fiscal and military reforms comparable to those in Lebanon, Egypt, and the central Ottoman state in the late eighteenth and early nineteenth centuries (Slama 1967). But there was generally less peasant resistance to the French colonial presence than in Algeria.

Rural rebellion, religion, and nationalism in the Balkans

In the Balkans, ethno-religious differences between peasants and landlords were common. Conflicts between Christian peasants and Muslim landlords came to be understood in national terms. Muslim peasants in Bulgaria and others whose identities were incompatible with this project were marginalized in the emergent Balkan national states.

Following the proclamation of the 1839 Gülhane Edict, Christian peasants in Vidin province on the banks of the Danube in modern Bulgaria refused to render compulsory labor service and other dues imposed on them in the eighteenth century by their Muslim landlords, former cavalrymen (*sipahi*s) who had privatized their military land grants. The central government did not assert control over the landlords. In 1850 the peasants rose up, demanding an end to landlord rule and title deeds to their lands. The pasha of Vidin supported them, but the central government proposed a more gradual solution. In 1851 the Istanbul authorities belatedly agreed to sell the landlords' land to the peasants, but they now demanded to receive land without payment. Unresolved peasant demands contributed to the 1876 nationalist revolt. Exaggerated reports of massacres of Christian peasants in that conflict amplified by the rhetoric of William Gladstone turned British public opinion against the pro-Ottoman foreign policy in effect since 1840 and prepared the way for military expeditions to occupy Ottoman territories in the following years (Quataert 1994a: 878–79; Shaw & Shaw 1976–77: II, 160–62).

In Bosnia and Herzegovina, Muslim holders of privatized military land grants and tax farms urged Muslim and Christian peasants to revolt against Ottoman land-registration measures in 1858–59. The peasants rose up, hoping to expropriate their landlords. However, the landlords maintained their holdings, their domination of the peasantry, and their control over a majority of the agricultural surplus. In 1875 Herzegovinian peasants revolted against Muslim tax farmers who demanded full payment of taxes despite the poor harvest. The revolt spread and, supported by the Three Emperors' League, led to the occupation of Bosnia and Herzegovina by the Hapsburg Empire (Quataert 1994a: 879; Shaw & Shaw 1976–77: II, 149–50, 158–60; Jelavich 1983: II, 352–61).

The 'Urabi revolt in Egypt

The formation of large estates in Egypt was accompanied by further revolts in the Delta and Minya in 1846, Giza in 1854, the Abu Tig district of Asyut province in 1863–65, Suhag and Girga in 1877–79, and the rice-growing region of the Delta in 1880. In 1882 tenants of the khedive's estate at Zankalun in Sharqiyya went on strike. Government orders to plant rice, demands for corvée labor, high taxes, economic hardship due to the collapse of the cotton boom, dispossession from lands, and poor wages were the targets of these peasant risings. The 1865 Abu Tig rebellion was led by Shaykh Ahmad al-Tayyib who claimed to be the *mahdi* and was hailed by peasants as a saint. The Islamic dimension of this movement resembles the upper Egyptian revolts of the 1820s (Baer 1982: 253–323).

Peasant grievances against large landowners were an element of the 1881–82 'Urabi revolt: a movement against khedivial autocracy, European economic control, high taxes, and discrimination by Turco-Circassian elites against indigenous Arabic-speaking army officers. However, peasant collective action in support of the 'Urabi revolt was less important than the role of guilds, freemasons, cosmopolitan intellectuals, and other urban elements. The leaders of the revolt were not themselves interested in peasant issues, and village headmen, not poor peasants, were 'Urabi's principal rural supporters. Once peasants were mobilized, they took the opportunity of the 1882 British invasion in support of Egyptian autocracy and the interests of European bondholders to seize the lands and confiscate the crops of landlords, sometimes led by their village headmen (Cole 1993: 259–68; Brown 1990: 193–94; Richards 1987).

Radical peasant movements in greater Syria

Kisrawan and the plain of Hawran were the sites of the largest peasant revolts in greater Syria. Export-oriented agriculture predominated in these regions. But merchants or local notables exploited the land and the peasants without establishing fully privatized estates.

The peasant revolt against the Khazin notables (*muqata'ajis*) in the Kisrawan district of Mount Lebanon in 1858–61 was one of the most radical nineteenth-century anti-landlord movements in the Arab provinces. Contraction of silk exports during the French Revolution impoverished the Khazins. When the trade resumed, European merchants began reexporting silk processed in Marseille to be spun in mechanized spinning mills in the Shuf and Matn closer to the port of Beirut than Kisrawan. The economic decline of Kisrawan impelled the Khazin shaykhs to sell lands to peasants and seek to recoup their income by increasing taxes and dues. The new Ottoman administrative regime established in 1845 allowed Christian peasants subject to Druze shaykhs to appeal to a Christian delegate (*wakil*) to protect them from such abuses. The peasants of Kisrawan had no such recourse because they and their Khazins shaykhs were Maronites. They rose up in rebellion when the Khazins refused to redress their grievances. On Christmas Eve 1858 they chose Tanyus Shahin, a village blacksmith who may have known something about the French Revolution, to lead their movement. With tacit but inconstant support from the Ottoman authorities and the lower Maronite clergy, the peasant rebels drove out the Khazins, seized their property, divided it among themselves, and proclaimed a republic. They demanded not only an end to the dues and payments recently introduced

by the Khazins, but abolition of all personal dues, better tenancy conditions, an end to shaykhs' rights to flog and jail peasants, and full social
equality: in short, a revolution against the *iqta'* system of Mount
Lebanon. The rebels did not demand the abolition of private property
altogether, perhaps because many of them were small owners who hoped
to extend their holdings. Although the most radical aspects of the
Kisrawan revolt – the peasant republic and the expropriation of all
Khazin lands – were beaten back, the administrative regulations promul-
gated when Ottoman control was restored in 1861 proclaimed equality of
all before the law and abolished the personal dues formerly received by
the *muqata'ajis*. The power of the Khazin family was sharply curtailed (al-
'Aqiqi 1959; Porath 1966; Touma 1972: I, 259–78; Baer 1982: 266,
271–79; Dahir 1988: 188).[6]

The reassertion of the power of the central Ottoman state curtailed the
most egregious abuses of the Khazin landlords and thus contained
peasant radicalism in Kisrawan. After the Crimean War, the Istanbul
authorities also sought to extend their reach in frontier areas of greater
Syria which had previously been only nominally or marginally under their
control. This prompted rebellions of peasants in Jabal Druze and Hawran
in the 1880s and 1890s and bedouin around Karak in 1910 (Rogan 1999:
184–217). In both places, the rebels opposed the Ottoman drive to regis-
ter land, which they quite reasonably feared would result in higher taxes
and conscription. The peasant revolt in Jabal Druze in 1888–89 also had
a sharp anti-landlord character comparable to the Kisrawan revolt.

During the Crimean War, wheat exports from Hawran grew along with
an increase in the size of managerial, but not necessarily production or
ownership, units. Holders of usufruct rights (*shaddads*) did not need to
own the land in order to extract its surplus. They controlled the strategic
points in the wheat trade by establishing sharecropping contracts with
peasants and relationships with urban grain dealers, millers, and money
lenders. After the 1860s an informal cartel of Damascene merchants
dominated wheat production, though the land remained under state
administration (*miri*) (Schilcher 1991a: 185–89).

Grain exports declined during the Great Depression, and the local
economy reached a trough in 1887–89. The Ottoman state continued to
extend its presence by introducing direct taxation in 1879, a plan for a
railway in 1882, and an attempt to conduct a census in 1886. In response
to the new tax system, Druze and Christian peasants sought guarantees
that they would not become wage workers on the lands they cultivated. In
1888–89 they set up a commune (*'ammiyya*) and attempted to distribute
cultivation rights among themselves while retaining three-quarters of the
harvest (rather than the traditional two-thirds) in sharecropping contracts

with newly elected shaykhs. The Ottoman government crushed the rebellion and built a railway in 1892–94 to increase its control of the region. The first registration of lands in 1892–93 provoked new revolts. Bedouin and peasants did not pay taxes in 1894. The next year the state responded by launching a military campaign to isolate the Druze, regain control of the Hawran, and impose a new tax calculated at 10 percent of the average crop over five years (takhmis). Sunni peasants rallied to the Druze and bedouin rebels and abandoned cultivation in 1897. The government discontinued the new tax in 1898 and issued a general amnesty in 1900. Twenty years of resistance to Ottoman direct rule and higher taxes allowed the Hawranis to retain a measure of rural autonomy. Peasants succeeded in obtaining a portion of the lands hitherto controlled by the Druze shaykhs, and some obtained property rights over the lands they cultivated. But this did not prevent the consolidation of a new social hierarchy linked to commercial agriculture (Schilcher 1991b; Hanna 1990).

In Kisrawan and Jabal Druze, unlike in the Balkans, the common religious affiliation of peasants and shaykhs and the location of these districts in mountainous areas where direct Ottoman control was tenuous encouraged radical peasant movements with something of a class character. The similarity of the demands of Maronite peasants, who were exposed to French education, and the largely illiterate Druze peasants suggests that the ideas of the French Revolution were not necessary to inspire such revolts.

It is common to argue that peasant rebellions were rare in the Middle East and that the revolts that did occur were exceptional, inconsequential, and not motivated by a "proper" social outlook. Haim Gerber goes so far as to claim that "there were no known cases of revolt among the Syrian peasantry" (Gerber 1987: 134). In fact, from the late eighteenth century until the Syrian Revolt of 1925–27 there were over thirty Druze and 'Alawi peasant revolts and half a dozen or more revolts in Mount Lebanon and the coastal mountains of northern Syria (Batatu 1999: 111, 367, fn. 9, 10; Hanna 1990; Dahir 1988). Gerber's teacher, Gabriel Baer, is inclined to see more peasant rebelliousness and is more willing to notice similarities between Middle Eastern and European peasant movements. But they agree that the Kisrawan revolt is exceptional, and neither considers seriously the 1888–89 Jabal Druze revolt. Baer acknowledges the radical character of the Kisrawan revolt but compares its lack of an anti-clerical element unfavorably with European peasant revolts (Baer 1982: 277–78). Gerber agrees with Baer that Middle Eastern peasant movements "lacked not only clear demands for change of property relations but any well formulated ideology of social change," until the 1950s (Baer 1982: 273; Gerber 1987: 134).

Comparing Middle Eastern, East Asian, and European peasant movements is a useful exercise in principle. And it may be that Middle Eastern peasant movements were weaker and less numerous than those of imperial China, czarist Russia, and early modern Europe, although further investigation would be required to sustain this proposition. However, Baer and Gerber use this comparison to compile a list of Middle Eastern absences measured against a European norm. Thus, according to Baer, the exceptional nature of the Kisrawan revolt is due to Lebanon's more "European" social formation. Its "social features differed from those of all other areas in the Middle East: an agrarian system with feudal features and private property of land" (Baer 1982: 312). As I noted in chapter 1, this is a problematic characterization of Mount Lebanon. In this context, it deflects attention from grasping the social and cultural dynamics of Middle Eastern peasant movements in their own terms. When they turn to the twentieth century, Gerber and Baer artificially separate the social and national–political aspects of peasant movements in Egypt (1919), Iraq (1920), Syria (1925–27), Palestine (1936–39), and Algeria (1954–62). Baer and Gerber's comparative and sociologically informed studies of peasant movements are a great advance over earlier Orientalist approaches. Their weaknesses result from viewing the trajectory of Europe as normative and perhaps also some anxiety, as Israelis, about the potential of Palestinian peasants for troublesome collective action.

Craft production, mechanized industry, and the gender division of labor

Soon after large quantities of European manufactured goods became available in Middle Eastern markets, European travelers and diplomats began predicting the imminent destruction of craft production and guilds (Owen 1981a: 93–95). Craft production, especially of textiles, the principal European manufactured import, did decline in the 1840s, but it was not permanently wiped out (Kurmuş 1981). By the 1850s, craft production began to recover and expand due to adaptive responses by urban guilds or reorganization of work outside the guild system.

These features of craft production in the second half of the nineteenth and early twentieth centuries are evident in the area around Salt in Transjordan (Rogan 1995). As part of its drive to assert control over the frontier areas of greater Syria, the Ottoman state established a new administrative district, al-Balqa', in 1867 and encouraged the reconstruction of nearly thirty water-powered flour mills in its villages. Historically, millers, like bakers and flour merchants, had a strong guild organization. These guild structures do not seem to have been restored along with the mills. The reconstructed mills were often owned by urban merchants or other wealthy men living outside the villages where they were located, but were operated by local craftsmen. In a frontier area of marginal interest to Europeans, local merchants were able to mobilize capital and labor to produce wheat for the local and export markets and thus bring about an integration of towns and villages comparable to the case of neighboring Jabal Nablus, discussed in chapter 1.

The nominal abolition of guild monopolies by the 1838 Anglo-Ottoman Commercial Convention was not strictly enforced. State-authorized certificates for practicing crafts (*gediks*) were used up to the 1860s. However, their number was allowed to increase, and shops were permitted to operate without them. The state's attitude towards guild monopolies was inconsistent. When the government adjudicated a juris-dictional dispute between two Istanbul guilds engaged in cloth printing, it did not protect the monopoly rights claimed by one of the guilds, although the cloth-printing guilds continued to operate through the 1880s. In other cases, the government defended guild monopolies. The motives for these contradictory policies are unclear (Quatert 1994b: 7, 54–55).

Militant textile journeymen and women's work in Damascus

Textile weaving in Damascus is a leading example of resurgent artisanal production within a guild framework. Some 10,000 Muslim, Christian, and Jewish Damascenes out of a population of 125,000 were involved in textile production in 1840. The leading commodity was a tie-dyed, luxury silk–cotton fabric: *alaja*. In the 1840s the number of looms fell from 5,000–6,000 to under 2,000 followed by a recovery that peaked in 1879 with nearly 7,000 looms and 4,000–5,000 journeymen members of the weavers' guild. Revival of the industry was accomplished by freezing journeymen's wages and relaxing enforcement of the requirement that workshop owners hold a government certificate. Merchants without cer-tificates reorganized the craft by putting out different stages of produc-tion through jobbers or establishing large workshops supervised by master weavers. Journeymen's wages recovered somewhat in the 1860s and 1870s, but living standards remained far lower than in the 1830s. In January 1879, 3,000 journeymen struck against the masters' imposition of a cut in the piecework rate, claiming that the masters had not upheld their duty to protect the interests of all guild members from the mer-chants, whose profit margins were at least 30 percent in the 1870s. Textile journeymen continued to strike frequently until the end of World War I (Rafeq 1983; Vatter 1993; Vatter 1994; Vatter 1995).

Typically, only men were permitted to join the Damascus textile guilds, though women did much of the cotton spinning, silk reeling, embroidery, and other finishing tasks. Many women lost their jobs when weavers began to use imported cotton yarns in the 1830s. In the 1870s, introduction of stocking-knitting and sewing machines, both outside the guild system, provided new sources of women's employment. Merchants provided women who worked at home with a machine on credit, and they repaid the loan from their wages. The system was ideal from the point of view of capital because it required no investment in a workshop, and female labor was cheap (Vatter 1995: 51–53).

Silk reeling and working women in Mount Lebanon

Women's work was also critical to the success of the Lebanese silk industry. Between 1840 and 1914 almost 200 mechanized silk-reeling factories, mostly owned by Lebanese Christians and perhaps fifteen Druze and Muslims, were established (Owen 1987). The first European-owned factories employed only men until 1858. By the early 1880s, 12,000 unmarried female workers, nearly a quarter of all women of working age, and 1,000 male supervisors were seasonally employed in mechanized silk reeling. The Maronite clerical hierarchy opposed the employment of women for ten years, but relented when women's wages became an essential part of family income. By the 1890s, male intermediaries no longer negotiated the terms of women's work; factory women began to deal directly with employers and retain control of their own wages. They also organized strikes to improve their appalling sweat-shop conditions: seventy to eighty women commonly worked ten to twelve hours a day in a 200-square-foot workshop with fifty fetid, steaming basins to unravel cocoons. Lebanese women's factory work transformed prevailing patriarchal social relations, but it was not generally perceived as liberating. Enhanced women's autonomy in factories coincided with a decline in silk prices, which increasingly drove Lebanese men to emigrate to the Americas seeking work. Young, married, working women were separated from their husbands for years, and single Christian women (no Druze until the 1920s) emigrated to find husbands because there were not enough eligible men at home. Factory work then, was part of a complex of social changes commonly perceived by women as undermining their economic and social well-being (Khater 1996).

Women's work in small workshops, households, and factories outside the guild system predominated in carpet knotting in Sivas, silk reeling in Bursa, tobacco sorting in Istanbul, Izmir, and Salonica, cotton and wool spinning in Salonica, Istanbul, Izmir, and Adana, and mohair weaving in Ankara. Expanded production of these commodities in the nineteenth century and their ability to compete with imported European goods depended on paying low wages to young, unmarried, Muslim, Christian, and Jewish women. Low wages were justified on the grounds that women's work was unskilled, temporary, and supplemental to the primary sources of family income. In fact, it was critical both in intensification of production using traditional methods and in early mechanized factories (Quataert 1991a; Quataert 1994b).

The uncertain formation of a "modern" working class

New transportation, communications, and urban utilities – the Suez Canal, railway and tramway lines, expanded port facilities in Salonica, Istanbul, Izmir, Alexandria, and Beirut, telegraph and telephone lines, water supply and gas lighting – created new occupations and social relations while previous institutions and relations of production persisted. The largest employer in Egypt at the turn of the twentieth century was the Egyptian State Railways. Its 12,000 workers operated and maintained 1,700 miles of track in 1914 including the first railroad in the Middle East, the Cairo–Alexandria line constructed in 1852–54. The Cairo Tramway Company, established in 1894 by a private Belgian entrepreneur, Baron Edouard Empain, operated over 63 kilometers of track and employed over 2,000 workers in the early twentieth century. Collective action of the railway and Cairo tram workers became an integral part of the Egyptian national movement after 1907 (Beinin & Lockman 1987: 38, 49–82; Lockman 1994b). The construction and operation of the Suez Canal and the port of Salonica demonstrate the complex amalgam of old and new social structures, practices, and mentalities that formed an emergent "modern" working class.

The Suez Canal: labor relations in a site of "modernity"

The Suez Canal was the most significant project of its kind during the mid-Victorian boom. When Sa'id Pasha (1854–63) authorized Ferdinand de Lesseps to build the canal, he also agreed to provide an annual corvée of 20,000 Egyptian construction laborers. The peasant/workers received pitiful wages, labored under harsh conditions, and thousands died during the ten-year construction period (1859–69).

Even more incongruous with the modern image of the Suez Canal was the continuation of slavery on its banks. The southern terminus of the canal, Suez, was major entry point for East African slaves into Egypt. As late as 1873, slaves were used on coastal sailing ships operating out of Suez (Baer 1969c: 166).

Dockers, coalheavers, and other unskilled workers along the Suez Canal were typically landless upper Egyptian (Sa'idi) peasants recruited by labor contractors (*khawli*s). The *khawli*s sometimes kept their laborers in debt peonage by functioning as money lenders. They served as the intermediaries between the peasant/workers and the subcontractors (shaykhs) who dealt with the foreign-owned port service companies (Beinin & Lockman 1987: 25–27).

The coalheavers of Port Said, a city founded when construction of the Suez Canal began, exemplify the uncertain identities and contradictory practices of working classes in formation. By the 1880s there were many guilds in the city, including both workers in traditional crafts and several categories of workers in new port service occupations, including coalheavers. In April 1882, the coalheavers struck for higher wages. Baer considers this the sole example of "a class struggle [which] developed between the workers and their shaykhs who had become contractors." In contrast, Zachary Lockman and I saw this strike as an early expression of modern, working-class collective action (Baer 1964: 136; Beinin & Lockman 1987: 27–31). Baer's understanding of this incident proceeds from his definition of a guild as a group of urban workers headed by a shaykh. From the point of view of the government, the coalheavers were organized as a guild (Najm 1987: 77–80). On this basis, both Juan Cole and Ellis Goldberg accept Baer's view (Cole 1993: 250, 317 fn. 52; Goldberg 1996: 171). This interpretation assumes that despite the novelty of nearly everything in Port Said, organizations called guilds and persons called shaykhs functioned as they had elsewhere a generation or more ago.

Lockman and I erred in suggesting that the significance of laborers engaging in a strike was similarly comparable across time and space. Coalheaving was a new occupation. The guild members were most probably Sa'idi peasants whose relations with their labor contractors and shaykhs were governed neither by the mutual obligations of guilds nor by the norms of "free" labor in a market economy. Reconsidering this issue, one of the few in Middle East labor history to have generated a scholarly debate, Lockman emphasized the persistence of the coalheavers' peasant identities and the ambiguous import of their actions. His reassessment, with its hint of the future role of urban workers in nationalist politics, applies to a broad range of relations between workers and employers in new transport and service industries in the late nineteenth and early twentieth centuries.

For the coalheavers themselves, the 1882 strike did not signal the emergence of a new self-identification as workers that replaced older identities as peasants or Sa'idis, nor does there seem to have been any significant shift in the course of the following decade and a half. Similarly, for Egyptian and foreign contemporaries, the 1882 strike did not signal the emergence on the social scene of a coherent and active working class. It was grasped as basically a local affair, one in which national politics may have played some part – it is likely that the coalheavers were emboldened to act by the fact that a sympathetic nationalist government was in power in Cairo – but not as a portent of things to come. (Lockman 1994c: 87)

The Jewish porters' guilds of Salonica

Port service workers in Salonica – the railhead of three railroads and along with Beirut the third busiest port in the Ottoman Empire after Istanbul and Izmir – were also organized in guilds. The porters (*hamallar*) were overwhelmingly Jews organized in guilds based on place of work or commodity carried and often controlled by one or another large Jewish family. Each porter belonged to a non-hierarchical group (*taife*) which kept accounts and organized members' social life, which centered around sunset prayers and drinking *rakı* at a pub after work each day. Wages were paid to a representative of the group who distributed each individual's share after deductions for charity and collective expenses, including drinks. Porters received sick benefits and funeral expenses from the guild. Sons had the right to replace their deceased fathers on the quay. A widow without sons could hire a permanent substitute who would be paid less than a full wage and keep the difference or sell her husband's right to work. To preserve their jobs, the porters' guilds attempted to block the modernization and expansion of the port, which was nonetheless completed around 1904. The power of the guilds was weakened in 1909 when the Salonica Quay Company agreed to allow trains onto the quay to load freight directly onto ships in the port. The porters who had previously carried goods from the train station to the port lost their jobs, though other categories of Jewish dockworkers continued to work at the port of Salonica for several more years (Quataert 1995: 59–61).

Mechanized industry and the industrial working classes

The development of industrial manufacturing was much less successful in the second half of the nineteenth century than transport and services. Little was left of Mehmed 'Ali's industrial program by the 1840s. The Ottoman central government embarked on a similar effort in the 1850s. About 5,000 workers including males, females, Christian orphans, and criminals convicted of misdemeanors were employed in state-owned armament and textile enterprises, most of which failed by the end of the decade (Clark 1974; Quataert 1994a: 899–900). Except for mechanized silk reeling in Mount Lebanon and Bursa and cotton ginning in Egypt, there was a hiatus in the development of new industrial manufacturing projects until the 1870s. We know little about the continuities, if any, between the first state-sponsored industrial efforts and later enterprises, many involving European capital seeking investment opportunities abroad during the Great Depression.

Khedive Isma'il renewed state-sponsored industrialization in Egypt, establishing some forty state-owned enterprises by 1873. The most substantial were twenty-two sugar-crushing mills which processed cane grown on the royal estates in upper Egypt (Owen 1981a: 149–51). Only ten or eleven of the sugar-crushing mills survived the state bankruptcy in 1876. Together with a sugar refinery established at Hawamdiyya in 1881, they were eventually acquired by La Société Générale des Sucreries et de la Raffinerie d'Egypte – a private firm involving French, British, and local Egyptian-Jewish capital built on the ruins of the state-owned sugar industry (Beinin 1998c: 256–59). The state bankruptcy and the British occupation of 1882 shifted the initiative decisively to such multinational investment groups.

Along with modern transport, the cigarette industry was the center of gravity of the emergent Egyptian working class. Cairo's cigarette-rolling industry was established after European creditors imposed a reorganization of the Ottoman tobacco monopoly to secure revenues to repay the state debt, prompting several Greek entrepreneurs to move to Cairo. By the early twentieth century, five Greek firms controlled 80 percent of the export trade and employed some 2,200 workers. Perhaps another 2,000 were employed by others, including smaller Armenian and European firms who supplied the local market (Shechter 1999: 64–65). The elite hand rollers were primarily Greek, but included Armenians, Syrians, and Egyptians.

The least skilled workers, the tobacco sorters, were mostly Egyptian women. The 1907 census, the first to enumerate industrial workers, undercounted the number of cigarette workers and barely acknowledged the presence of women in the labor force. It enumerated 3,162 cigarette-factory workers including only 15 women (Egypt. Census Department 1909: 280). A French investigator observed twenty women working in only one of the thirty-seven factories (Vallet 1911: 95–96). Cigarette-rolling factories in Istanbul, Salonica, and Izmir employed women as tobacco sorters (Quataert 1983: 18; Quataert 1995: 71). The same Greek families and production methods prevailed in Cairo. There is no reason to think that social norms in Egypt posed a greater barrier to women's factory employment.

The statistical error of the Egyptian census takers may reflect the ambivalence and uncertainty of state authorities about women working for wages in the public sphere and how to categorize a new urban social group still largely identified with foreigners. The Greek cigarette workers formed the first union and organized the first recorded strikes in Cairo. Their struggles were initially not considered to be an Egyptian social phenomenon (Beinin & Lockman 1987: 49–54).

Around 1879, the first successful privately owned cotton-spinning mill was established in Salonica, which became the most important industrial center in the Ottoman Empire until it was annexed by Greece in 1913. Twenty thousand workers, mostly Jews, were employed in over thirty enterprises producing textiles, alcohol, soap, tiles, bricks, nails, furniture, and cigarettes; 5,000 workers were engaged in the transport sector. Three-quarters of the cotton-spinning mill workers were girls aged twelve to eighteen. A Jewish girl usually worked until she accumulated a dowry and married at age fifteen. Cigarette manufacturing was the largest industry in the Salonica region and employed 4,000–5,000 workers, including many women (Quataert 1995).

In Anatolia, the major concentrations of factory production were Istanbul, Izmir, and the Adana area. Many factory workers, including most of the 1,400 workers in the Istanbul cigarette factory, were female. By 1913 there were 36,000 workers in at least 214 factories, 92 percent of which were privately owned (Quataert 1994b: 3; Quataert 1994a: 902–04).

In the early twentieth century the urban labor force in the Middle East consisted of guild workers struggling to maintain their livelihoods and social status, peasants recruited by intermediaries to work in construction and transportation services, female factory workers who received lower wages than males and were subject to patriarchal gender relations at work and at home, and a small elite of skilled workers, often comprising foreigners or minorities, such as the Greek cigarette rollers of Cairo. Their radically different life experiences and mentalities did not prevent some of them from engaging in strikes and other forms of collective action commonly associated with a modern working class. While craft and community were the primary basis for mobilizing early collective actions, trade unionism, socialism, and nationalism were already on the scene.

Peasants and urban working people did not know they were in need of reform. Hence, during and after the Tanzimat era they had to be cajoled or coerced to accept the enhanced presence of the state in their lives in the form of new taxes, enumeration, and military conscription along with legal equality. Because the Tanzimat was a project of bureaucratic elites with little interest in democracy and minimal social links to working people, it is not surprising that subalterns resisted or evaded aspects of the reforms that extended the reach of the Ottoman state, its European allies, and their administrative, economic, and cultural practices. The economic regimes and military expeditions of European powers became increasingly invasive in the course of the nineteenth century, culminating in outright colonial rule in Algeria, Tunisia, Egypt, Libya, and Morocco by World War I. The enhanced European presence both continued and amplified the contest over attempts to impose European-style modernity on subaltern subjects begun by indigenous state builders such as Mehmed ʿAli Pasha, Amir Bashir II, and Sultan Mehmed II and the Tanzimat bureaucrats.

3 The rise of mass politics, 1908–1939

The accelerated global circulation of capital, commodities, people, and ideas induced by the mid-Victorian economic expansion persisted through the Great Depression of 1873–96 until the start of World War I. However, the confluence of the London-centered recession of 1906–08 and the inauguration of the era of mass politics marks a divide in the period for the purposes of this book. Through collective actions precipitated by the Young Turk uprising against Sultan Abdülhamid II on July 23, 1908, the June 1906 Dinshaway incident in Egypt, and the 1905–06 Constitutional Revolution in Iran, Middle Eastern workers and peasants established a more salient presence and discursive legitimacy in the world of politics than had previously been the case. These events, their repercussions, and their international context constituted new and sometimes competing, sometimes overlapping social categories of citizen, worker, farmer, and believer that hailed subalterns as modern, national, political subjects.

Resumption of direct capital investment and increased market demand in the 1890s integrated parts of the Middle East even more closely into the world capitalist market. European capital created new, large-scale enterprises with large concentrations of wage workers in transportation, urban services, and a few manufacturing industries and became more actively engaged in expropriating and reconfiguring the peasantry. Concurrently, many middle-strata urban professionals educated in a western style adopted European conceptions of modernity and progress encompassing science, technology, education, social reform, and cultural revival. This was a newly constituted status group termed the *effendiyya* in Egypt and the *mutanawwirun* (men of enlightenment) in greater Syria. Turkist intellectuals associated with the Young Turks played a similar cultural role. From these circles emerged the principal publicists for a political program of secularism, liberalism (in the classical British sense), nationalism, and moderate women's emancipation.

European capital became more engaged than ever before in Egypt after the British occupiers imposed political and fiscal stability. Much of the

71

Nile Delta was transformed into a vast plantation. Cotton expanded from 18 percent of the cultivated area in 1886/87 to 27 percent in 1904/05–1908/09 – twice the rate of growth of the total cultivated area. The proportion of lands held in estates of over 50 *faddans* rose from 42.5 percent in 1894 to 44.2 percent in 1913. Cotton and cotton seeds grew from 75 percent of total exports in 1880–84 to over 92 percent in 1910–13 (Owen 1981a: 217–19). Britain received the bulk of Egypt's cotton exports.

The collapse in the price of silver in relation to gold during the economic crisis of 1906–08 sharply reduced the value of the 1908 and 1909 Egyptian cotton crop; the harvest of 1909 was the poorest in a decade of declining yields. Adversely affected large landowners concluded that cotton monoculture and European domination of the market exposed them to unacceptable risk. Several became leaders of the new nationalist political parties. Nationalist programs following the 1911 Egyptian National Congress advocated economic diversification and industrial development.

Mount Lebanon was similarly transformed into a monocrop export economy. By the 1890s, nearly half of the cultivated land was planted with mulberry trees, and silk thread constituted half of the total value of Beirut's exports. About half of all Maronite families earned a living cultivating mulberry trees or reeling silk. France was the principal market and the main source of capital for the Lebanese silk industry. But the silk-reeling factories were operated primarily by local Christian entrepreneurs. Their profitability depended on cheap women's labor, low capital investment, and obsolete technology. These structural weaknesses led to technical stagnation and inability to compete with Japan and China. Production peaked in 1910, declined rapidly during World War I, and briefly revived in the 1920s before disappearing in the 1940s (Owen 1981a: 249–53; Owen 1987; Khater 1996).

The Public Debt Administration controlled as much as one-third of all Ottoman state revenues from 1881 to 1914. The Ottomans sought to loosen the grip of Anglo-French financial domination by granting a concession to build the Anatolian Railway to the Deutsche Bank in 1888. By establishing trading companies that imported and sold agricultural machinery on credit to farmers along the Anatolian Railway, especially in the cotton-growing plain of Çukurova (see chapter 2), the bank aspired to transform the economy of Anatolia, as British and French capital had transformed lower Egypt and Mount Lebanon. As a late entrant in the race for empire, German capital could not accomplish this objective in the few years before World War I.

Declining profitability of Lebanese silk after 1907 and unwillingness of peasant men to do "women's work" for low wages in the silk-reeling factories were among the factors prompting the emigration of some 100,000 mainly Christian men to North and South America between 1884 and World War I (Khater 1996: 340). Perhaps as many as 100,000 more peasants from greater Syria emigrated to the Americas from the 1880s until the adoption of the US Immigration Act of 1921. Parallel processes led Iranian workers to migrate to Russia; their numbers peaked at 275,000 in 1913. About 10,000 Algerian Berbers legally sought work in France between 1906 and 1914; many more migrated illegally (Owen 1989: 33). During World War I, nearly 120,000 Algerians were recruited to work in French industry.

Middle Eastern integration into markets and modernity centered in Europe was advanced by further territorial conquests. Italy invaded the Ottoman provinces of Tripolitania and Cyrenaica in 1911. On the flanks of the Ottoman Empire, Britain and Russia partitioned Iran into zones of influence in 1907, and France declared a protectorate over Morocco in 1912. The British protectorates established over Bahrain (1892), Kuwait (1899), and Qatar (1916) confirmed the Persian Gulf as a British lake. The Ottoman alliance with the Central Powers in World War I sharpened the discrepancy between nominal and actual sovereignty in Egypt. His Majesty's Government resolved this anomaly by declaring Egypt a British protectorate in December 1914. After the war, European imperial rule was consummated by the establishment of mandates – colonial regimes supervised by the League of Nations – in several former Ottoman provinces. The British held mandates in Iraq, Transjordan, and Palestine; the French in Syria and Lebanon. Related processes led to separation of most of the remaining Ottoman territories in the Balkans: Bosnia and Herzegovina (1908), Bulgaria (1909), Macedonia (1913), and Albania (1912).

From rabble to citizens of the nation

In the Ottoman lexicon "Turk" commonly meant a crude Anatolian Muslim peasant or nomad. Alternative positive connotations began to appear in the 1860s. During the reign of Sultan Abdülhamid II (1876–1909), Turkist intellectuals began to promote the language of Anatolian peasants as the ideal to be emulated and to acclaim them as the backbone of the Ottoman state, the heroes of the Turkish nation, and the guardians of Islam and the Anatolian homeland (Shaw & Shaw 1976–77: II, 263; Kushner 1977: 20–21, 54). Yusuf Akçura, the leading proponent of Turkism, considered peasants "the basic matter of the Turkish nation" who deserved the greatest attention of the government (Ahmad 1983: 287). While he regarded the bourgeoisie as the "foundation of the modern state," Akçura considered the "Turkish people" to comprise small landowners or landless peasants, small artisans and merchants, and wage earners and workers (Berkes 1964: 425, 427).

Celebration of Anatolian Turkish peasants was linked to Marxist ideas and anti-imperialist struggle by the Russian-Jewish revolutionary Alexander Israel Helphand (Parvus), an influential theorist and journalist of the Second International. From 1910 to 1914, Parvus lived in Istanbul and wrote regularly on economic topics in several Turkish periodicals. He contributed three articles on "The Peasants and the State" to the leading Turkist organ *Türk Yurdu* (Turkish Homeland), edited by Yusuf Akçura. Parvus was well connected to the Committee of Union and Progress (CUP), though the extent of his direct political influence over the Young Turk regime is uncertain. Despite its pro-peasant rhetoric and the populist views of its minority elements, the CUP generally accommodated large landlords. However, the economic policies of the future Turkish republic owed something to Parvus (Berkes 1964: 335–37, 425; Zeman & Scharlau 1965: 128; Ahmad 1980: 336–37; Ahmad 1983: 288; Arai 1992: 110–40; Ahmad 1993: 41–43).

The early twentieth-century Egyptian nationalist *effendiyya* transformed their conception of the social contours of their political community even more definitively than late-Ottoman-era Turkists. Like the Ottomans, they first regarded peasants, the urban lower classes, and urban wage workers as the most backward and morally corrupt section of the people. One of them described the young women who worked in Cairo's cigarette-rolling factories as "the most wicked of girls in their behavior and the most reprehensible in their souls, the more so as it is said that a large number of them are illegally married to Greek boys" (Lockman 1994a: 167). To overcome the backwardness of the masses of poor Egyptians, the *effendiyya* sought to reform and uplift the lower orders. With proper education and discipline they would be reconstituted as workers and peasants fit for citizenship in the modern Egyptian nation. This pedagogical project enhanced the social power of the *effendiyya*, who saw themselves as the sector of Egyptian society best able to understand the European sources of modernity and nationalist political theory and to transmit them to the lower orders.

The vision of nationalist modernity embraced by the *effendiyya* spread to a mass audience for the first time during the anti-British upsurge following the Dinshaway incident in June 1906. Five British officers shooting pigeons in the Delta village of Dinshaway accidentally wounded the wife of the village prayer leader and set fire to a threshing floor. Outraged peasants attacked the soldiers, wounding two of them. One subsequently died of sunstroke. A hastily convened military tribunal tried fifty-two peasants on the preposterous charge of premeditated murder. Thirty-two were convicted, four were hanged, and the rest were sentenced to flogging or prison. Nationalist writers denounced the verdict in the pages of *al-Liwa'* (The Standard) and other newspapers, hailing the peasants of Dinshaway as heroes of the Egyptian nation. Mahmud Tahir Haqqi's melodramatic, fictionalized reconstruction of the events featuring a peasant girl as the hero, *The Virgin of Dinshaway*, quickly became a best seller (Haqqi 1906; Haqqi 1986). Poetry and journalism about Dinshaway by the nationalist *effendiyya* integrated peasants and the urban lower classes into a new conception of the Egyptian nation (Lockman 1994a: 179–81). The popular anti-British mobilization prompted the editor of *al-Liwa'*, Mustafa Kamil, to form the Nationalist Party (al-Hizb al- Watani) in December 1907; the gradualist–nationalist People's Party (Hizb al-Umma) and its journal, *al-Jarida* (The Newspaper), were founded several months earlier.

The leading intellectuals of the People's Party – Ahmad Lutfi al-Sayyid, Muhammad Husayn Haykal, Qasim Amin, Fathi Zaghlul, and ʿAbd al-ʿAziz Fahmi – were the sons of rich peasants or village headmen (*ʿumda*s) whose parents had realized the value of a European-style education. Their village origins allowed them to present themselves as authentic Egyptian peasants, unlike the Turco-Circassian elites. They were familiar enough with peasant life to speak to and for the peasantry, and their understanding of the representational politics of modernity and nationalism led them to believe that it was their right and duty to do so. They were also highly conscious of the superior status conferred by their landed property and modern educations.

Their sensibility and relationship with the peasantry are expressed in *Zaynab*, a novel of education and social reform written by Muhammad Husayn Haykal while he was studying law in Paris in 1910–11 (Haykal 1963; Haykal 1989). Its publication by *al-Jarida* in 1914 marks Haykal's status as an *effendi* aspiring to national political leadership and gave *Zaynab* the imprimatur of the sector of the *effendiyya* most fully committed to secular, liberal nationalism. *Zaynab* criticizes the seclusion of women, arranged marriage, popular forms of Islam, and other "backward" village customs, and acclaims the liberatory power of western-style education. Hamid, the narrator and Haykal's alter ego, leaves his village to become a student in Cairo. Education allows him to observe and understand his village as both the peasants and the large landowner cannot. He contests the right of Sayyid Mahmud, the large landowner, to lead the peasants and by extension the nation because his only concern was to sell the cotton at the highest price and rent out his land for the highest rate while exploiting the farm workers . . . It never occurred to the proprietor to extend a helping hand to them or to lift them up from their enslaved condition as if he did not realize that this working mass would be more efficient if their standard of living were improved. (Haykal 1963: 22–23)

Yet Hamid feels superior to the peasants, whose improvement he ostensibly seeks, commenting that migrant agricultural workers were "used to eternal bondage and submitted to its power without complaint"(Haykal 1963: 22). Even more revealing is Hamid's self-reproach after a sexual encounter with an unnamed peasant girl: "How could I descend from the heights of the sky . . . to the level of people who do not think?"(Haykal 1963: 181).

Like *The Virgin of Dinshaway*, *Zaynab* exemplifies the social–romantic literary genre that lauds peasants as the quintessentially authentic Egyptians who must be lifted up by the educational work of the *effendiyya*. Other canonical works of this genre are Tawfiq al-Hakim's *Return of the Spirit* and ʿAbd al-Rahman al-Sharqawi's *Egyptian Earth* (al-Hakim 1938; al-Hakim 1989; al-Sharqawi 1990). Despite their iconic status in nationalist literary history, these novels contain few peasant voices. Like Hamid in *Zaynab*, the narrators are peasants who have left their villages to become students. This genre expresses both the centrality of peasants in the discourse of Egyptian nationalism and the success of the *effendiyya* in excluding actual peasant voices from that discourse.

The Syrian *mutanawwirun* also thought of themselves as the educators of the nation. Their writings and activities shaped an Arabist discourse and set the political agenda of the Arab government that ruled in Damascus from October 1918 to July 1920. The leading Arabist publicist, Muhibb al-Din al-Khatib, observed: "The great mass of the nation is composed of working people who dwell in villages and mountains, those who are breaking the soil and planting. It is to these that the educated must devote their zeal, to enlighten their hearts and advance their talents and intellectual abilities" (Gelvin 1998: 202).

One of these *mutanawwirun*, Shukri al-ʿAsali – a member of a prominent Damascene family, district governor (*qaʾimmaqam*) of Nazareth, and subsequently a founder of the Arab Club of Damascus – established his political reputation by making defense of Palestinian peasants from the encroachments of Zionist settlers a major political issue well before a Palestinian nationalism was fully articulated. Ilyas Sursuq of Beirut acquired 230,000 *dunam*s in Marj ibn ʿAmr (the Valley of Jezreel) from the Ottoman state in 1872. In 1910 he sold the lands of al-Fula (ʿAfula) to the Jewish National Fund (JNF). The peasants refused to vacate their plots, and al-ʿAsali supported them by defying the order of the provincial governor to deliver the title deed to the new owners. Al-'Asali published several anti-Zionist articles in the newspapers of Damascus, Haifa, and Beirut, linking the dispossession of the peasants with patriotic appeals. He even sent troops to drive off armed Zionist settlers who tried to occupy al-Fula. In January 1911, the governor intervened, expelled the peasants, and allowed the Zionist settlers to occupy the land. Al-'Asali's support of the peasants of al-Fula became the emblem of his campaign to represent Damascus in the Ottoman parliamentary by-election that month. He won the seat and became a leading parliamentary opponent of Zionism. Unfortunately, the existing accounts of these events do not present the voices of the peasants who were their subjects and whose interests were at their center (Mandel 1976: 106–07; Khalidi 1997: 106–09).

The discursive articulation of nations as legitimate political communities led nationalist intellectuals throughout the Middle East to revalorize peasants and workers as fully human subjects. "The masses are thereby endowed with a potential for agency: they become a constituency which can be mobilized by the nationalist movement, and their interests and demands can be subsumed within the national struggle" (Lockman 1994a: 181). Political interest, paucity of evidence, and the difficulty of unraveling multiple and contradictory popular consciousnesses foster a proclivity for nationalist intellectuals and historians to obscure the agency, interests, and demands of peasants and workers. The formation of new classes and political agendas was not solely due to the discursive work of the intelligentsia. In addition to the social structural factors at work, peasants and urban working people contested the political programs of intellectuals and legitimized their own social demands through their participation in nationalist movements (Gelvin 1998; Ahmad 1993; Ahmad 1995; Batatu 1978; Swedenburg 1995; Beinin & Lockman 1987). Popular conceptions of the boundaries of political communities, the collective interest, and the capacity to realize them were formed and reformed through experience in specific political and economic contexts.

Urban workers and the 1908 Young Turk Revolution

Local struggles over declining wages, loss of jobs, crop failures, food shortages, and high prices during 1906–08 formed the social context of the Young Turk Revolution of July 23, 1908 (Quataert 1983: 103–13; Quataert 1979; Karakışla 1992: 156). The revolution was initiated by the actions of units of the Macedonian army linked to the Salonica-based Committee of Union and Progress followed by an upsurge of popular collective action. Despite Sultan Abdülhamid II's "Declaration of Freedom" restoring the 1876 constitution, he was deposed following a failed counter-revolution in April 1909. Thereafter, the CUP ruled indirectly through its influence on the government and directly after the coup d'état of January 1913.

Workers and urban crowds construed the Declaration of Freedom as a warrant to advance their economic and social demands and launched an unprecedented wave of strikes and demonstrations. There were some fifty recorded strikes in the Ottoman territories from 1872 until July 24, 1908. From July 24 to the end of the year there were 111 strikes concentrated in Istanbul (39), Salonica (31), and Izmir (13). As many as 100,000 of the 200,000–250,000 urban wage laborers throughout the empire went on strike during 1908. Most sought higher wages, overtime pay, or paid vacations to compensate them for the decline in real wages since 1903 and price increases of 20 to 30 percent in the two months following the revolution. The strikes were partially successful in this respect. Average daily wages in Anatolia rose 15 percent from 1905 to 1908; white-collar workers generally did better than blue-collar workers. Union recognition and an eight-hour day were also common demands (Karakışla 1992: 154–55, 159).

The incipient labor movement encompassed several different forms of struggle and organization. Strikes against foreign concessionary enterprises – the railways, the Istanbul Quay Company, and the Zonguldak coal mines operated by the Ereğli Company – were among the fiercest, most violent, and most successful. The foreign character of these enterprises inclined the CUP and the government to support the workers. But fear of social disorder led them to break strikes with bloody consequences at the coal mines, the Aydın Railway, and the Tobacco Régie factory in Samsun. Strikers at the Istanbul Tramway Company and the Anatolian Railway demanded the removal of foreign directors: an expression of anti-imperialist opposition to foreign capital, xenophobia, and naive personalization of grievances, or all three simultaneously.

The union of the Anatolian Railway workers founded in October 1907 was led by a Greek doctor, Arhengelos Gabriel, and represented predominantly Ottoman Christian, white-collar employees. They were the most insistent in demanding the removal of the Swiss director of the company during the September 1908 strike. Muslim laborers recruited from villages were more interested in higher wages. The least-skilled workers may not have been members of the union at all. These divisions allowed the Deutsche Bank and the government to split the workers and break the strike and the union, although both white-collar employees and laborers won wage increases (Quataert 1983: 71–93).

In contrast to the ethno-religious disunity of the railway workers, the tobacco workers of Salonica and its environs were among the first to establish a class-conscious trade union in the wake of the Young Turk Revolution. Their organization of about 3,200 members included 2,000 Jews, 500 Greeks, 400 Turks, and 200 Bulgarians – a veritable proletarian international. The tobacco workers' union was the bulwark of the Socialist Workers' Federation founded in 1909 by Sephardi Jews and Bulgarians. It operated a workers' club and published a newspaper in Ladino, Bulgarian, Turkish, and Greek. Fourteen trade unions affiliated with the federation, enabling it to mobilize 7,000 workers for a May Day demonstration in 1911. The federation was the most important socialist organization in the Ottoman Empire until Salonica and Macedonia were annexed by Greece in 1913 (Velikov 1964: 31, 35–38; Harris 1967: 17–18; Dumont 1980: 384–88; Quataert 1995: 73–74).

The workers most effective in winning their demands under the new regime were not trade unionists, but the members of the porters' and lighter boatmen's guilds of Istanbul. Like the porters of Salonica, they had been struggling against the French-owned Istanbul Quay Company's plan to the modernize the port and eliminate their jobs since 1894. They were virtually defeated after striking in June 1907. The government abandoned their cause and acceded to the demand of the company and the European powers to implement the port modernization in exchange for increasing the Ottoman customs rate from 8 to 11 percent. Forty-two porters seized the occasion of the 1908 revolution to reclaim their jobs, and the largely Jewish boatmen forced the company to use their lighters rather than its new floating docks to load and unload ships. The CUP supported the porters and the boatmen, though it forcefully suppressed a strike involving all the port workers on August 13, 1908. The porters and lighter boatmen retained their power on the docks of Istanbul until 1924, when the republican government dissolved their guilds (Quataert 1983: 95–120).

The government's exceptionally sympathetic treatment of the Istanbul port workers was partly due to discovering that they could help achieve its political objectives. On October 5, 1908 the Hapsburg Empire annexed Bosnia–Herzegovina, which had been autonomous since 1878. In response, crowds in Istanbul blocked entry to Austrian shops, initiating a commercial boycott that lasted until the end of February 1909, when the Ottoman government accepted an indemnity in exchange for recognizing the annexation. The main force behind the boycott was a coalition of the CUP and Young Turk supporters and port workers' guilds in Istanbul, Salonica, Trabzon, Tripoli, Beirut, and Jaffa. In Izmir, where foreign merchants predominated, the boycott was less popular. Muslim Turkish and Kurdish port workers used the boycott to secure their jobs at the expense of Greeks and Armenians, who were less committed to the action. The Young Turks were prepared to ally with the porters' and boatmen's guilds because they served the government's interests and did not seem to pose the same threat as trade unions, with their foreign workers and new ideas (Quataert 1983: 121–45).

Striking workers who appealed to the CUP and the government to support their demands – the traditional stance of guild members towards the Ottoman state – were generally disappointed. The modern Young Turk regime considered strikes an infringement of public order. CUP members attempted, with some success, to mediate strikes and persuade workers to return to work, but the government did not hesitate to suppress strikes forcefully if that failed. The CUP responded to the strikes of September 1908 that paralyzed the Anatolian, Rumelia, Aydin, Oriental, and Beirut–Damascus–Hama railways by proposing a law banning strikes in public enterprises (Karakışla 1992; Quataert 1983: 113–18). The legislation enacted on October 10, 1908 slowed but did not break the strike wave. Moreover, despite strict government control over workers' associations, fifty-one trade unions and artisans associations were established in Istanbul alone from 1910 to the end of World War I (Ahmad 1995: 76).

Nationalism and an Egyptian working class

Unlike the Young Turks, Egyptian nationalists did not yet rule a state. This may explain why some of them were more willing to recognize and embrace the social power of urban wage workers. The Nationalist Party sought to organize and educate urban working people in ways comparable to the relationship of the People's Party with peasants. The champion of the pro-labor orientation of the Nationalist Party was Muhammad Farid, who became party leader after Mustafa Kamil's death. He maintained ties with Keir Hardie, leader of the British Independent Labor Party, and other European socialists and trade unionists.

In 1908 the party established a network of people's schools (*madaris al-sha'b*) where student party sympathizers instructed urban craftspeople and wage workers in literacy, arithmetic, hygiene, history, geography, religion, ethics, and, by extension, modern, national identity. At the four Cairo night schools, "the carpenter, the shoemaker, the stonecutter, were shoulder-by-shoulder with the cook, all seeking education" (al-Rafi'i 1961: 151). Commingling members of different guilds in the schools encouraged them to develop a new understanding of themselves as a working class and as citizens of the nation possessing inalienable rights.

The Nationalist Party used its base in the people's schools to form the

Manual Trades Workers' Union (MTWU – Niqabat 'Ummal al-Sana'i' al-Yadawiyya) in 1909. Craft workers and proletarians, notably workers at the Egyptian State Railways, joined the MTWU. The combination of these elements is suggested in the name of the organization, which combines the usual modern Arabic term for workers (*'ummal*) and terminology suggesting manual craft work (*al-sana'i' al-yadawiyya*). The MTWU was one of the first workers' organizations to use the word *niqaba*, which subsequently became the common term for trade union.

The distress caused by the 1906–08 economic crisis, the effects of which lasted until World War I, prompted workers at the Cairo Tramway Company and the workshops of the Egyptian State Railways to engage in well-publicized strikes. With a new understanding of the political potential of the lower classes in the aftermath of the Dinshaway incident, these actions were embraced by the nationalist movement (Beinin & Lockman 1987: 57–82). Workers at both enterprises protested against twelve-hour days, low pay, favoritism, arbitrary fines, promotions, and dismissals. They also complained that the foreign inspectors and managers beat and verbally abused them. The railway workshop workers struck in October 1910, and the tramway workers struck in October 1908 and again in July–August 1911 supported by the Nationalist Party. *Al-Liwa'* congratulated and exhorted the tramway workers after their second strike, writing:

Your cause is the cause not only of the tramway workers, but of all the workers in Egypt. Your strike coming after that of the [railway workshop] workers is proof that a new power has emerged in Egypt that cannot be ignored – the awakening of the power of the working class (*tabaqat al-'ummal*) in the countries of the East and their becoming conscious of their interests and rights and desire to be men like other men . . . Unite and strengthen yourselves and increase your numbers through combination and through unity with the European workers, your comrades; form unions and finance them to provide a large permanent fund from which you will benefit in time of need. (Quoted in al-Ghazzali 1968: 45–46)

The suppression of the Nationalist Party and the exile of Muhammad Farid in 1912 temporarily suspended the reciprocal relationship of the Egyptian nationalist and trade union movements. It resumed with greater intensity after World War I.

World War I, the Russian Revolution, and the end of the Ottoman Empire

The war years were catastrophic for working people. Martial law was proclaimed in both the Ottoman Empire and Egypt. Strikes and other forms of economic protest were suppressed. Peasants and their draft animals were conscripted. Over 1.5 million Egyptian peasants served in the Labor

Corps or the Camel Transport Corps; many were killed or wounded during the Gallipoli campaign or the battle for the Suez Canal (Schulze 1991: 185). Service was ostensibly voluntary, but village headmen used coercive methods to fill quotas they were given by British authorities (Lloyd 1933–34: I, 241–42). From 1914 to 1919 the cost-of-living index for basic foods rose from 100 to 239 in Cairo; in Istanbul the retail price index soared from 100 in 1914 to 1279 in 1923 (Beinin & Lockman 1987: 85; Shaw & Shaw 1976–77: II, 373). Replacement of food crops with cotton grown to take advantage of high prices due to military demands caused a food-supply crisis in Egypt in 1917. There was famine in greater Syria due to a series of natural disasters in 1914–16 and the Entente naval blockade; rationing was imposed in 1916. Poor nutrition and the breakdown of municipal services exposed the urban population to a series of epidemics (Gelvin 1998: 22–23). The deportation and annihilation of over a million Armenians in 1915–16 violently rent the social fabric of Anatolia. Banditry became a major problem by 1917.

The political framework of Ottoman sovereignty was destroyed by World War I. A new configuration of national states and Anglo-French imperial rule took its place. Two rival notable families of the Arabian Peninsula – the Hashemites of the Hijaz and the Al Sa'uds of the Najd – allied with Britain against the Ottoman sultan. The correspondence between Sir Henry McMahon and the Hashemite sharif of Mecca, Husayn ibn 'Ali, during 1915–16 on the one hand and the treaty negotiated between the India Office and 'Abd al-'Aziz Al Sa'ud in 1915 on the other promised each of the Arab parties quasi-independent rule over much of the same territory at the end of the war. After capturing al-Hasa from the Ottomans in 1913, the Sa'udis fought the pro-Ottoman Rashid tribe of the north central Arabian Peninsula during World War I, thus protecting the southwest flank of the British force that occupied Basra and Baghdad in 1917–18. The Arab army led by the Hashemite scion, Faysal ibn Husayn, and guided by T. E. Lawrence covered the eastern flank of the British expedition that conquered Palestine and occupied Damascus on October 1, 1918. French troops landed in Beirut in 1919, poised to occupy Lebanon and Syria in accord with the 1916 Sykes–Picot agreement that envisioned partitioning the Arab provinces of the Ottoman Empire between France and Britain. Greece seized the opportunity of the Ottoman defeat to invade Anatolia with British, French, and American naval support in May 1919. Encouraged by misleading British and French promises and endorsement of the right of nations to self-determination by both Woodrow Wilson and V. I. Lenin, Arab, Zionist, Armenian, Azerbaijani, and Kurdish nationalists claimed pieces of Ottoman territory.

The Russian revolutions of 1917 made socialism part of the global political lexicon. Iranians who had migrated to Russia in search of work learned something of socialism which was expressed in the short-lived Soviet Socialist Republic of Iran established in the northern province of Gilan in 1920 by an alliance of the newly formed Communist Party of Iran and the Jangalis – a guerrilla movement of small landowners led by a Muslim cleric (Abrahamian 1982: 111–12, 116). Turkish workers and students in Germany participated in the revolutionary uprising of the Spartakusbund in January 1919; the Workers' and Peasants' Party of Turkey was founded in Berlin later that year (Ahmad 1993: 134). The first Iraqi Marxist, Husayn al-Rahhal, was also living in Berlin in 1919 and discussed the revolutionary uprising with his schoolmates, some of whose parents participated in the events (Batatu 1978: 390). The Communist Party of Egypt and its associated trade union federation, the Confédération Générale du Travail, were established in 1921, led by a Palestinian-born Russian Jew, Joseph Rosenthal. In the early 1920s the Confédération was the leading force in the Alexandria labor movement (Beinin & Lockman 1987: 137–54).

By the mid-1920s there were 100,000 Algerian migrant workers in France, living culturally and economically on the margin of French society. The communist-sponsored Union Intercoloniale convened a congress of North African workers in December 1924. This led to the establishment of North African Star (ENA – Etoile nord-africaine) – the first Algerian nationalist organization – in 1926. By 1928 it grew to 4,000 members; the leadership consisted primarily of communists or members of the communist-led trade union federation (Ruedy 1992: 136–38).

Russian Jews immigrating to Palestine after the 1903 Kishinev pogrom developed the theory and practice of labor Zionism (Shafir 1989; Lockman 1996). In 1909, settlers of this second wave of immigration (*'aliya*) founded the first kibbutz – the emblematic Zionist colonization and settlement institution. Labor Zionism was organizationally consolidated in the next wave of emigration with the establishment of the General Federation of Hebrew Workers in the Land of Israel (Histadrut) in 1920.

Resistance to European plans to partition the Ottoman Empire and demands for political independence intersected with the economic grievances of peasants and urban working people which had been exacerbated by war. Nationalist movements, armed mobilizations, strikes, demonstrations, and newly formed socialist parties were part of the international popular upsurge inspired by the Russian Revolution. They were not, however, orchestrated by Moscow in the way that British and French imperial officials often suspected. The roles of workers and peasants in nationalist movements depended on local configurations of forces.

Resistance to the Greek invasion that culminated in the secular Turkish republic in 1923 regrouped elements of the Ottoman military and bureaucratic apparatus and infused them with the recently articulated Turkish secular nationalist ideology. Military victory legitimized this ideology and the leadership of Mustafa Kemal Atatürk. This and the substantial continuities between the Young Turk era and the republic made the new regime relatively independent of popular collective action. The friendly attitude of the Bolsheviks to Turkish nationalism led Atatürk to tolerate briefly the Communist Party of Turkey, established in 1920, and other radical forces that sought to extend the anti-Greek resistance into a rural social revolution.

At the end of World War I, political figures previously associated with the gradualist People's Party formed a delegation (Wafd) under the leadership of Sa'd Zaghlul Pasha and sought to place the demand for immediate Egyptian independence on the agenda of the Versailles peace conference. The Wafd leadership recognized the need to mobilize the lower classes in order to prevail over the British Empire's determination to maintain its occupation. Although its leaders were primarily large landowners, the Wafd adopted a populist image. Zaghlul proudly called himself a "son of the rabble" (*ibn al-dahma'*).

In Syria, Iraq, and Transjordan the Hashemite family's ability to redeem the promises it received in the Husayn–McMahon correspondence depended on collaborating with the British. The Arab government established in Damascus by Faysal ibn Husayn during October 1918–July 1920 was wary of popular sentiment. After being ousted from Damascus by the French, Faysal was installed as king of Iraq, where he had no popular support. The demise of the Arab regime in Damascus led Palestinian nationalists to begin organizing independently, rather than as Arabs or southern Syrians.

Socialism and the formation of the Turkish republic

During the resistance to the Greek invasion of Anatolia a peasant guerrilla force known as the Green Army (Yeşil Ordu) formed in the Eskişehir region controlled by partisan units commanded by the communist leader, Nejat Ethem. Green Army officers advocated an amalgam of socialism, nationalism, and Islam. When Atatürk felt threatened by the Green Army, he engineered a split in the Communist Party, declared Ethem a traitor, and attacked the troops that remained loyal to him (Harris 1967: 67–89).

The military campaign against Greece coincided with an upsurge of working-class organizational activity, followed by a wave of strikes in the second half of 1923. Students and munitions workers returning from study in Germany and influenced by Marxism formed the Turkish Workers' Association (Türkiye İşçi Derneği) in 1919; Greeks and Armenians formed a Union of International Workers (Beynelmilel İşçiler İttihadı) the same year. Building from a base among the Istanbul tramway workers, a General Workers' Federation of Turkey (Türkiye Umum Amele Birliği) with thirty-four constituent unions and 44,000 members was established in 1923 (Ahmad 1993: 134–37; Ahmad 1995: 79–86; Yavuz 1995: 102–03; Harris 1967: 39–41, 127). The Workers' and Peasants' Socialist Party (Türkiye İşçi ve Çiftçi Sosyalist Fırkası), the Istanbul transplant of the party formed in Berlin in 1919, adopted a more confrontational policy towards the republican government. In 1923, after the victory over Greece, it organized the first large May Day demonstration in Istanbul. The regime responded by dissolving the Union of International Workers and arresting socialist workers and intellectuals.

Atatürk was sufficiently cognizant of the contribution of urban workers to the national struggle and their potential as a social force to invite their representatives to the 1923 Izmir Economic Congress. Despite the regime's efforts to manipulate and coopt them, the "Workers' Group" articulated an independent program calling for an eight-hour day, a paid weekly day off, and an annual vacation after one year's service in an enterprise. It also asked that the 1909 anti-strike law be modified, that trade unions be recognized, and that May 1 be recognized as the holiday of Turkish workers. The Workers' Group sought public recognition of the emergence of a new social class by proposing that the term for worker be changed from *amele*, connoting general, unskilled physical labor, to *işçi*, the word commonly used in Turkish today.

Some of these demands were reiterated on May 1, 1924 in a demonstration in front of the Grand National Assembly in Ankara. The government reacted by arresting workers' leaders, closing pro-labor journals, and enacting a law making May 1 the Spring Festival. The General Workers' Federation of Turkey ceased activity due to political obstacles. Its successor, the Workers' Advancement Society (Amele Teali Cemiyeti), was less militant and operated within the confines allowed by the regime until it was banned in 1928.

The early Turkish socialist movement was composed primarily of intellectuals. A salient exception is Yaşar Nezihe, the daughter of an unemployed municipal worker. Despite her father's opposition, she learned to read and write. None of her three husbands supported her; she worked her entire life. Eventually she began publishing poems. Her ode celebrating May 1, 1923 appeared in the socialist weekly, *Aydınlık* (Light) (Ahmad 1993: 135–336; Ahmad 1995: 80–82). This excerpt from her poem for May 1, 1924 shows that, although the Turkish working class was fragile and largely dispersed in small-scale enterprises, the ideals of the international socialist movement were beginning to be meaningful for some working people.

> Oh workers! May Day is your day of freedom
> March forward, there's light [*Aydınlık*] to lead you.
> The workshops are silent as though the world sleeps.
> The exploiters shake, in fear.
> Today the Red Flag spreads its inspiration
> Opening the path to liberation tomorrow.
> Don't tire of demanding your just rights.
> The bourgeoisie always deceive with their lies.
> . . .
> The greatest celebration will come only when you seize your rights.
> What a sweet thought is liberation from exploitation!
> Always be united and show your strength!
> Don't abandon unity if you want victory.
> You are no plaything in the patrons' [bosses'] hands.
> Raise your head and make them bow before you. (Ahmad 1995: 81)

All oppositional political activity was banned after the outbreak of the Kurdish rebellion led by Shaykh Said in February 1925. The left-wing press supported suppression of the rebellion because it was motivated primarily by opposition to secularism. Nonetheless, the left was banned along with conservatives inclined to support the rebels.

Peasant rebellion and labor upsurge in Egypt

British authorities refused to permit Sa'd Zaghlul and the Wafd to attend the Versailles peace conference. To demonstrate their popular mandate, nationalist students gathered signatures from workers, peasants, and the *effendiyya* on petitions authorizing Zaghlul and the Wafd to present Egypt's demand for independence. Nonetheless, Wafd leaders were surprised by the extent of the popular upheaval set off by the arrest and deportation of Zaghlul and his colleagues on March 8, 1919. Within days, demonstrations and strikes by workers, students, and lawyers broke out in Cairo and Alexandria.

Peasants joined the movement, and for two months the countryside was in revolt. Attacks on the railway system were the most prominent peasant challenge to British authority: sixty-three railroad stations were burned down and the line was damaged at over two hundred points. Ellis Goldberg proposes a rational-choice explanation for the peasant insurrection, arguing that it was motivated by food shortages and high food prices in rural areas due to requisitioning of supplies for the British army and resentment over conscription of draft animals to the Camel Transport Corps and peasant men to the Labor Corps during World War I. Thus, attacks on the railroad line were a "rational" effort to keep foodstuffs and men in the countryside (Goldberg 1992b). These grievances are expressed in a popular song of the period.

> Woe on us England
> Who has carried off the corn [wheat]
> Carried off the cattle
> Carried off the camels
> Carried off the children
> Leaving us only our bare lives
> For the love of Allah, now leave us alone!(McPherson 1985: 150,
>   variant in Goldberg 1992b: 271)

Goldberg avoids the extravagant claims common among proponents of rational-choice theory. His attribution of peasant motives is more plausible than the view that the peasants were aroused by antipathy towards non-Muslims or xenophobia, or the claims of some British officials that the uprising was a Bolshevik plot (Safran 1961: 104–5; Vatikiotis 1980: 265). But rational choice does not explain many peasant actions directed against the institutions of rural power and social structure.

Peasants destroyed some one hundred villages, police stations, and large estates, including nearly every 'izba in Daqahliyya province. They robbed banks, wrecked irrigation works, and inundated fields. Reinhard Schulze argues that peasants in the major cotton-growing areas of the central and inner Delta – where 'izbas prevailed and 70 percent of the cultivated area was owned by large landowners – directly attacked the cotton economy and the 'izba system in an effort to restore their economic positions. Peasants and bedouin in other regions sought their own local objectives (Schulze 1991). Inequities of the rural social structure explain peasant attacks on the cotton-growing 'izbas of the Delta, but do not account for aspects of the revolt directed against British imperial rule.

Nathan Brown notes that many peasant attacks against railroads, telegraph lines, and government buildings were led by rural notables who had economic grievances similar to those of peasants and encouraged them to direct their anger at the British regime. During the war peasants evaded the demands of the British rulers to the extent they could – a common "weapon of the weak" (Scott 1985). With the emergence of the Wafd, nationalist rural notables signaled to peasants that they were authorized to rebel against the British. Brown emphasizes that the 1919 events were a nationalist uprising, not simply economically motivated, minimizing the significance of radical peasant actions against landlords. While acknowledging the centrality of peasant actions in 1919, he concludes: "The role of notables and local officials was critical in assuring peasants that they could act and even in selecting targets for them" (Brown 1990: 213).

Because peasants rarely leave records explaining their actions, Goldberg and Schulze must ultimately rely on functionalist explanations of peasant motives, while Brown directs our attention to the motives of rural notables. Goldberg's emphasis on rationality does not account for the full range of peasant collective actions. But his insistence that peasants responded reasonably to their experiences as they understood them is sound. Schulze emphasizes the intersection of rural class struggle and rural nationalism and suggests that peasants had more capacity for independent social and political thought than either Goldberg or Brown acknowledge. Some peasants very probably did feel aggrieved by disruption of the village moral economy due to the spread of cotton-growing *'izba*s, but their capacity to act was limited by the character of their leadership and the broader political context. Fear of the radical social potential of a sustained peasant revolt probably inhibited rural notables and the *effendiyya* from leading a peasant-based nationalist revolution like those in China, Mexico, Vietnam, or Algeria. Hence, the framework of the nationalist movement both enabled and limited the extent of peasant actions.

The peasant insurrection lasted about two months. Then the focal point of nationalist struggle returned to Cairo and Alexandria. Concurrently with the peasant uprising, a strike wave during March–April 1919 encompassed the Cairo, Heliopolis, and Alexandria tramways, the railway workshops and printing press, the Government Press, the arsenal, government workshops, the Helwan electric railway, the Cairo electric company, post office, port, lighthouse, customs employees, and taxi and carriage drivers. Wafdist lawyers installed themselves as counselors to trade unions and encouraged workers to strike and participate in urban demonstrations against the British. The initial wave of strikes following Zaghlul's arrest was followed by another in August 1919. By the end of the year dozens of new trade unions had been organized (Beinin & Lockman 1987: 83–120).

Until the 1930s, most wage workers in large-scale enterprises in Egypt were employed and supervised by foreigners or permanently resident Greeks, Italians, Armenians, Syrian Christians, and Jews (*mutamassirun*). Consequently, both workers and the general public commonly perceived strikes and economic demands made on such enterprises as part of the nationalist movement. Workers in large-scale urban enterprises comprised a highly concentrated mass relatively easily mobilized through their trade unions for nationalist political action. The economic demands of urban workers posed less of a threat to large landowners, who were prominent among the nationalist elites, than peasant demands. Conse-

quently, a strong reciprocal relationship between the nationalist movement and the trade union movement developed, and national and
working-class identities became closely intertwined.

After failing to reach an agreement with the Wafd, in 1922 the British
unilaterally declared Egyptian independence, subject to four reserved
points. The close relationship between the labor movement and the
national movement established by the events of 1919 rendered trade
unions an important component of the Wafd's urban political base by the
time the party first assumed office in January 1924. In March–April 1924
ʿAbd al-Rahman Fahmi Pasha, one of Zaghlul's lieutenants, organized a
General Federation of Labor Unions in the Nile Valley under Wafd patronage, the first of many Wafd attempts to exercise tutelage over the trade
union movement.

Muhammad Kamil Husayn, a lawyer identified with the Nationalist
Party, was one of several non-Wafd *effendi*s and workers who contested
Wafd's role in the labor movement. He had emerged as a leader of the
Cairo Tramway Workers' Union during the strike of August 1919. In
February 1924, misjudging the popularity of the new Wafd government,
Husayn and several tramway workers attempted to organize a strike.
They were arrested for violating public order and insulting the prime
minister. Saʿd Zaghlul was unwilling to countenance anything that might
discredit the Wafd government or his claim to lead the nation. The Wafd
similarly smashed the Communist Party and the Confédération Générale
du Travail after they organized a series of strikes and factory sit-ins in
Alexandria in February–March 1924 (Beinin & Lockman 1987: 110,
113–15, 128–35).

The Wafd believed that the labor movement should be subordinated to
the nationalist movement, of which it was the sole legitimate representative. Workers should join in strikes and demonstrations against the British
and their Egyptian collaborators when authorized by the Wafd to do so.
But they should submit to the Wafd's vision of an orderly, bourgeois,
nationalist, modernity, as ʿAbd al-Rahman Fahmi stated clearly.

We want the worker in his factory to be like a soldier on the field of battle. There is
a time for work and a time for leisure. At work there should be devotion, diligence,
and sacrifice, at leisure freedom and renewal. We want him properly behaved,
moderate in his habits, sincere in his desires and relationships, pious in all situa-
tions, pure and clean in his actions. He should respect law and order and preserve
peace and public security, meritorious in the eyes of men and rewarded by God.
(Beinin & Lockman 1987: 161)

From 1930 to the middle of World War II the most prominent alternative to Wafd leadership in the trade union movement was Prince ʿAbbas
Halim, a cousin of King Fuʾad (r. 1917–36), who cultivated a populist

image as a manly, workers' prince. Nonetheless, the prince saw himself as a beneficent intercessor on behalf of his social inferiors, and like the Wafd, 'Abbas Halim saw the labor movement as an adjunct of the nationalist movement (al-Shantanawi 1935). He began his checkered career as a labor leader by collaborating with the Wafd to revive trade union organizations weakened by the repressive regime of Isma'il Sidqi Pasha (1930–33). The Wafd attempted to control the trade union federation led by 'Abbas Halim, provoking a split in 1935 that seriously weakened the labor movement.

As modern transport and industry expanded the ranks of urban wage laborers, the Wafd and its rivals used trade unions to mobilize an urban constituency. Workers, Wafdist *effendis*, and Prince 'Abbas Halim engaged in a complex tug of war in which each party attempted to use the others to establish its legitimacy and achieve its own ends. In the process, trade unions became a permanent fixture of urban life, the "labor question" was inscribed on the public political agenda, and the existence of a social collective designated as the working class was affirmed.

Peasants, Druze communalism, and Syrian nationalism

Because the popular classes of Damascus were not unanimously enthusiastic about Faysal's Arab government of 1918–20, the regime and the Arab Club sought to mobilize urban guilds to support the Arabist cause while preventing independent political action on their part. In May 1919 the Damascus municipality organized a demonstration of the guilds to welcome Faysal on his return from France. Each guild was directed to carry a banner with the slogan "Long Live Arab Independence" and to cheer "Long Live the Amir" as Faysal arrived. Police monitored the demonstration to ensure compliance. Representatives of over fifty guilds testified before the King–Crane Commission in favor of Syrian independence. But Christians of Aleppo complained that some of these guilds were fronts for the Arab Club and composed exclusively of Muslims, whereas many of the crafts they purported to represent included Christians and Jews (Gelvin 1998: 231–33).

When economic conditions deteriorated in late 1919 and early 1920, urban working people did not restrain their economic demands in solidarity with the Arab government. Railway and tramway workers, printers, glass and textile workers, electric company workers, and artisans launched a wave of strikes demanding higher wages. In February 1919, Aleppo natives attacked the Armenian refugee community, killing forty-eight and wounding two hundred. The motives for the riot included resentment over alleged preferential treatment accorded to the refugees by the Arab government and its foreign allies and the unemployment, overcrowding, and economic competition resulting from the influx of refugees. One refugee camp alone contained 4,000 hand looms. In the spring of 1920 urban rioters in Hama and Aleppo demanded lower prices for bread and creation of a grain reserve (Gelvin 1998: 44–45).

Faysal's dependence on British good will and his own social conservatism led him to avoid embracing the anti-Ottoman rebellions of Druze and 'Alawite peasants that broke out towards the end of World War I (Hanna 1975–78: I, 268; Hanna 1990: 254–58). Moreover, these peasants' heterodox religious identities and the orientation of the 'Alawite region and much of northern Syria towards Anatolia rather than Damascus put these movements on the margin of Faysal's sense of Arab identity. Even had Faysal allied with them, he was unlikely to have averted defeat by French forces at the Battle of Maysalun in July 1920 and the imposition of the French mandate regime over Syria.

The Great Syrian Revolt of 1925–27 and the Moroccan Rif Rebellion of 1921–26 were the strongest challenges to French imperial rule between the two world wars. Both began as regional revolts, and that is primarily how the French authorities and historians who adopt their outlook understand them (Andréa 1937; Miller 1977). Contesting this imperial perspective, nationalist historians seamlessly integrate these revolts into the grand national narrative (Rabbath 1982; Hanna 1978: II, 94–95). These peasant-based insurrections did become part of the Moroccan and Syrian national movements, but in ways that elude both French imperial and uncritical nationalist understandings.

The Syrian Revolt was set off by the aggressive drive of the French governor of Jabal Druze to impose private-property relations on the traditional agrarian system (agricultural land was annually reapportioned, and the Druze shaykhs received one-third of the best lands) and to forcibly recruit peasants to work on road construction and other modernization projects. Moreover, the autonomy of Jabal Druze was undermined by the imposition of a French governor on the district in violation of the 1923 Franco-Druze treaty, which stipulated that a Druze would occupy the post (Khoury 1987: 152–67). The leader of the Druze revolt, Sultan al-'Atrash, had been in contact with nationalist figures in Damascus since 1916, but did not coordinate his actions with them in advance. The primary element in al-'Atrash's appeal to Druze peasants as he toured the villages to win support for the revolt was "saving the honor of the Druze community" (Batatu 1999: 116). He undoubtedly also sought to preserve his family's leading position in Jabal Druze.

Afer the revolt broke out, peasants of the Ghuta oasis on the outskirts of Damascus joined in, as did nationalist politicians and disaffected lower-class elements in Damascus and Hama (Khoury 1987: 168–204). Nonetheless, the revolt was not an undivided expression of the national aspirations of the Syrian people. Sectional rivalries limited its extent largely to the south and Hama. In the Ghuta, small peasant proprietors enthusiastically supported the revolt, whereas landless peasants did not (Batatu 1999: 115). Thus, the 1925–27 revolt was not unambiguously national in character. Nationalists subsequently appropriated it for the cause. However, it did mark a change in the configuration of political communities. The Druze leaders who initiated the revolt embraced the nationalist political figures of Damascus, forging an alliance beyond their traditional ambit. The peasants of Jabal Druze and the Ghuta jointly bore the brunt of the French suppression of the revolt; this encouraged them to think they shared something in common. Through the revolt and subsequent opposition to French rule, a new Syrian political community was forged, even as the territorial boundaries of that community were imposed by France.

Shi'a peasant rebellion and the formation of Iraq

As in Syria, the working people and local elites of Iraq were not eager to embrace the Hashemite family and its Arab nationalist ambitions. At the end of World War I Britain occupied the former Ottoman provinces of Basra and Baghdad. It sought to establish a mandate regime including them and oil-rich Mosul, though the latter had been promised to France in the 1916 Sykes–Picot Agreement. Approval of this objective by the April 1920 San Remo Conference and the experience of direct British rule, taxation, and water-management practices that harmed the rice crop prompted a tribal rebellion from July to October 1920. Like the Great Syrian Revolt, this uprising was subsequently appropriated by Iraqi nationalists. But Iraqi nationalism barely existed when it erupted, and the borders of the future Iraqi state were still highly contested.

The revolt was led by large landowners of the shi'a Shamiyya tribe who claimed descent from the Prophet (*sadah*). They did not seek national independence, but "freedom to rule over their estates and peasants in the way to which they had been accustomed, that is, by and large as they pleased" (Batatu 1978: 174). Moreover, "the nationalists of this period were . . . 'tribal nationalists,' . . . numerically insignificant nationalists [attempted] to use the tribes for nationalist ends" (Batatu 1978: 119). The revolt drew the shi'a Arabs of the south closer to the sunni Arabs of central and northern Iraq. But Kurds and Assyrians living within the borders of the future Iraqi state were beyond the purview of the infant nationalist movement.

After defeating the tribal revolt, the British installed Faysal as king of Iraq in 1921. Faysal understood that his task was simultaneously to create an Iraqi nation and to keep it from threatening the imperial air route to India and British oil interests. More populist political figures had a different agenda. Ja'far Abu al-Timman, a shi'a merchant who had attempted to turn the 1920 revolt into a national movement, led the establishment of the National Party in 1922. It drew support from handicraft workers and small merchants of Baghdad. The government banned the party soon after its formation. Abu al-Timman went into exile until 1928, when he returned to reactivate the party.

The revived National Party initiated an Artisans' Association (Jam'iyyat Ashab al-Sina'a) in 1929 led by Muhammad Salih al-Qazzaz, a mechanic who became Iraq's first labor leader. Its members included handicraft workers and merchants as well as workers in the Baghdad headquarters of the Iraqi Railways, the largest enterprise in the country. Like the Egyptian Manual Trades Workers' Union, the Artisans' Association combined aspects of a guild and a trade union and commingled working-class and nationalist identities and politics. It organized a fourteen-day general strike in July 1931 against new municipal taxes that mobilized country-wide opposition to the British-sponsored monarchy. The government responded by banning the association and arresting al-Qazzaz.

In 1932 al-Qazzaz founded the first Iraqi trade union federation, the Workers' Federation of Iraq. Like the Artisans' Association, the federation was broken after organizing a month-long boycott of the British-owned Baghdad Electric Light and Power Company in December 1933–January 1934. The government banned trade unions and arrested their leaders, and the labor movement suffered a decade of repression until it was revived under the leadership of the Communist Party of Iraq (Batatu 1978: 295–97; Farouk-Sluglett & Sluglett 1983: 147–49).

Islamic revivalism, peasant revolt, and Palestinian nationalism

Palestinian Arab opposition to the Balfour Declaration, which enunciated the British policy of "the establishment in Palestine of a national home for the Jewish people" was led mainly by urban notables, large landowners, and religious figures organized in the Arab Executive. They believed that dialogue with Britain would secure Arab interests in Palestine. Even al-Hajj Amin al-Husayni, who became the most prominent elite nationalist leader, adopted this strategy and accepted appointments from the British Mandate authorities as grand mufti of Jerusalem and head of the Supreme Muslim Council.

Popular mobilization against Zionist colonization was inspired by Muslim religious sentiment as well as Arab and local Palestinian nationalism. Palestinian Muslims gathered annually for a week-long popular religious festival (Nabi Musa) and a pilgrimage to a mosque near Jericho believed to be the tomb of Moses. Arab nationalists sought to turn the April 1920 celebration into a demonstration of support for Faysal, recently crowned king of Syria. After hearing speeches supporting extension of Faysal's rule over Palestine, the crowd, including some Christians, marched through Jerusalem. A bomb of unknown provenance exploded as the procession passed the Jaffa Gate, and the crowd responded by attacking the Jews of the city.

The salient example of the fusion of religious and national sentiments is the conflict over dispute the Wailing Wall/al-Buraq in Jerusalem. In August 1929, intensified by right-wing Zionist provocations, a dispute over Muslim and Jewish rights at the site erupted into countrywide Arab riots and attacks on Jews and the British. Amin al-Husayni at first tried to restrain the violence. Ultimately, he was propelled into national leadership by this outburst of popular rage (Mattar 1988: 33–49).

A British investigation concluded that dispossession of Arab peasants as a result of Zionist land purchases was a major factor underlying the violence. The 1930 Passfield White Paper advocated sharp restrictions on Jewish immigration and land purchases. Prime Minister Ramsay MacDonald repudiated these recommendations in a February 1931 letter to Chaim Weizmann, which was denounced by Arabs as the "Black Letter."

The Black Letter and sharply increased Jewish immigration after Hitler's rise to power in Germany in 1933 radicalized Palestinian Arab sentiment. The ineffectiveness of elite nationalist leaders, some of whom had actually sold lands to the Zionist institutions, and the increasing economic distress of the peasantry widened the cleavage between the elites and the peasant majority (Stein 1984: 229–39; Khalidi 1987). Shaykh 'Izz al-Din al-Qassam addressed the frustrations and anger of the popular classes: peasant tenants distressed by high rents, falling commodity prices, heavy debts, and the possibility of losing their livelihoods altogether should their lands be sold to the Jewish National Fund; seasonal migrants seeking industrial work; and permanent workers fearing loss of their jobs because of the labor Zionist policy of imposing exclusively Hebrew labor ('avodah 'ivrit) on employers whenever they could (Meswari-Gualt 1991: 16–42).

A graduate of al-Azhar and an adherent of conservative–populist Islamic revivalism, al-Qassam participated in armed resistance to the imposition of French rule over Syria and then fled to Haifa in 1921. In the

Istiqlal mosque, established to serve the needs of Haifa's growing number of industrial and port workers, al-Qassam preached against the political impotence and factional rivalries of the nationalist elites. He amplified his message by organizing literacy classes after prayers and circulating in villages around Haifa in the course of his duties as a marriage registrar. As early as 1925, he began recruiting workers and peasants to become fighters (*mujahidun*) in a militant movement of resistance to British rule and Zionist settlement. In opposition to the moderation of al-Husayni and other elite nationalist leaders, al-Qassam called on "the bootblack to exchange his shoebrush for a revolver and to shoot the Englishmen rather than polish their shoes" (Kimmerling & Migdal 1993: 62).

In November 1935 he led a band of followers to the hills near Jenin. They planned to begin guerrilla warfare against the British and inspire a peasant uprising. Within a week British forces discovered and attacked the group, killing al-Qassam in combat. His death debilitated the movement, though surviving Qassamites continued political and military action. The shaykh's status as a nationalist symbol was secured by the participation of thousands of workers and peasants in his funeral procession.

'Izz al-Din al-Qassam's movement was the harbinger of the Arab Revolt of 1936–39. The revolt was ignited on April 15, 1936 when three Qassamites seeking to commit a robbery to raise money for the movement ambushed a caravan of cars and killed two Jews in the attack (Farah 1991: 77). Zionist militias retaliated by killing two Arabs. Further beatings and killings sparked Arab protests throughout the country. Nationalist committees comprising Qassamites and other radical forces formed in several towns and, adopting a tactic used earlier in the year by the Syrians, proclaimed a general strike. Seeking to put themselves at the head of this popular upsurge, on April 25 elite nationalists formed the Arab Higher Committee and endorsed the strike (Mattar 1988: 69–70). Arab port workers of Jaffa, the Vehicle Owners' and Drivers' Association led by Hasan Sidqi al-Dajani, and other Arab workers who had previously cooperated with the Histadrut participated actively in the strike (Lockman 1996: 240–41). Peasant guerrilla bands, several led by Qassamites, began operating in the Galilee and the hill country of what is today called the West Bank in May. The general strike ended on October 12, 1936 after Arab rulers promised to intercede with "our friend Great Britain, who has declared that she will do justice" (Mattar 1988: 80). Not coincidentally, the strike was halted before the orange harvest season began, preserving the incomes of Palestinian Arab citrus growers. The elite nationalists failed to provide countrywide coordination and leadership for the revolt; many virtually abandoned the movement after the initial upsurge.

In response to a British proposal to partition Palestine, the banning of the Arab Higher Committee, and the removal of Amin al-Husayni from his religious offices, peasants in the hill country resumed armed struggle in the fall of 1937. In its last phase, in addition to its anti-British and anti-Zionist aspects, the revolt had a strong anti-landlord and anti-elite character. Peasant rebels imposed a moratorium on all debts, canceled rents on all urban apartments, and seized the property of wealthy urbanites who had fled and sold it at a mock public auction for nominal prices, leading the British high commissioner to conclude that "something like a social revolution on a small scale is beginning" (Porath 1977: 269). On August 26, 1938, when the peasant movement was at its height and had gained control over several towns, rebel leaders decreed that all Palestinian women should wear headscarves and men should adopt peasant headdress: the *kufiyya* (or *hatta*) and *igal*. This allowed peasant rebels to circulate in towns without being easily identified and captured. It also humbled the urban middle and elite classes who had to abandon the fez (*tarbush*), which had become a symbol of modernity, education, and *effendi* status. The social conflict signified by the imposition of peasant headgear is expressed in a ditty of the Nazareth *kufiyya*-sellers (Swedenburg 1995: 30–37):

> *Hatta, hatta* for ten *qurush* [piasters]
> Damn the father of whoever wears a *tarbush*

Class was not the only social cleavage to be exacerbated in the latter stages of the revolt. Tensions among Muslims, Christians, and Druze also sharpened (Swedenburg 1995: 91–94; Porath 1977 269–73). Muslim–Christian unity was restored. But the murder of twenty Druze shaykhs of Shafa ʿAmr by a rebel commander and rebel attacks on the Druze villages of Mount Carmel, which had cooperative relations with the Zionist Haifa Labor Council, led most Druze to withdraw from the Palestinian national movement and to collaborate with the Zionists in 1948 and beyond.

The Arab Revolt was suppressed by the combined force of some 25,000 British soldiers, 3,000 Jewish "Colony Police," and special night squads comprising labor Zionist militia (Haganah) members trained in commando operations by Captain Orde Wingate. With the banning of the Arab Higher Committee by the mandate authorities, the elite nationalist leadership was defeated and disoriented. Amin al-Husayni fled the country and did not return until 1949, when he briefly headed the All Palestine Government based in the Gaza Strip. The general strike allowed Hebrew labor to enter sectors of the economy previously dominated by Arabs. The special night squads became the core of the future elite unit of the Zionist armed forces (Palmah). These developments prepared the way for the Zionist victory in 1948.

The events described above and their meaning have been fiercely debated. Most Palestinian and Arab narratives assume the nationalist character of the Qassamite uprising and the Arab Revolt but de-emphasize al-Qassam's Islamic revivalist teachings, the role of peasants, their conflicts with landowning elites, and tensions with the Druze ('Allush 1978; Kayyali 1978; al-Hut 1981). Left nationalist accounts acknowledge that peasants were the main force in the revolt and criticize the timidity of the elite leaders but cast doubt on the capacity of peasants to organize and initiate political and military action independently of urban elites (Kanafani 1972; Farah 1991). In nationalist discourse, the elites or the infant left are the representatives of modernity and the nation who were unable to overcome the traditionalism and backwardness of the peasants.

Standard Zionist accounts deny the national and radical social content of the Qassamite movement and the Arab Revolt and describe the peasant rebels as gangs of bandits, rioters, or terrorists (Elpeleg 1978; Arnon-Ohanna 1982; Lachman 1982). Yehoshua Porath, author of a standard history of the Arab Revolt, has a more positive view of peasants. Nonetheless, he regards their prominence as one of the causes of the failure of the revolt and criticizes them and the entire Palestinian nationalist movement for failing to adopt the same vanguardist practices as Zionism: "If one considers the broader aspects of this abortive attempt at a revolution, one finds a confirmation of the basic tenets of Leninism: there is no revolutionary action without revolutionary ideology and a revolutionary party" (Porath 1977: 269).

More critical Israeli historians, who have become prominent since the late 1970s, acknowledge the national and social character of the Arab Revolt. Meira Meswari-Gualt argues that peasants were part of the nationalist movement, but participated on terms derived from their understandings of their own experiences.

Peasants joined the national revolt only when it suited them, i.e. in May and June [1936] after the harvest, and they chose to participate only in methods that were appropriate to their own motives and way of life . . . An armed attack was . . . suitable for peasants because they could involve themselves in it between harvesting and planting and because they already had a long tradition of rural resistance either as bandits or guerrillas . . . they were [not] completely devoid of nationalist ideology . . . their nationalism was not based solely on the modern secular ideology of the upper classes . . . Palestinian peasant nationalism during this period was based on their economic experience in the villages and towns, experience made bitter by their own landlords, the British government, and Zionist colonialism. The ideology of Islam[ic] populism brought to them by preachers like . . . al-Qassam rang familiar and comfortable. (Meswari-Gualt 1991: 58–59)

This explanation rectifies the marginalization of peasants in Palestinian Arab and Zionist nationalist histories but gives too much coherence and clarity of purpose to peasant actions. To avoid this pitfall, Ted Swedenburg adopts Gyatri Spivak's dictum that "if the story of the rise of nationalist resistance to imperialism is to be disclosed coherently, it is the role of the indigenous subaltern that must be strategically excluded" (Spivak 1987: 245, quoted in Swedenburg 1995: 18). Swedenburg elucidates the social conflicts and subaltern voices intimated by the incoherent and contested memories of the Arab Revolt refracted by subsequent historical events without attempting to reconstruct a "true" past. He explores both the central role of peasants and conflicts among the religious communities, instances of Arab collaboration with the Zionists, and internecine violence in the Arab Revolt that marked the revolt as it unfolded. Actions of this sort are inevitable in mass social movements because subalterns do not discipline their behavior with respect to elite norms. But Swedenburg does not consistently uphold Spivak's injunction. Ultimately, he quite reasonably maintains that the Arab Revolt of 1936–39 was an expression of the Palestinian nationalist movement and that armed actions of peasants were a central component of the revolt. Although Swedenburg's primary purpose is ethnographic investigation of memory and not comprehensive historical reconstruction, his effort demonstrates the possibility and value of writing histories of workers and peasants into national narratives while exercising care not to conflate the two.

The formation of new national political fields in the wake of the demise of the Ottoman Empire both enabled and constrained the political expression of hitherto marginalized social groups: peasants, workers, and women. Elite nationalists acknowledged these subalterns as functionally differentiated elements of the nation and sought to discipline them and contain their collective actions within the boundaries of the national project as they understood it. The discourse of nationalism limits the political participation of subalterns to domains and issues authorized by nationalist leaderships. Contests over the boundaries of political action and the "true" understanding of the national interest define the terrain of the nationalist movements.

4   Fikri al-Khuli's journey to al-Mahalla al-Kubra

Despite this book's focus on workers and peasants, their voices have made only minor appearances in the text so far. In part this is because a synthetic overview of any subject, by attending to "the big picture," is predisposed to emphasize large-scale structures and historical trends at the expense of microsocial histories which might allow more scope for subaltern voices. It is also because working people were commonly illiterate before the twentieth century and have left very few records. Often, the best that can be done is to reconstruct their presence in historical processes through the reports of elite and middle-class sources. Even when working people gained access to education in the late nineteenth and twentieth centuries, the great majority of those who did record their experiences and understandings of the world around them did so using the language and conceptual categories of modernist, nationalist, or religious elites.

There are many published autobiographies and labor histories by trade union leaders demonstrating that they were not simply manipulated by the elite and middle-class elements of twentieth-century nationalist movements (al-ʿAmara 1975–76; al-ʿAskari 1995; ʿIsawi 1969; Kamil 1985; al-Mudarrik 1967–69;ʿUthman 1982–94). They describe the efforts of trade unionists to assert their own agendas and carve out zones of autonomy from the political forces that competed for the loyalties of the labor movement. These accounts also indicate that many trade union leaders did orient their lives and their understandings of themselves around the modern, national categories and institutions promoted by the political classes. They may have disagreed with the policies of one or another sector of those classes. But their identities and life activities as they report them are extensively enmeshed with vocational training schools, large-scale transportation and industrial enterprises, foreign capital, trade unions, political parties, nationalist movements, and the state. Authors of autobiographies and histories who represent their experience primarily as a relationship with the institutions of modernity – schools, capitalist enterprises, and the nation-state – have in some important respects transcended their social origins and are no longer, strictly speaking, subaltern subjects.

99

Subaltern experience and consciousness are, by their nature, not wholly coherent (Gramsci 1971: 52, 54–55). They are not primarily composed of politically conscious resistance to domination, but include accommodation, everyday subversive acts, and hybrid attitudes and understandings that simultaneously reflect participation and alienation from elite and middle-class modernity. Subalterns have no access to the press and other communications media. They do not win public office or address national political forums. Consequently, they are almost always represented by others – in police reports, personnel records of enterprises where they are employed, government legislation, and accounts of erstwhile subalterns who rise above their origins. Does the near impossibility of recovering unmediated subaltern voices mean that we have no access to subaltern experiences and consciousnesses?

Other than occasional colloquial poems, I am aware of only one text by a worker or peasant author who does not present his/her life and its historical circumstances primarily in terms of the categories, institutions, and narratives of modernity. *Al-Rihla* (The Journey) is an autobiographical memoir/novel in three volumes by Fikri al-Khuli, an Egyptian peasant boy who became a worker at the Misr Spinning and Weaving Company in the Nile Delta town of al-Mahalla al-Kubra (al-Khuli 1987–92). This narrative has affinities to other works of colloquial poetry and prose that became popular as the Egyptian reading audience expanded in the 1920s. Such works often addressed aspects of popular experience and culture outside the ambit of the subjects approved by nationalist elites and the *effendiyya*, such as prostitution or petty gangsterism (Yusuf 1920; al-Usta Hanafi [1923]; ʿAtiyya 1926). But *al-Rihla*'s sustained attention to the daily experience of work in large-scale industry is unique.[1]

Al-Khuli eventually became a communist and composed *al-Rihla* while he was imprisoned at Kharga oasis during 1959–63 together with most of the other Egyptian communists. The author's political commitments and the distance between the date of the text's composition and the events it relates raise questions about its reliability. Is this merely an ideological justification of al-Khuli's political path or a clichéd exercise in socialist realism? Doesn't al-Khuli's political consciousness at least partially attenuate his subaltern status? Some of the misrepresentations that might result from these circumstances may be partly corrected by the fact that al-Khuli's explicit motive for writing *al-Rihla* was to correct his communist comrades' illusions about the modernity of the Misr Spinning and Weaving mill. In an introduction to an unpublished and highly abridged English translation of *al-Rihla*, he explained:

In prison there is plenty of spare time, so we used to meet together and tell stories ... One day one of us was telling of an outing he had gone on ... to al-Mahalla al-Kubra. He described the textile factory, how fine it was, and how there was housing for the workers and a hospital. He described the huge buildings and the beautiful modern machines ... He came to al-Mahalla as an outsider and marveled at the town and the factory and enjoyed it all, but I listened to what he said and I was shattered. Here was a worker like myself, yet he saw the factory in a completely different way from mine.

I began to speak and tell them that it was not as simple as it seemed, and that the factory was really quite different from the way my colleague described it. (El-Messiri 1980: 386)

During the 1970s, as part of the rollback of the policies of President Gamal ʿAbd al-Nasir, the Egyptian government permitted the publication of many memoirs and histories of the communist movement by communists who had been imprisoned in the Nasirist era. However, *al-Rihla* was not published until the late 1980s and early 1990s, and then by a tiny enterprise operated by Kamal ʿAbd al-Halim, a former leader of the Communist Party of Egypt on bad terms with the party and many former members. The only public acknowledgment of its existence until then was the partial translation previously mentioned, which eliminates much of the cultural specificity of its language and offers little explication of the text or its significance.[2]

Why wasn't the publishing house associated with the Communist Party of Egypt (Dar al-Thaqafa al-Jadida) or another of the more established progressive presses interested in a book written by a working-class comrade? In addition to whatever personal and political rivalries may have been a factor, three reasons come to mind. First, *al-Rihla* is a long and rambling narrative that cannot be considered a great work of art by prevailing aesthetic standards.

Second, *al-Rihla* is written largely in colloquial Egyptian Arabic, reinforcing its status as "not good art" among most intellectuals. While its language is closer to actual usage than any other available account of modern Egyptian workers, this may actually have embarrassed even left intellectuals. Even leftists who embrace colloquial poetry, which can be consigned to a niche on the margin of modern Arabic literature as "popular culture," usually have little tolerance for colloquial prose. As part of the *effendiyya*, they participate in the project of educating workers in nationalism and modernity, albeit in different terms than those the Wafd and other bourgeois nationalists employed. Moreover, since the 1950s Marxists and other leftists have usually insisted on writing in standard Arabic as a cultural expression of their commitment to pan-Arab nationalism. Writing in colloquial Egyptian Arabic undermines Egypt's Arab identity and its claim to leadership of the Arab world.

Finally, *al-Rihla* reveals aspects of the experience of workers at Mahalla that may disrupt the expectations of Marxists as much as those of bourgeois nationalists. Al-Khuli preserves the earthy sense of humor, the fierce local rivalries, the plebeian sense of manliness, and the fatalism that were part of the world of workers at Mahalla but are missing from the narratives of most labor leaders. He lovingly portrays the quotidian particulars of life in the mill and the petty incidents that unexpectedly explode into struggles, transforming the situation. He also relates in intimate detail taboo topics such as prostitution, the unsanitary toilet facilities used by the workers, and flirtatious dalliances with peasant girls during his return to his village (al-Khuli 1987–92: I, 91–108, 212–24).

Al-Khuli and the colloquial poet Salah Hafiz, who wrote the introduction to the first volume, regard *al-Rihla* as an authentic, unmediated record of al-Khuli's subaltern experience. This is a naive appreciation. No evidence can have this character. It is, however, a singular text that refuses to conform to the expectations of prevailing literary forms or organized currents of political opinion. Consequently, *al-Rihla* is a highly subversive work in many different contexts. Situating the subjects of the text in relation to other sectors of Egyptian society and bearing in mind the conditions of its publication enable us to use it to uncover something of the presence of peasant/workers, their discourse, and the social relations of production at Misr Spinning and Weaving, and by implication other enterprises like it, that would otherwise be totally inaccessible.[3]

The Misr Spinning and Weaving Company

Bank Misr was established in 1920 during the high point of the nationalist movement. It proclaimed itself "an Egyptian bank for Egyptians only" and announced the intention of breaking the monopoly of foreign financial capital in Egypt and providing capital to establish Egyptian-owned, large-scale, industrial enterprises. Hence, the bank was regarded as an expression of the nationalist movement. Tal'at Harb, the founder and managing director, vigorously promoted the industrial ventures financed by Bank Misr in the 1920s and 1930s, arguing that their particular interests, such as a protective tariff on imported cotton goods that raised the price of cloth for poorer consumers, served the national cause (Harb 1939: 68–73, 98–101, 138–44). In practice, Bank Misr and its enterprises were not nearly as nationalist as Harb's proclamations (Beinin 1998a:

326–27). Nonetheless, Bank Misr and its flagship industrial enterprise, Misr Spinning and Weaving Company, were the emblems of economic nationalism between the two world wars.

Misr Spinning and Weaving Company – the first mechanized textile enterprise owned by Muslim Egyptians – was established in 1927 in al-Mahalla al-Kubra. The firm undertook the entire textile-manufacturing process including spinning, weaving, and dyeing. Soon after beginning full-scale operations, it employed some 15,000 workers. By the end of World War II, Misr Spinning and Weaving employed over 25,000 workers and was the largest industrial enterprise in the Middle East. Bank Misr established two other major mechanized textile enterprises at Kafr al-Dawwar, near Alexandria, in 1938 employing some 11,000–12,000 workers. Both were joint enterprises with British firms, but the social relations of production were similar to the mill at Mahalla.

Launching Misr Spinning and Weaving required the company to recruit peasants and train them to become factory workers, raising their educational level, self-discipline, productive capacity, and patriotic consciousness in the process. Tal'at Harb touted his firm's commitment to the social advancement of its workers. Of course, the active agents of progress were to be the managers of the company and the political leaders of the country. Just as 'Abd al-Rahman Fahmi Pasha and others had suggested (see chapter 3), workers and peasants were to be the disciplined beneficiaries of instruction and improvement.

Peasants, workers, Egyptians

Bank Misr chose al-Mahalla al-Kubra as the site for its spinning and weaving mill partly because it was a traditional center of handicraft textile production. The company hoped to draw on the expertise of the craftsmen, and they did become an important part of the production and marketing complex that grew up around the mammoth mechanized mill. However, the great majority of unskilled and semi-skilled workers at Misr Spinning and Weaving were former peasants from villages around Mahalla.

The *effendi* who came to Fikri al-Khuli's village of Kafr al-Hama to recruit peasants to work in the mill explained Misr's mission of national economic development:

Bank Misr has established a factory to spin the cotton you grow. It will make it into cloth that you can wear. For a long time we grew cotton and the English took it from us. Today, we will grow cotton and turn it into cloth. We are the ones who will plant the cotton, spin it, weave it. It will all be Egyptian-made – a national industry. (al-Khuli 1987–92: I, 17)

In 1928, at the age of eleven, al-Khuli went to work at Misr Spinning and Weaving shortly after the mill opened. Adults in his village knew something about national politics and the economics of growing and marketing cotton (al-Khuli 1987–92: I, 207). But al-Khuli claims he had no political consciousness: "I had heard of Sa'd Zaghlul and the demonstrations against the English . . . I heard my mother and other women in the village trill for Sa'd and the Constitution, and the men applauded the Wafd when it returned to power [in 1927]. [But] I was not aware of what went on around me" (al-Khuli 1987–92: I, 15). Though he had attended the village school (*kuttab*) and knew how to read and write, al-Khuli was unaware of the geography of the nation. Tanta, the largest city in the Delta, lay only 3 kilometers from his village, and he had to pass through it on his journey to work at the mill. But he wrote, perhaps exaggerating the isolation of peasant life, that he did not know where it was (al-Khuli 1987–92: I, 18).

Arriving in Mahalla young Fikri noticed that people on the street wore clothing similar to that worn by people in his village (al-Khuli 1987–92: I, 22). If *al-Rihla* were written as a teleological allegory of the nation coming into its own in the style of many other writings of Egyptian trade union leaders, this recognition of similarity might be developed into a recognition of national identity. But al-Khuli undermines this expectation by repeatedly reporting that the dominant basis of identity in and around the mill was the sharp antagonism and rivalry between the local residents of Mahalla (*mahallawiyya*) and the peasants recruited to work at the Misr enterprise (company men, or *shirkawiyya*) (al-Khuli 1987–92: I, 55ff). The *shirkawiyya* identified themselves by their villages of origin, as non-Mahalla residents, and as Muslims. Even when they came to believe they had common interests and to act on them, they often regarded the Mahalla residents as their enemies as much as the Misr company management.

Similar frictions developed among the workers when the company decided, perhaps to undermine unionization efforts that had recently begun (see below), to employ females in the mill. Most of the males fiercely opposed the entry of females to their workplace. Some even physically attacked them (al-Khuli 1987–92: III, 51–64).

The *mahallawiyya–shirkawiyya* rivalry was so intense that in one of the central scenes of the first volume of *al-Rihla*, it explodes into a violent brawl between the two factions (al-Khuli 1987–92: I, 145–53). The fight provided an occasion for 'Abd al-'Azim to establish himself as a leader of the *shirkawiyya* by organizing self-defense "just the way we do things in the village . . . If the Mahalla people are united by the desire to get rid of us, we are also united by making our living" (al-Khuli 1987–92: I, 145).

The potential for class and national consciousness is evident in this statement. But al-Khuli does not allow the political commitments he ultimately developed to interfere with acknowledging that at the time of this incident in the late 1920s, local identities clearly predominated over class or national identities. The voice of the desired future is present, but secondary, in the narrative. When the *shirkawiyya* asked ʿAbd al-ʿAzim to organize them to beat up the *mahallawiyya*, he refused, saying, "We have the same concerns as they. All of us are one country and have one interest, but that is a matter that will become clear tomorrow" (al-Khuli 1987–92: I, 158).

The matter does begin to be clarified in the course of the first strike at the mill (al-Khuli 1987–92: II, 33–44). The workers wanted a wage increase to enable them to buy blankets so that they could sleep through the cold nights. Al-Khuli, by this time a respected mechanical loom operator despite his youth, initiated the strike by stopping his machine while an engineer was walking through his section of the mill. Other workers followed his lead and presented their demand to the engineer. After conferring with the general manager, the engineer returned and reiterated the educational mission of the *effendiyya* as it applied to the mill: "We've brought you here from the village. Every one of you is from a different village. We brought you here to train you" (al-Khuli 1987–92: II, 41).

The company did not agree to a general wage increase, which would have acknowledged and conceded to the collective interests and power of the workers, something managers of private enterprises are nearly always loath to do. Instead it established a new piece-rate wage system. Piece rates tend to pit workers against each other: younger and quicker against older and slower, veterans acquainted with the production system against unseasoned newcomers, and so on. Employers commonly prefer piece rates because they allow them to treat workers as individuals without regard to the social context: seniority, disability, etc. Individuals are the units of modern society. As consumers in the capitalist market and citizens of the nation they possess equal rights in principle, but vastly unequal capacities to realize those rights. Treating people of unequal capacities equally multiplies injustice. Workers at the Misr firm seem to have understood this, and opposed the transition to piece-rate wages. After hearing the engineer one concluded:

They've tricked us, and now they're going to make us sweat blood . . . They say we'll be paid according to production. What production? Is that better than a daily rate? We'd know how much we were going to make and plan accordingly. Now they've confused our world. They haven't given us a raise or left us in peace. They've left us with our same miserable life. (al-Khuli 1987–92: II, 42)

This worker believed that he and his mates would be better off being paid a daily (or hourly) rate and that solidarity among workers is better than competition. He may have formed this opinion based on his understanding of his experience in the mill; or, he may have adapted a previously held moral economy outlook, which would have been common among both peasants and urban guild workers, to the new circumstances of industrial wage labor.

The prince and the workers

In 1936, Prince ʿAbbas Halim visited al-Mahalla al-Kubra to organize the Misr Spinning and Weaving workers into a union under his leadership. Amidst much fanfare, the prince, borne on the shoulders of workers, entered a marquee where he was to address an assembled crowd. When he began to speak in a stammer, al-Khuli and the other workers were distressed that they could not understand him. "What's he saying? Is he speaking Polish?" they asked each other. "Is he speaking to us? He's speaking to the mechanics." One said, "He's speaking a foreign language." Another said, "Of course he's ignoring us, man. Why should he talk to us? He'll speak to people who understand him" (al-Khuli 1987–92: III, 31).

Like many members of the royal family from Khedive Ismaʿil on, ʿAbbas Halim had spent much of his childhood in Europe. He was educated in Germany and never perfected his Arabic. On this formal occasion he may have thought it appropriate to address the workers in standard Arabic rather than colloquial Egyptian. The better educated skilled mechanics probably understood his language far better than uneducated or minimally educated unskilled workers. Stammering in imperfect standard Arabic would only have compounded the comprehension difficulties of the less educated. At the conclusion of ʿAbbas Halim's speech, in response to a worker's complaint that he had understood nothing, one of the prince's aides summarized his words in colloquial Egyptian. Although the prince's stammer and flawed Arabic complicated matters, many Misr workers apparently had difficulty understanding the national language of Egypt if that language was to be modern standard Arabic rather than colloquial Egyptian, as the great majority of the *effendiyya* believed was proper.

The problem was not only lexical. After ʿAbbas Halim departed, the workers carried on a lively debate about whether he or anyone else who lived in Cairo could help them. Those in al-Khuli's circle had not known that ʿAbbas Halim was to visit them and were skeptical of what he could accomplish for them. But reluctant to pass up an offer of assistance, they agreed to pay their dues and join the union (al-Khuli 1987–92: III, 35). In fact, 'Abbas Halim never returned to Mahalla; this effort to organize a union was unsuccessful. The workers eventually resolved to write up their grievances themselves (al-Khuli 1987–92: III, 81).

Workers and others

The social distance and mutual incomprehensibility between the Misr workers and 'Abbas Halim is normal in any situation involving subalterns and a royal personality. But the workers also had little confidence in and no identification with any of Egypt's Cairo-centered national institutions – the government, political parties, or trade unions. They believed that bringing their problems to the attention of the government was useless: "Who does the government belong to? We're in one valley and they're in another. Do we know any of them? What did they do when [our fellow worker] was seized and beaten to death?" (al-Khuli 1987–92: II, 13). The workers were also alienated from the management *effendi*s they saw every day. When one of the foremen died in a work accident, al-Khuli was amazed that the company did not stop the machines even for a moment to acknowledge the dead man. "They must be different from us," he thought. "All their lives they've lived apart from us. They live in palaces. They're sons of village headmen (*wilad 'umad*). No one has ever insulted them or beaten them. They've made their lives by beating up other people" (al-Khuli 1987–92: II, 18). The behavior of the supervisors appeared arbitrary, cruel, and calculated to break the workers' spirit and human dignity. The harsh system of fines deducted from workers' wages for even the most minute infraction, beatings of workers by foremen, and other aspects of the administration of discipline in the mill appeared unreasonable to workers compared to the norms of their villages. When al-Khuli was cheated out of his wages because he was falsely accused of spoiling a bolt of cloth, some workers not only felt that it was humiliating to complain to management about the problem, but useless as well, because "no one would take sides with poor people like us" (al-Khuli 1987–92: I: 189).

Labor, capital, and the nationalist movement

Like many others in similar circumstances, workers at the Misr mill did eventually come to feel a collective solidarity which they directed against their immediate supervisors and the company management. On July 18, 1938 they struck in support of their demand for a higher piece rate and an eight-hour day in place of the twelve-hour shifts they had been working – a much larger and more comprehensive strike than the one previously mentioned (al-Khuli 1987–92: III, 165 ff). The intensity of the strike took the company by surprise. It closed down for forty-five days during which the weaving mill was reorganized into smaller workshops to diminish the danger of future collective action. About a hundred workers were arrested for their role in the strike and paraded through town as an example; fifty-five were convicted for participating in the strike. The judge who presided over their case articulated the prevailing sentiment of Egypt's political classes in expressing the court's

> strong regret and astonishment at this foolish action on the part of the weaving workers of the Misr Spinning and Weaving Company at Mahalla . . . they have departed from fulfilling their duty toward a company which helped them, supported them, and opened a door for them which they might enter while they were still ignorant . . . The workers must . . . cooperate with the company for production and sacrifice every personal interest in order to serve the fatherland, develop its commerce, and not lose the fruits of that gigantic effort because of the influence of dangerous opinions which we do not like to see among the workers, whatever the reason . . . strikes and destruction have nothing to do with Egyptians. These acts are completely repulsive to them by virtue of their education, their circumstances, and their religion, which is based on forgiveness, cooperation, and nobility of character. This young company, one of the pillars of our current renaissance, did not overwork the workers and did not ask more than their capacity, wages being determined in accordance with output. (Quoted in Eman 1943: 183–84)

According to the court and those who shared its outlook, ignorant peasants should be grateful for the opportunity to become industrial wage workers. This enabled them, perhaps unwittingly, to participate in the great project of modern, national economic construction, which required them diligently and obediently to sacrifice their personal interests for the good of the nation. Only the workers' susceptibility to subversive outside agitators obstructed their recognition of these truths.

A simulacrum of modernity?

Why were most Egyptian elites and *effendiyya* of the interwar period so unable to appreciate the aspects of work and life at Misr Spinning and Weaving reported by Fikri al-Khuli? The political classes sincerely desired certain cultural, social, and institutional changes associated with modernity, nationalism, and economic development. However, the privileges they acquired and maintained through the projects of the newly established nation-state and large-scale capitalist industry prevented them from engaging with the necessarily disorderly and dirty daily processes in specific modern institutions such as textile mills. Consequently, the judge who convicted the striking workers and very probably had shared interests with the Misr managers was unable to appreciate the conditions that motivated their action.

Outright denial was also a factor. During King Faruq's visit to Misr Spinning and Weaving in 1937, Tal'at Harb expressed his pride that the company "did not spare any effort . . . to advance [its workers'] health and social conditions by insuring them against work accidents and building first aid stations and a mosque devoted to the performance of religious obligations" (Harb 1939: 40). These claims are totally contradictory to Fikri al-Khuli's account of working conditions in the mill.

Another barrier to understanding was the development of modern representational techniques that defused idealized images of mechanized textile mills as citadels of modernity, national progress, and economic development very broadly throughout Egyptian society during both the monarchy and Nasirist periods, even among Fikri al-Khuli's communist comrades. Néstor Garcia Canclini argues that in Latin America "[modernity is] a simulacrum conjured up by elites and the state apparatuses . . . they only ordered some areas of society in order to promote a subordinate and inconsistent development; they acted as if they formed national cultures, and they barely constructed elite cultures, leaving out enormous indigenous and peasant populations" (Canclini 1995: 7). If Canclini means that the simulacrum of modernity is consciously conjured up by elites, then his approach is too conspiratorial to explain broad social and cultural structures.

However, some of Tal'at Harb's promotional efforts did portray Misr Spinning and Weaving literally as a simulacrum of modernity. The third volume of his collected speeches contains a $9^{1}/_{2} \times 15^{1}/_{2}$-inch fold-out, full gray-scale photograph of the mill at Mahalla (Harb 1939: following 138). On close examination, this turns out not to be a picture of the mill at all; it is a photograph of an architect's model of the facilities. The photograph has an eerie quality and contains no human beings or any other sign of life or motion. It eliminates all the messiness associated with industrial manufacturing in favor of an image bearing only a shadowy resemblance to the production process and its attendant social relations.

Such images were appropriated and circulated to a wide audience by the mass media. *Sayyidat al-Qitar* (Lady of the Train) – a film produced in the last months of the monarchy and screened shortly after its demise – is an outstanding example of the popular idealization of mechanized textile production (Chahine 1952). It features two major figures of twentieth-century Egyptian mass culture – director Youssef Chahine at the beginning of his career and singer/actress Layla Murad towards the end of hers. As the convoluted plot approaches resolution, Layla Murad, who is (as a woman, most improbably) "head of the workers" (*ra'isat al-'ummal*) in a mechanized textile mill owned by her family, appears on the shop floor singing a romantic, nationalist ballad to the machinery – "Dur ya mutur" (Turn, motor!).[4] The lyrics echo Tal'at Harb's message about the national character of the mechanized textile industry: "Free Egypt would rather go naked than dress in imported fabric." As Layla Murad sings, automated spindles and looms thump away in time with the music. The operators are well-dressed men and women who love their supervisor, who has graciously organized a party for their benefit. No element of social realism impinges on this idyllic scene.

The pedagogy of modernity

The repressive measures of the Misr Spinning and Weaving management succeeded in maintaining stable labor relations at al-Mahalla al-Kubra for several years. In 1941 Tal'at Harb was removed as director of Bank Misr. The new management team are dubbed compradors in Egyptian nationalist historiography. There was a brief strike in June 1946. Then, in September 1947 there was a massive strike – the largest collective action in the history of the Egyptian labor to that date (Beinin & Lockman 1987: 353–56). Although this was a major episode in the radicalization of the post-World War II nationalist movement, and communists were heavily involved in organizing the workers and promoting their cause, it is not included in *al-Rihla*. The narrative breaks off in 1942 when al-Khuli stopped working in the mill, undermining the teleological nationalist understanding of workers' collective action as part of the resistance to British rule and its local allies.

After the 1947 strike, the Misr company and the state authorities collaborated to repress all expressions of independent trade unionism at Mahalla. However, Misr's harsh labor policies ignited a fierce strike at its Fine Spinning and Weaving Mill in Kafr al-Dawwar in August 1952, shortly after the Free Officers' coup of July 23, 1952 which put an end to the Egyptian monarchy. The striking workers hailed General Muhammad Naguib and the Revolutionary Command Council, believing that the new order would be more responsive to their demands than the old regime had been. But the government repressed the strike and rapidly convened a military tribunal that sentenced two of the leaders to death by hanging (Beinin & Lockman 1987: 421–26).

Despite its harsh repressive actions at Kafr al-Dawwar, the new regime was concerned about conditions at the Misr mills and similar enterprises throughout Egypt. Acting out of the same corporatist and paternalist understanding that had informed the relations between most of the *effendiyya* and workers, it sought to introduce reforms that would obviate the need for independent trade unions and collective action initiated by workers. The regime and the company cooperated with William Carson, who undertook a study of labor relations at Misr Spinning and Weaving in 1953 funded by a grant from the Ford Foundation. Although couched in the language of value-neutral social science, Carson's report criticized the Misr company management harshly.

Full production cannot be realized under the present conditions because of the chaotic system of supervisory discipline and the complete absence of production incentives for the worker. The present labor control system in the mill conspires to maintain a constant state of tension among the workers and an ever present danger of strife.

The superior is expected to maintain production through the agency of a rigid disciplinary system which is the consequence of the opinion that the workers are "too ignorant to understand" and therefore must be ruled through fear . . . Communication has come to mean punishment and for this reason the worker stays away from his supervisor . . . The disciplinary system . . . reduces all production to the level of the poorest worker rather than raising it to the level of the good or excellent worker.

. . . Negative pressure has now created a feeling of solidarity and common cause in the labor force and antagonism toward the company.

Workers consider the present level of wages low and as an insufficient reward for their work. It is apparent that a large number are not receiving proper diet because of low income and high number of dependents . . . the workers tend to resent strongly the large differential between themselves and their supervisors and higher management whom they believe receive these salaries at their expense. It amounts to open accusation of starving them and their families. Undernourished workers are not capable of full production. (Carson 1953: 1–3)

Carson's report suggests that the *effendiyya* and upper management failed in their mission to instill national loyalty and modern attitudes in its workers at al-Mahalla al-Kubra. Any feelings of national identity and solidarity that existed among the workers in the plant were directed against them. The *effendiyya* and upper management also failed in their national economic construction mission. Building the mill and others like it was a substantial achievement, but the transformative capacity of these enterprises proved to be much less than Tal'at Harb and others hoped. The original machinery at Misr Spinning and Weaving was purchased second hand from European firms who were moving on to technologically more advanced equipment. The number of workers per loom at Misr's enterprises was far greater than in European and American textile mills. Low labor costs generated little incentive to increase efficiency. Maintaining a larger than necessary labor force and controlling it by harsh discipline was economically "rational" in the short term. Most managers probably did not believe that the peasants recruited to work in the mill were capable of understanding the tasks they were expected to perform. Certainly, they did not think workers might offer proposals to increase productivity.[5] The material limitations of capital and technology and culturally structured disdain for subalterns undermined the capacity of the *effendiyya* to achieve their national and economic objectives. In a typically pragmatic, American, liberal fashion, Carson advised that better communication between management and labor, paying workers adequately, and treating them respectfully would improve economic efficiency and, by extension, promote nationalist modernity.

Tal'at Harb, the judge who sentenced the participants in the 1938 Misr Spinning and Weaving strike, the producers of *Sayyidat al-Qitar* and dozens of other films with comparable themes, and the Egyptian elites and *effendiyya* promoted a specific bourgeois vision of modernity and nationalism that inspired many concrete achievements, such as the Misr Spinning and Weaving mill. It also established and reinforced their positions of social privilege and by extension the existing social hierarchy. For them, nationalism and modernity entailed ending the British occupation and maintaining their own leading positions in the process of remaking Egypt in Europe's image.

The difficulties in publishing *al-Rihla* were, at least in part, likely due to its disruption of the idealized images of mechanized textile production which were central to this vision of modernity: its blurring of the boundaries between peasants and industrial workers, between the village and the city, between Egypt's past and its desired future. The view of the condition of workers in the mill articulated by Tal'at Harb and the judge who convicted the striking workers and lectured them about their national duty stands in sharp contradiction with Fikri al-Khuli's accounts of the prevalence of work accidents, lung disease, restrictions on the use of toilets during work hours, physical beatings of workers by foremen, and the like. We can not determine the absolute truth of any particular incident related in *al-Rihla*. But clearly al-Khuli and his mates at Misr Spinning and Weaving thought they were working in a very different sort of place from the one imagined by the judge at the 1938 strike trial, Tal'at Harb, Youssef Chahine, or Layla Murad.

Thus, like all historical circumstances, Egyptian modernity emerges as a hybrid and untidy phenomenon incorporating attitudes and practices that its Egyptian and Euro-American promoters labeled "traditional," "backward," "premodern," etc. In the specific semi-colonial situation of Egypt, "modern" institutions and practices – such as the cultivation and export of cotton for the world market or the local manufacture of cotton goods – depended heavily on the persistence of "premodern" institutions and practices – such as the *'izba* system, with its extra-economic means of surplus extraction, and the coercive labor-control practices at Misr Spinning and Weaving. This hybrid structure was kept in place from 1923 to 1952 by the collaborative interaction of the Egyptian monarchy, its affiliated elites, most of the *effendiyya*, the British imperial presence, and privileged permanently resident foreigners. The gap between the pristine theory of nationalism, industrial development, and modernity and the power that accrued to their promoters in the course of its hybrid practice blocked the managers of Misr Spinning and Weaving and those associated with them from apprehending the experience of workers in the mill as reported by Fikri al-Khuli.

Therefore, modernity and the nation might best be understood as ensembles of materialities, institutions, practices, and ideas, and fields of social struggle that are not created or constrained solely by state-centered individuals, institutions, and ideologies. Fikri al-Khuli is, of course, not an authentic or objective chronicler but a participant in that social struggle. By injecting the presence, experience, and consciousness of subalterns into a leading site of Egyptian modernity and economic nationalism, he exposed its "impure" character and the daily struggles over production processes and social hierarchy which the elites and *effendiyya* were unwilling and unable to acknowledge.

5   Populist nationalism, state-led development, and authoritarian regimes, 1939–1973

Until the mid-1930s the majority of the political classes of the Middle East espoused liberal projects of cultural and social reform and political and economic development that they expected would set their countries on what they understood to be the historical trajectory of France and England (Hourani 1962). These projects recruited peasants and workers to send their children to schools where they would learn to be productive citizens of secular nation-states, to work to build the national economy, and to participate in national political life on terms determined by their social betters. Higher wages, access to agricultural land, and other social issues were to be postponed in the name of the national cause. Liberal economics, politics, and culture were undermined by the depression of 1929–39, the impoverishment of the peasantry, the social demands of expanding urban working classes, the growth of an underemployed, young intelligentsia, the challenges of communism, fascism, pan-Arab nationalism, and Islamism, and the glaring discrepancies between liberal theory and Anglo-French imperial practice.

The Palestinian Arab Revolt of 1936–39 exemplifies the transition between political and social movements of the liberal era and the subsequent period. Palestinian notables did not initiate the revolt; they tried, but failed, to contain it; and their failure sparked a peasant-based struggle that challenged Zionism, British imperialism, and their own social and political dominance. The 1939 White Paper limited Jewish immigration and land purchases and attempted to accommodate Palestinian Arab demands without abandoning British rule or the principle of establishing a Jewish national home. Refusing to grant immediate independence to the Arab majority and imposing restrictions on Jewish immigration when the Jews of Nazi-ruled Europe were already imperiled convinced many Arabs and Jews alike that British liberalism was a facade for a morally and politically bankrupt imperialism.

The nominally independent states formed in the former Ottoman Arab provinces exercised limited sovereignty. Iraq became independent in 1932, but the Anglo-Iraqi treaty of 1930 allowed British forces to remain as guardians of the oilfields and the imperial air route to India. The limits of Iraq's independence were demarcated in the wake of the April 1941 coup d'état that installed Rashid ʿAli al-Gaylani as prime minister and prompted the flight of the regent, ʿAbd al-Ilah, and the leading pro-British politician, Nuri al-Saʿid. Al-Gaylani refused to declare war on Germany or break diplomatic relations with Italy, and he attempted to prevent the British from expanding their base at Basra. Consequently, British forces reoccupied Iraq, reinstated ʿAbd al-Ilah as regent, and restored the power of Nuri al-Saʿid. The collaboration of the monarchy, the political elite, and the large landowning shaykhs with Britain increasingly discredited the regime.

The Anglo-Egyptian treaty of 1936 expanded the scope of Egypt's independence but did not eliminate British preeminence. The prevailing relations of power were exposed by the infamous incident of February 4, 1942. As German troops advanced towards Alexandria, British tanks surrounded the royal palace, and the British ambassador demanded that King Faruq appoint the reliably anti-Nazi Wafd leader, Mustafa al-Nahhas Pasha, as prime minister. Collaboration with the British occupation, inability to enact a land reform, urban economic distress, and internal schisms diminished the Wafd's popular appeal during the last ten years of the monarchy.

Despite the proclaimed anti-imperialism of the Socialist and Communist parties, the 1936–38 Popular Front government of France could not agree to grant independence to Syria and Lebanon or overcome *colon* opposition to extending the franchise to the 25,000 "evolved" Algerian Muslims who had adopted French culture. North African Star, the nationalist organization based among Algerian workers in France, criticized the proposal to extend the franchise as inadequate and demanded independence. Consequently, in January 1937, the movement was proscribed. Its tactically more moderate Algeria-based successor, the Algerian People's Party, was also banned in 1939. Disappointment with the Popular Front's colonial policy led two Syrian Sorbonne graduates, Michel ʿAflaq and Salah al-Din al-Bitar, to form the circles of students who became the nucleus of the Baʿth Party.

Depression and world war: the beginnings of state-led industrial development and the growth of urban working classes

The open economies imposed on the Middle East by the 1838 Anglo-Ottoman Commercial Convention remained in effect until the depression of the 1930s. Declining industrial production in Europe and North

America reduced exports to the Middle East and created space for development of local industry. Turkey, Egypt, and to a lesser extent other countries adopted state interventionist industrial policies and experienced counter-cyclical economic growth along with an increase in the number and social significance of urban wage workers.

Turkey's new economic policy of state-led industrialization and autarkic development was embodied in the Five-Year Industrial Plan adopted in 1934. It featured a huge textile mill in Kayseri opened in 1935 with machinery and technical assistance provided by the Soviet Union and an iron and a steel complex established in 1938 with British financial assistance. Manufacturing output doubled from 1932 to 1939. A quarter of the production came from some twenty state-owned industrial and mining enterprises. Still, at the start of World War II, only about 10 percent of the labor force was employed in manufacturing, utilities, and mining (Keyder 1987: 110; Owen & Pamuk 1999: 18, 244).

Harsh labor-control measures accompanied state-led industrial development. Istanbul workers were fingerprinted in 1932. The Labor Laws of 1934 and 1936 established a corporatist regime modeled on Italian fascist legislation. Trade unions and strikes were banned. Instead of unions (*sendika*) workers were encouraged to form corporations (*birlik*). Class-based associations were banned in 1938 (Ahmad 1993: 99; Ahmad 1995: 92; Yavuz 1995: 100–01; Keyder 1987: 104).

Following the abolition of the Capitulations in 1937, Egypt enacted protective tariffs and initiated new industrial enterprises, including joint ventures with foreign firms. Except during the despotic Sidqi regime (1930–33), trade unions and workers' collective actions were repressed less severely than in Turkey, though unions were not formally legalized until 1942. The Cairo suburb of Shubra al-Khayma became a center of the textile industry and radical, working-class collective action. In 1937–38, dissatisfied with the tutelage of the Wafd and Prince 'Abbas Halim over the labor movement, Muhammad Yusuf al-Mudarrik and other trade unionists from the Shubra al-Khayma area founded the Commission to Organize the Workers' Movement. The commission advocated trade union independence from party politics – an articulation of its aspiration to assert the autonomy of the working class as a social force.

World War II accelerated state-led industrial development and the growth of working classes. Revived European and North American manufacturing served Allied military needs and did not compete with nascent Middle Eastern industries. The Anglo-American Middle East Supply Center established in Cairo in 1941 encouraged local industrial development in order to reduce nonmilitary imports into the region.

Private entrepreneurs and the Allied forces employed local workers for military production, transport, and auxiliary services, especially in Egypt and Palestine, the principal British bases in the Middle East. In late 1943, Allied forces employed 263,000 workers in Egypt. By 1945, in a nonagricultural wage labor force of approximately 2.5 million, there were some 623,000 industrial workers, including 165,000 still employed by Allied forces (Beinin & Lockman 1987: 260–61). The largest employer of urban wage labor in Palestine until World War II was the Palestine Railways; its Arab–Jewish workforce peaked at 7,800 in 1943. Consolidated Refineries in Haifa began production in 1940 and employed over 2,000 Arab, Jewish, and British manual and clerical workers. By 1944 there were 100,000 Arab non-agricultural wage workers, about 35,000 of whom were employed at British military bases along with 15,000 Jewish workers (Lockman 1996: 12, 267, 292, 351). Perhaps another 80,000 Arabs and Jews were employed in war-related activities (Owen & Pamuk 1999: 69).

Even in Saudi Arabia, war-related oil production brought a tiny working class into existence. The Arabian American Oil Company (ARAMCO) began production in 1939. After an initial cutback, output was expanded in 1943 to provide fuel for Allied forces in east Asia. Consequently, ARAMCO's workforce grew from 2,882 in 1943 to 11,892 in 1945, including nearly 7,500 Saudi nationals (Owen & Pamuk 1999: 87).

As a neutral country, Turkey did not benefit from Allied-sponsored industrial development. Industrial and agricultural production dropped sharply during the war, while inflation soared. Social unrest was controlled by martial law and the National Emergency Law in 1940, which virtually militarized the economy. Workers in mining and industry were required to work overtime and forbidden to leave their workplaces. An eleven-hour day was imposed, even on women and children. Weekly days off were banned (Güzel 1995).

The Democrat Party (DP) regime of 1950–60 loosened the state's grip on labor somewhat. In the 1950 election campaign the DP pledged to legalize strikes, but it failed to fulfill this promise (Işıklı 1987: 315). With assistance from the American Federation of Labor and the International Confederation of Free Trade Unions, the DP encouraged the formation of the Confederation of Turkish Trade Unions (Türk İş – Türkiye İşçi Sendikaları Konfederasyonu) in 1952. The DP insisted that this be an apolitical, business union led by one of its supporters.

The peasant question

Rural poverty and inequitable distribution of agricultural land placed the peasant question on the agenda of local reformers and international development agencies in the 1940s (Warriner 1948). In Egypt, Iraq, and Syria inability to enact land reform came to be considered a salient failure of the newly independent regimes. Land distribution was most inequitable in Algeria, but no reform was possible under colonial rule. Ironically, Turkey, which was least in need of an agrarian reform, was the first country to enact one, though it was not primarily directed at redistributing large holdings.

Egypt: landed power and political paralysis

In 1939, 53 percent of all rural households in Egypt neither owned nor rented land and subsisted solely on wage labor. By 1950, 60 percent of the rural population, 1.5 million families, was landless. Two million families, 72 percent of all landowners, held 13 percent of the land in plots of less than 1 *faddan*; about 12,000 families, less than 0.5 percent of all landowners, held 35 percent of the land in plots of over 50 *faddan*s (Radwan & Lee 1986: 7).

Population pressure on agricultural land induced steady migration from the countryside to the cities. The combined population of Cairo and Alexandria, 1.24 million in 1917, rose to over 3 million by 1947 – over three times more rapid growth than that of the overall population. Only a small fraction of new urban dwellers found work in manufacturing.

Despite these appalling conditions, the political dominance of large landowners prevented land redistribution from receiving serious consideration in the 1930s. 'A'isha 'Abd al-Rahman, the first woman from a peasant background to attend Cairo University, worked with the Wafd on rural questions for a time and wrote two books bitterly protesting against the misery of the peasants (Bint al-Shati' 1936; Bint al-Shati' [1938]). Mirrit Ghali and Hafiz 'Afifi, representing the views of "enlightened" landowners and industrialists respectively, published widely acclaimed calls for social reform (Ghali 1938; 'Afifi 1938). All these manifestoes ignored or opposed redistributing agricultural land.

At the end of World War II, Mirrit Ghali altered his stand and endorsed agrarian reform as a way to direct capital from agriculture to manufacturing and commerce, deepen the domestic market, and ensure "economic independence and social dignity" (Ghali 1945: 9). Neither the minority governments of 1944–50 nor the Wafd regime of 1950–52 seriously considered this. The Wafd could not adopt policies inimical to landed interests because village headmen and local notables were the basis of its rural strength, and party strongman Fu'ad Sirag al-Din Pasha owned 8,000 *faddan*s. No other significant political force took up the peasants' cause. Ahmad Sadiq Sa'd, a leader of the New Dawn communist group, wrote a pamphlet advocating agrarian reform, but the Marxists concentrated their attention on urban workers (Saʿd 1945).

The preponderant power of landed wealth and lack of effective urban allies prevented peasants from organizing a coherent social or political movement. They did clash with landlords, local officials, merchants, tax collectors, and the police over rents, evictions, taxes, illegal drugs and arms, and water rights. Partial and unsystematically compiled reports indicate that there were twenty or twenty-one such collective actions from 1924 to 1936, and thirty-seven from 1944 to 1952: a marked increase in peasant collective action in the last twelve years of the monarchy compared to its first twelve years (Brown 1990: 128–47). Moreover, in the earlier period only five actions appear to have been aimed directly against landlords, while in the later period there were twelve openly anti-landlord actions. They were concentrated during the three successive upsurges of the nationalist movement: fall 1945 to July 1946; fall 1947 to May 1948; and mid-1951 to January 1952. During the Wafd regime of 1950–52, peasant collective actions increased sharply on large estates in the outer Delta, including several strikes demanding lower rents or higher wages. The minister of social affairs, Dr. Ahmad Husayn, reported "unmistakable signs of revolution" in the countryside (al-Ishtirakiyya, September 15, 1950, Quoted in Brown 1990: 108).

These words seem to anticipate the uprising on the al-Badrawi family estate (ʿizba) at Buhut in June 1951. After an overseer attempted to collect extra rent, peasants marched to the al-Badrawi mansion to air their grievances. One of the al-Badrawis fired on the crowd. Peasants responded by torching the mansion and other estate property. This incident was especially politically salient because the al-Badrawis were the largest landowners in Egypt outside the royal family and were related by marriage to the minister of interior, Fuʾad Sirag al-Din Pasha.

Iraq: tribal shaykhs, political elites, and rural poverty

The British Mandate and the Iraqi monarchy encouraged the growth and legal recognition of a large landowning class comprised of shaykhs who privatized the holdings of their tribes and political elites who acquired large plots. The cropped area expanded nearly five times from 1913 to 1943 due to increased used of irrigation pumps, facilitated by a 1926 law that exempted crops on newly pump-irrigated land from taxes for four seasons. Installation of pumps allowed shaykhs and others with wealth to privatize state-administered (miri) land, and this was further encouraged by the land settlement laws of 1932 and 1938. By the 1950s, 72.9 percent of all landholders held only 6.2 percent of the agricultural land in small

plots of less than 50 *dunum*s, while 55.1 percent of all privately held agricultural land was held by less than 1 percent of all owners in large plots of
over 1,000 *dunam*s. Some 600,000 rural household heads out of a total
rural population of 3.8 million were landless. Property holding was most
concentrated in the southeastern provinces of Kut, ʿAmara, and other
regions where irrigation pumps and barrages had recently been introduced and tribal social relations remained strong (Batatu 1978: 54–56;
Farouk-Sluglett & Sluglett 1987: 31–32). There were five peasant revolts
in these areas from 1952 to 1958, though we know little about them (Haj
1997: 162).

Landless peasants, especially from ʿAmara, migrated to Baghdad and
Basra. From 1947 to 1957 the population of greater Baghdad increased
from 515,000 to 793,000. In the early 1950s some 92,000 recent
migrants to Baghdad lived in 16,400 huts made from palm branches
(*sarifa*s). Many impoverished *sarifa* dwellers from ʿAmara found employment in the Baghdad police force. Hence, they found themselves repres-
sing the popular uprisings of January 1948 and November 1952 in which
many of their compatriots participated prominently (Batatu 1978:
133–36; Farouk-Sluglett & Sluglett 1987: 34).

Syria: large landlords and peasant politics

French mandatory rule in Syria accelerated trends that had begun earlier
and encouraged the consolidation of a large landholding class by abolishing tax farming, strengthening private property rights, and fostering a pro-
French landed elite. The expanded use of mechanical pumps and tractors
from 1948 to 1952 and the cultivation of cotton on the middle Orontes
River forced many sharecroppers off the land and turned them into seasonal workers (Batatu 1999: 129). By the early 1950s, owners of plots of
more than 100 hectares constituted less than 1 percent of the agricultural
population but held half the cultivable area, while 60 percent of the agricultural population owned no land at all (Hinnebusch 1989: 88, 119–20).
Substantial peasant ownership of small plots of 10 hectares or less persisted in the provinces of Hawran (47 percent of the land), Latakia (32
percent), and Jabal Druze (30 percent). At the other end of the spectrum,
56 percent of the land in Hama province was held in plots of over 100 hectares, while only 2 percent was held in plots of 10 hectares or less. Small
and medium peasants held the majority of land around Damascus,
Aleppo, and Homs. Large landowners were less entrenched in Syria than
in Egypt and Iraq, but they formed the most powerful economic interest
group and the largest bloc of parliament members during the Mandate
and the first decade of independence (Gerber 1987: 97, 101).

The extreme concentration of agricultural land in the Hama region in the hands of the Barazi, ʿAzm, and Kaylani families motivated the formation of an exceptional peasant-based political movement (Batatu 1999: 124–30). In 1939 a pan-Arabist lawyer from Hama, Akram Hawrani, formed the Youth Party (Hizb al-Shabab). The other founding party leaders were also members of the urban new middle class, but peasants were its main supporters. In 1943, the party adopted a radical pro-peasant, anti-landlord orientation expressed by its slogan "Fetch the Basket and Shovel to Bury the Agha and the Bey." Some 800 party members volunteered to fight in the 1948 Arab–Israeli War. Hawrani returned from Palestine convinced that "feudalism" was the cause of the Arab defeat and that the agrarian question and the Arab national cause were closely linked. The party marked its transformation into the Arab Socialist Party (ASP) in 1950 by convening a peasant congress in Aleppo attended by at least 40,000 people. The ASP's 10,000 members included sunni and Christian horticulturalists and sharecroppers from Hama and other regions, ʿAlawis, and Druze, making it an all-Syrian class-based peasant party. The ASP supported direct parliamentary elections and a secret ballot so landlords could not intimidate peasant voters; it also used violence against landlords who abused their sharecroppers. In 1952 the ASP merged with the Baʿth Party. Though only eighty leading ASP members formally joined the Baʿth, Hawrani's peasant followers remained loyal to him and lent a popular character to the Baʿth, which had had a very limited and primarily student following until then.

Algeria: colons and landless peasants

The distribution of agricultural land was most inequitable and the status of peasants most dire in Algeria. By 1954 some 22,000 French landowners held over 2.7 million hectares of the best land, the great majority in large plots of over 100 hectares. The 631,000 Muslim landowners held almost 7.7 million hectares, mostly in small and medium-sized plots of 50 hectares or less. As grapevines replaced wheat as the leading crop, landless peasants shifted from sharecropping in wheat to wage labor in viticulture, which required five times more work days per hectare than wheat. This created a large, seasonally employed, agrarian semi-proletariat whose numbers peaked at 571,000 in 1954 (Bennoune 1988: 61–62; Wolf 1968: 231).

Underemployment of the rural population accelerated migration to Algiers, Oran, and other cities. Between 1936 and 1954 the total number of urban Muslims rose from 722,800 to 1.6 million. Many peasant migrants who failed to find work in the cities continued on to France, especially after the 1947 legislation permitting free movement between Algeria and France. The annual number of Algerian migrants peaked at nearly 202,000 in 1955, when there was a total of 400,000 Algerian workers, mostly former peasants, in France (Bennoune 1988: 69, 77–78).

Turkey: peasant family farms and rollback of Kemalism

Unlike the Arab countries, 72.6 percent of Turkish agricultural holdings were owner operated in 1950, rising to 85.3 percent in 1963. Most of these were peasant family farms of less than 10 hectares (Margulies & Yıldızoğlu 1987: 276, 283). The Land Distribution Law of 1946 permitted redistribution from large to small owners. But the great majority of the 3.15 million hectares distributed to small holders and landless peasants between 1947 and 1959 consisted of state lands and communal pastures. Marshall Plan aid financed the importation of tractors and other machinery, which primarily benefited rich peasants and large landowners. Land distribution and mechanization increased the cropped area by 55 percent, which contributed to the spurt of growth in agricultural production from 1947 until the end of the Korean War in 1953 during which both peasant family farms and large landowners prospered (Hansen 1991: 341; Owen & Pamuk 1999: 106–10). These favorable conditions allowed the Democrat Party to leaven its pro-business, agriculture-led economic policy with a certain populism. Seeking to roll back Kemalism, the DP ended the most substantial intervention of the state in village life: the village institutes established in 1940 to instruct peasants in secular modernity (Ahmad 1993: 83–84). Hence, the DP was popular among peasants despite its pro-business outlook.

Declining crop prices after the Korean War and hopes for a better life in the city led one out of ten Turkish villagers to migrate to an urban area from 1950 to 1960. The size of the four largest cities increased by 75 percent, and urban dwellers grew to 26 percent of the total population (Keyder 1987: 137). In the early 1960s some 45–60 percent of the population of Ankara, Istanbul, and Adana and 33 percent of the population in Izmir lived in squatter settlements known as *gecekondus* (Karpat 1976: 11).

Nationalism and urban social radicalism

The prominence of the Soviet Union in the international anti-fascist coalition brought Marxism to the attention of many intellectuals in the 1930s and 1940s. The concepts of class, exploitation, and imperialism offered a plausible explanation for the dismaying conditions of peasants and urban working classes and the collaboration of large landowners and other elites with European political and economic domination. Allied wartime promises raised expectations for a postwar era of independence and economic development. Coalitions of intellectuals and urban workers infused postwar demands for independence with a new social radicalism. In addition to Palestine, Egypt, and Iraq which are discussed here, there were comparable developments in Sudan and Iran (Warburg 1978; Abrahamian 1982).

Palestine: Marxism and national conflict[1]

The Palestine Communist Party (PCP) spoke in the name of both the Arab and Jewish working classes and sought to provide an alternative to the contending nationalisms. Opposition to Zionism and the leadership of the Arab Higher Committee marginalized the party in both communities, and Arab–Jewish unity was badly strained by the 1936–39 Arab Revolt. The growth of the Arab working class during World War II allowed Marxism to become a significant force in the Arab labor movement, while the Soviet Union's leading role in the anti-Nazi struggle after 1941 made it attractive to a larger Jewish audience than before.

There were four trade union organizations in Palestine in the 1940s. The Histadrut was the central institution of labor Zionism and the entire Jewish community and the vehicle for implementing the labor Zionist policy of promoting exclusively Hebrew labor. It included the great majority of Jewish workers except known communists, and many non-workers as well. Inspired by the labor Zionist notion that Jewish settlement would bring economic development to Palestine and liberate Arab society from domination by the landed notables, the Histadrut tried half-heartedly to organize Arab workers in the Palestine Labor League (Ittihad 'Ummal Filastin/Brit Po'alei Eretz Yisra'el). Some Arab workers cooperated with the Histadrut in certain circumstances. Even they were justifiably suspicious that it would eventually seek to place Jews in their jobs.

The Palestine Arab Workers' Society (PAWS – Jam'iyyat al-'Ummal al-'Arabiyya al-Filastiniyya) was established in Haifa in 1925. Its core was comprised of the Arab members of the short-lived Arab–Jewish railway workers' union who left the joint organization when the Jews refused to sever their ties with the Histadrut. In 1942, new branches were established, some led by communists and other leftists who preferred to remain in the PAWS despite its conservative social orientation and the undemocratic leadership of Sami Taha. The nominal national membership of the PAWS in the mid-1940s was about five thousand, though less than five hundred paid dues.

In 1942 young Marxist intellectuals led by Bulus Farah, who had recently been expelled from the PCP for his nationalist views, established the Federation of Arab Trade Unions and Labor Societies (FATULS – Ittihad al-Niqabat wa'l-Jam'iyyat al-'Arabiyya). By the end of the year, it recruited 1,000–1,500 members, including workers in the Haifa-area petroleum sector, the Haifa port, and the British military camps. Thus by 1943 Marxists led much of the organized Arab working class.

The cost-of-living index rose from 100 in 1936 to 103 in 1939, 269 in 1943, and 295 in 1945, sharply eroding real wages. Government workers received a cost-of-living allowance (COLA) in late 1941. This proved inadequate as prices continued to rise. Wages and working conditions at the British military bases were worse than average, and the camp workers did not receive the COLA. In April 1943 the Histadrut began competing with the PAWS to organize and speak for both Jewish and Arab camp workers. The Histadrut decided not to cooperate with the PAWS and unilaterally proclaimed a strike on May 10 to obtain the COLA. Thousands of Arab workers joined the strike, but the majority refused to follow the Histadrut's leadership and responded to the PAWS appeal not to strike. The issue of Arab–Jewish cooperation faded away in June when the government announced that it would grant a new COLA that would apply to camp workers.

The May 10 camp workers' strike was the proximate cause of the demise of Arab–Jewish unity in the PCP. Arab communists active in the PAWS, in accord with party policy, tried to convince the Arab workers not to strike. Most Jewish communists, though critical of its unilateral action, sought to rejoin the Histadrut and refused to ask Jewish workers to break the strike.

The camp strike and the dissolution of the Comintern the same month encouraged young Arab intellectuals in the PCP influenced by Bulus Farah to assert a more national orientation. They provoked a split by distributing a leaflet describing the PCP as an "Arab national party." By early 1944, most Arab Marxists regrouped in a new Arab organization – the National Liberation League (NLL – 'Usbat al-Taharrur al-Watani), which adopted as its organ the previously established weekly of the FATULS, *al-Ittihad* (Unity). The NLL was a social movement representing the young, mostly Christian intelligentsia and the nascent working class: social strata that were marginal to the existing Palestinian Arab political system. Its program advocating working-class social demands, democracy, and national liberation was a common post-World War II communist strategy.

Both the FATULS and the left wing of the PAWS supported the NLL. When Sami Taha attempted to dictate the composition of the PAWS delegation to the founding congress of the World Federation of Trade Unions in August 1945, the left wing of the PAWS joined with the FATULS in forming the Arab Workers' Congress (AWC – Ittihad al-'Ummal al-'Arab), which quickly became the largest and most important Arab labor organization in Palestine. It claimed 20,000 members in 1945 and was the leading Arab union federation in Jaffa, Gaza, Jerusalem, and Nazareth. In Haifa, it challenged the historic primacy of the PAWS. Two AWC leaders – Fu'ad Nassar, the former head of the Nazareth PAWS branch, and Khalil Shanir, a veteran communist and former head of the Jaffa PAWS branch – joined the NLL central committee.

Because of the internationalist background of many of its leaders, the AWC was amenable to joint action with the Histadrut on economic issues. In September 1945, the two unions organized a seven-day strike of 1,300 workers at the British military workshops outside Tel Aviv. They demanded union recognition, payment of the COLA, relaxation of disciplinary rules, and rehiring of unjustly fired workers. Arab and Jewish strikers established picket lines at the work site and marched through Tel Aviv chanting in Arabic and Hebrew, "Long live unity between Arab and Jewish Workers."

The partial success of this strike encouraged the Histadrut to collaborate with the AWC in addressing the demands of the camp workers. The PAWS was stronger than the AWC among the Arab camp workers and less inclined to work with the Histadrut. But prompted by the announcement of a new round of layoffs, the three unions agreed to call a one-day strike of the 40,000 workers on May 20, 1947. The Histadrut leaders declined further joint action because they feared that a protracted strike might advance the Arab nationalist cause just as the United Nations Special Committee on Palestine was due to arrive in the country. They believed Sami Taha was an ally of the exiled titular head of the Arab Higher Committee, al-Hajj Amin al-Husayni.

In fact, a rift between Taha and al-Husayni had been developing since late 1946, when the PAWS adopted a resolution endorsing a vague socialism. Taha had begun to speak about forming an Arab labor party and to explore the possibility of a compromise with the Zionists. On September 12, 1947 he was assassinated. The assailant was never identified but was widely presumed to be acting on behalf of Amin al-Husayni.

The AWC and the NLL were severely weakened by splits in the wake of the Soviet Union's support for the UN proposal to partition Palestine into an Arab and a Jewish state. Unlike all the other Arab political forces, the NLL recognized the civic rights of Jews in a future democratic state of Palestine and distinguished between Zionism and the Jews of Palestine. But it envisioned a unitary state whose character would be determined by the fact that there was a large Arab majority in Palestine up to 1948. The split over the partition question, the closure of *al- Ittihad* by the British authorities in 1948, and the expulsion and flight of over 700,000 Palestinian Arabs during 1947–49 incapacitated the AWC and NLL. The left-national movement they promoted was too young and the Arab–Jewish working-class solidarity they aspired to build too limited to withstand the force of the Arab–Zionist conflict.

Egypt: the rise and limits of working-class radicalism[2]

Towards the end of World War II, some 250,000 Egyptian workers were dismissed from war-related jobs. Unemployment was exacerbated by sharp fluctuations in production and intensified mechanization in the textile industry. The cost-of-living index rose from 100 in 1939 to 331 in 1952, and real wages did not keep pace. These conditions, along with the escalating agrarian crisis, the military defeat in Palestine, the debauchery and corruption of King Faruq, and the continuing British occupation informed the amalgam of radical trade union and nationalist mobilization that contributed to the demise of the monarchy.

By 1942, the Shubra al-Khayma textile workers' union, led by Taha Sa'd 'Uthman, Mahmud al-'Askari, and their allies in the future New Dawn communist group, established itself as the most militant and politically independent-minded group of Egyptian workers. In September 1945 the textile union leaders, along with Muhammad Yusuf al-Mudarrik and the labor lawyer Yusuf Darwish, founded the Workers' Committee for National Liberation (Lajnat al-'Ummal lil-Tahrir al-Qawmi) and a newspaper, *al-Damir* (The Conscience). Alarmed by these developments, the police and army instituted heavy patrolling of Shubra al-Khayma in mid-December, precipitating a nine-day strike in January 1946 that targeted both the government and continuing layoffs in the textile industry. The Society of Muslim Brothers challenged the leadership of the Marxists and their allies during this strike and afterwards. Despite support from the government, they achieved only limited and temporary successes.

A police attack on a student demonstration demanding evacuation of British troops on February 9, 1946 prompted the formation of the National Committee of Workers and Students (NCWS – al-Lajna al-Wataniyya lil-'Ummal w'al-Talaba) – a coalition supported by the communist groups – New Dawn, Iskra, and the Egyptian Movement for National Liberation (EMNL – al-Haraka al-Misriyya lil-Tahrir al-Watani) – and the radical wing of the Wafd, the Wafdist Vanguard. The NCWS called for a general strike and demonstration on February 21,

1946, designated as "Evacuation Day." Thousands of workers from Shubra al-Khayma joined a crowd estimated at between 40,000 and 100,000 in the Cairo demonstration.

The fusion of radical trade unionism and militant nationalism embodied in the NCWS inspired efforts to establish a national trade union federation. After some initial factional contention, trade unionists linked to the EMNL and New Dawn agreed to join forces, just as a second strike broke out at some nineteen textile mills in Shubra al-Khayma in May 1946. The united federation, the Congress of Trade Unions of Egypt (Mu'tamar Niqabat 'Ummal al-Qatr al-Misri), called for a general strike on June 25 to support the Shubra al-Khayma strikers and to demand a government campaign against unemployment, restoration of all fired workers to their jobs, and immediate evacuation of all British forces from the Nile valley. This was far more than a newly formed, Cairo-centered organization could realistically attain. Isma'il Sidqi Pasha had been reappointed prime minister in February with the understanding that he was to crush the working-class and nationalist upsurge. When the labor radicals overextended themselves, he struck. On July 11 he arrested the labor federation leaders and proscribed all the left and labor periodicals and associations, including the nascent trade union federation.

Despite this setback, a new wave of labor and radical nationalist collective action began in the fall of 1947 after the Sidqi–Bevin talks failed to renegotiate the 1936 Anglo-Egyptian treaty. The most dramatic event of this period was the strike of the 26,000 workers at the Misr Spinning and Weaving mill in al-Mahalla al-Kubra in September 1947 in response to layoffs and the harsh and paternalistic regime of labor control. This upsurge was ended by the declaration of martial law on May 13, 1948, two days before the Egyptian army invaded Palestine.

From mid-1951 until January 1952 suburban Cairo textile workers once again emerged as the center of gravity of the radical current in the workers' movement. Their most prominent leaders, Muhammad 'Ali 'Amr and Muhammad Shatta, were members of the Democratic Movement for National Liberation (DMNL – al-Haraka al-Dimuqratiyya lil-Tahrir al-Watani), formed by the merger of Iskra and the EMNL in 1947. Communists also established themselves in other sectors, including the Congress of Egyptian Joint Transport Drivers' and Workers' Unions founded in June 1951 and led by DMNL members Hasan 'Abd al-Rahman and Sayyid Khalil Turk. Trade union and nationalist struggle converged once again when the 71,000 workers employed at the British base in the Suez Canal Zone went on strike to support the Wafd government's abrogation of the 1936 Anglo-Egyptian treaty on October 8, 1951.

In this atmosphere of popular mobilization, DMNL trade union leaders formed the Preparatory Committee for a General Federation of Egyptian Trade Unions (PCGFETU – al-Lajna al-Tahdiriyya lil-Ittihad al-ʿAmm li-Niqabat ʿUmmal Misr). This effort to build a national trade union federation by promoting working-class-inflected nationalism won the DMNL many new allies. By December, 104 unions with nearly 65,000 workers – nearly half of all union members – adhered to the PCGFETU. The organization planned a founding congress for a national trade union federation on January 27, 1952. The Cairo fire of January 26 and the proclamation of martial law prevented the conference from convening and signaled the impending end of the monarchy.

The DMNL was the only communist group to support Gamal ʿAbd al-Nasir and the Free Officers who overthrew the Egyptian monarchy on July 23, 1952, but its hope to exercise influence over the new regime was quickly disappointed. The Free Officers' first act in the realm of economic and social policy was to suppress the strike of textile workers at Kafr al-Dawwar in August 1952 and hang two of its leaders. ʿAbd al-Nasir refused to allow the founding congress for a national trade union federation to convene until 1957, after several campaigns of arrests eliminated communists from most of their positions of influence in the trade unions.

Iraq: communism and the end of the monarchy[3]

The number of Iraqi industrial and transport workers employed in enterprises of one hundred or more increased from 13,140 in 1926 to 62,519 in 1954, or 375 percent. Over half of them were employed in greater Baghdad or Basra. Maldistribution of oil wealth augmented normal wartime inflation, making the gap between the wealthy few and the poor majority exceptionally wide. From 1939 to 1948 the price-of-food index rose 805 percent, while average wages of unskilled workers increased only 400 percent. Salaries of civil servants, teachers, clerks, journalists, and army officers also lagged far behind the rate of inflation. These rapidly growing sectors of the urban population, along with students, formed the base of support of the Communist Party of Iraq (CPI). Led by Yusuf Salman Yusuf (Fahd), the CPI became the only truly national political party and the best-organized force in the trade union movement in the 1940s.

Twelve of the sixteen trade unions legalized during 1944–46 were led by the CPI. The largest and most important of these, the Railway Workers' Union, enrolled a third of the 10,800 railway workers; its president was the communist locomotive driver ʿAli Shukur. On April 15, 1945 most of the 1,265 workers at the Schalchiyya railway workshops in Baghdad and some workers outside the capital struck the British-managed Railway Directorate demanding a 30–50 percent wage increase. The strike committee was arrested and the union suppressed, but the workers won wage increases of 20–30 percent. Lack of a recognized union did not deter the railway workers from responding to further strike calls from the CPI on February 27, 1946 and three times in March–May 1948.

The 3,125 members of the Basra Port workers' union, 60 percent of the total workforce, were led by the communist ʿAbd al-Hasan al-Jabbar. They struck for five days in May 1947, demanding higher wages. The government responded by dissolving the union and arresting the leadership. The union was broken after three additional strikes in April–May 1948.

The oil industry employed 12,750 blue- and white-collar workers in 1946. After their request to form a union was denied, a committee led by four communist workers organized a strike on July 3, 1946. Some 5,000 workers, most of the local labor force, marched peacefully through Kirkuk on July 4. On July 12, mounted police attacked workers who had gathered in a garden to hear news of the strike, killing ten and wounding twenty-seven. This unprovoked police attack radicalized the oil workers even though they received a daily wage increase from 200 to 310 *fils*, and the CPI's organizational capacity was weakened by the arrest of the strike committee.

Leadership of these strikes prepared the CPI to play a major role in the largest popular insurrection of the monarchy: the *wathba*, or leap, of January 1948. As in Egypt, British refusal to accept full Iraqi independence combined with urban social distress to forge a coalition of students and workers. On January 16, 1948 the Portsmouth Agreement, extending the presence of the British air bases in Iraq, was announced. The Student Cooperation Committee, led by communists and supported by the other opposition forces, responded with three days of strikes and demonstrations. On January 20 the students were joined by the Schalchiyya railway workers and poor migrants to Baghdad from ʿAmara and the southeast. Police fired on the demonstrators, who returned the next day to face the bullets once again. The massive popular response forced the regent's renunciation of the Portsmouth Agreement and the resignation of the prime minister.

The social mobilization of the *wathba* continued with a strike of over 3,000 oil workers at the K3 pumping station near Haditha in April 1948. They demanded wage increases of 25–40 percent. After striking for three weeks, the workers, led by the CPI, began to march towards Baghdad on May 12. They were warmly supported by the people of Hit and Ramadi. At Falluja, some 70 kilometers from Baghdad, the police intervened and arrested the strikers. Despite its failure, the Great March became a legend in Iraqi politics and enhanced the CPI's prestige among workers and other opponents of the regime.

The CPI was seriously weakened by successive waves of repression in the 1950s. Nonetheless, it retained sufficient strength to participate in the nationalist upsurges of 1952 and 1956. It was a key component of the civilian coalition that supported the Free Officers led by ʿAbd al-Karim Qasim who overthrew the monarchy on July 14, 1958.

Armed struggle in Algeria and Yemen

The post-World War II Algerian nationalist movement differed from those of Palestine, Egypt, and Iraq due to its peasant base, the marginal role of communists, and the armed struggle. North African Star and its successors infused Algerian nationalism with a strong working-class, Marxist-influenced element. Its leader, Messali Hadj, never joined the National Liberation Front (FLN), which launched the armed struggle for independence on November 1, 1954, though most of his followers did.

The dire situation of peasants and agricultural wage workers impelled the radical orientation of Algerian nationalism. Even the relatively moderate Manifesto of the Algerian People drafted by Ferhat Abbas after the Allied landing in North Africa in November 1942 demanded "the abolition of feudal property by a major agrarian reform and the right to well being of the immense agricultural proletariat" (Ruedy 1992: 146). The political program formulated by the FLN at its Soummam Valley Congress in 1956 endorsed agrarian reform and a vague commitment socialism. To the extent that the FLN's armed struggle succeeded, it was a peasant-based movement.

Workers' economic struggles became a component of the nationalist movement because most employers were *colons*. In response to the refusal of the communist-affiliated trade union federation to address the national demands of Muslim Algerian workers, Messali Hadj founded a nationalist union federation in February 1956. The next month the FLN established the Union Générale des Travailleurs Algériens (UGTA), seeking to outflank its rival. The UGTA functioned as the legal urban arm of the FLN, though its leadership was more consistently left wing. It organized a general strike in January 1957 to coincide with the debate on Algeria at the UN. After the FLN defeat in the Battle of Algiers, the UGTA went underground, and its leadership went into exile. It remained neutral in the factional violence that tore the FLN apart as it came to power at the end of the French colonial regime in 1962 (Alexander 1996a: 61–62).

The South Yemeni struggle against British colonial rule is the only other case of a successful armed struggle against colonial rule. Urban workers were more prominent in South Yemen than in Algeria, and the post-colonial regime was more firmly committed to socialism. The Aden Trades Union Congress, formed in 1956 with twenty-five constituent unions, combined trade union and nationalist struggle. It supported the armed struggle that began in 1963 and ousted the British from South Yemen in 1967; and it was a champion of the socialist policies of the People's Democratic Republic of Yemen (Murshid 1981).

Post-colonial, authoritarian-populist regimes

The grievances and collective actions of workers, peasants, and their allies among the intelligentsia popularized the notion that truly independent national governments would serve the needs of workers and peasants. Except in Algeria and South Yemen, they were not the decisive forces that dislodged the colonial and semi-colonial regimes and the structure of landed power. In the monarchies of Egypt and Iraq and the newly independent republic of Syria, in which the landed classes remained dominant, the old regimes were overthrown by army officers, many of whom, especially in Syria, had their roots in rural areas. Even in Algeria, the regular armies based in Morocco and Tunisia during the revolutionary war, not the peasant-based guerrillas, became the dominant power after independence.

Egypt under Gamal 'Abd al-Nasir, Syria under several military regimes, especially Ba'th rule since 1963, Iraq after the Free Officers' overthrow of the monarchy in 1958, and independent Algeria were authoritarian-populist regimes speaking in the name of "the people," "the toilers," or the "popular classes." The political discourse of these regimes was infused with the vocabulary of class, exploitation, and imperialism drawn from the Marxist lexicon. Like similar ideologies in Africa and Latin America, Nasirism, Ba'thism, and other varieties of Middle Eastern authoritarian-populism rejected the notion of class struggle in favor of corporatism. Trade union and peasant federations were linked to the state apparatus. Collective actions of workers and peasants that exceeded authorized boundaries were quashed. The magnanimity of the state, not popular initiative, was the source of improvements in the standard of living and social status of workers and peasants.

The key economic and social policies of these regimes were state-led development, agrarian reform, import-substitution industrialization, and social benefits for workers and white-collar employees in a greatly expanded public sector – a package commonly designated "Arab socialism." This was often accompanied by a commitment, if only rhetorical in many cases, to pan-Arab nationalism. This political orientation became so popular that even Tunisian president Habib Bourguiba, distinguished by his pragmatic pro-western views, authorized a "socialist experiment" during the 1960s, albeit with a rather anti-labor and pro-business, pro-landowner orientation.

Because of the absence of a colonial past, political currents in Turkey differ from those in the Arab countries, but its course of economic development after 1960 is comparable. Economic growth stalled after the Korean War, and the Democrat Party was compelled to adopt some statist measures. A coup by junior army officers on May 27, 1960 reinstated state-led, import-substitution industrial development and economic planning. The 1961 constitution guaranteed workers' rights to unionize, to strike, and to engage in collective bargaining for the first time. Nearly 300,000 of the 869,000 eligible workers were union members at this time (Işıklı 1987: 316). The more permissive atmosphere allowed the formation of the Turkish Labor Party (TLP – Türkiye İşçi Partisi) in 1961, though the Communist Party remained illegal.

Land reform in Egypt, Syria, Iraq, and Algeria

The coup of July 23, 1952 ended the Egyptian monarchy and was popularly legitimized by the land reform enacted in September 1952. The law set a rather high ceiling of 200 *faddan*s on land ownership (300 for a family), gradually reduced to 50 *faddan*s (100 for a family) by 1969. Accompanying measures – an agricultural minimum wage, tenancy reforms, and limiting agricultural rents to seven times the land tax – probably contributed more than land redistribution to raising peasants' standard of living. The reform was substantial, but not revolutionary. It broke the political power of the large landowners. But their property was not expropriated, and the agrarian system continued to be based on highly unequal distribution of privately owned land. Large owners were allowed to sell all their lands over the limit. The buyers were primarily middle and rich peasants, whose numbers increased as a result of the reform. After the 1952 reform, 94.4 percent of landowners held 46.6 percent of the land in plots of less than 5 *faddan*s; 0.4 percent of owners held 20.3 percent of the land in plots of 50 *faddan*s or more. About 15 percent of the cultivable land was redistributed, and the landless rural population was reduced from 60 percent in 1950 to 43 percent in 1970. The share of the agricultural income received by wage workers and owners of less than 5 *faddan*s doubled. Government-sponsored cooperatives replaced large landowners in organizing production and marketing, providing credits, and supplying seeds and fertilizers (Abdel-Fadil 1975; Hinnebusch 1985: 27; Radwan & Lee 1986: 8–9).

Land reforms in Syria and Iraq had similar social and political effects, though somewhat more land was confiscated from large owners. Syria enacted a modest land reform after joining with Egypt in the short-lived United Arab Republic (1958–61). The Ba'th regime that came to power in 1963, and even more so the radical Ba'th rule of 1966–70, reduced the ceilings on ownership, accelerated the pace of reform, and ultimately confiscated 22 percent of the cultivated land. Large landowners retained 15 percent of the cultivated area, including much of the best land (Hinnebusch 1989: 87–100; Batatu 1999: 29–37, 162–70).

The Iraqi land reform of September 1958 limited individual holdings to a generous 1,000 *dunum*s of irrigated or 2,000 *dunum*s of rain-fed land. The March 1959 uprising of Nasirist army officers demanding that Iraq join Egypt and Syria in the UAR briefly led 'Abd al-Karim Qasim to ally more closely with the communists. The CPI used this opportunity to organize extensively among peasants. The regime authorized the establishment of peasant societies, and Qasim addressed the founding congress of the Federation of Peasant Societies on April 15. By the end of 1959, communists had won leadership of 2,267 of the 3,577 peasant societies. The spread of communist influence in the countryside was stemmed by Qasim's rebuff of the communist bid to share power and the repression of the party afer Kurdish communists participated in a massacre of Turkmens in Kirkuk in July 1959. The second Ba'th regime that seized power in 1968 initiated more radical and sophisticated measures, canceling compensation payments to large landowners, reducing the ceilings on ownership, and recalculating the size of plots to be redistributed to take into consideration fertility and access to water. By 1973, 22.7 percent of the cultivable land was redistributed to peasants and 34.5 percent was rented out to peasants by the State Organization for Agrarian Reform. The Iraqi land reform was more radical than those of Egypt and Syria, in part because of the influential role of the communists in 1958–59. Nonetheless, in 1972, 2.7 percent of all landowners still owned 31.3 percent of the cultivable land, including much of the most fertile lands (Gabbay 1978: 108–20, 129–31; Batatu 1978: 1116–20; Farouk-Sluglett & Sluglett 1987).

Redistribution of land in Algeria began as a revolutionary initiative of agricultural workers. During 1962, the UGTA encouraged workers to seize the farms and businesses of departed *colon*s and manage them as cooperatives. At its height, this experiment in self-management (*autogestion*) encompassed 30 percent of the cultivable land. The FLN originally embraced *autogestion* but abandoned it after 1965. The land became state property, and farms were centrally managed by the state apparatus. The 1971 Charter of Agrarian Revolution abolished sharecropping, canceled sharecroppers' debts, and proclaimed that absentee owners of more than 5 hectares were to be expropriated. But by 1977 only a third of some 3 million eligible hectares had been transferred to the agrarian reform sector, largely due to the resistance of medium and large landowners. Algeria was much less successful than Egypt, Syria, and Iraq in redistributing land and raising agricultural productivity (Clegg 1971; Pfeifer 1985; Ruedy 1992: 221–23).

The Kamshish Affair: agrarian reform in a culture of fear

The authoritarian-populist regimes broke the political dominance of the landed elite through land reforms, but middle and rich peasants were the main beneficiaries. In many cases, families from the second stratum of local notables under the old regimes preserved much of their wealth and influence. Agrarian bureaucracies deepened state intervention in rural life more than they empowered poor peasants. The salient example of these outcomes is Egypt's Kamshish Affair (Ansari 1986: 19–49).

The Fiqqis were local notables in the village of Kamshish north of Cairo who had become became large landowners in the nineteenth century. In the 1950s, Salah Husayn Maqlad, a member of the Muslim Brothers who had a property dispute with the Fiqqis, led the peasants in confronting the Fiqqis' local power. The breakup of the UAR in 1961 led the Nasir regime to adopt a new ideological orientation – Arab socialism – and a new single party – the Arab Socialist Union (ASU). The new course included more radical measures against landed property; the limit on land ownership was reduced to 100 faddans. The Fiqqis' lands were sequestered and redistributed to 200 of the 576 poor peasant families in Kamshish, each receiving an average of 2 faddans. Most of the Fiqqis were exiled from the village. Salah Husayn Maqlad was politically rehabilitated in late 1965. He became an ASU activist and resumed his campaign against the Fiqqis. This aroused the ire of the State Security Services, who accused Maqlad of spreading Marxism and advocating collectivized agriculture. On April 30, 1966, as he was returning from Cairo, where he had urged the ASU Secretariat for Peasant Affairs to expropriate the Fiqqi mansions and turn them into educational and health facilities, Salah Husayn Maqlad was assassinated.

In response to the assassination, the Higher Committee to Liquidate Feudalism was formed and charged with investigating the extent to which "feudalists," such as the Fiqqis, had undermined land reform and Arab socialism. Members of the two recently dissolved communist parties and other leftists hoped that this signaled a firmer commitment to socialism by the regime. In fact, it was the high-water mark of Arab socialism, both locally in Kamshish and nationally.

Authorities in Kamshish opposed efforts to hold memorial meetings for Salah Husayn Maqlad, led by his wife Shahinda. In January 1967 local authorities clashed with peasants protesting against the governor's dismissal of the local ASU secretary and arrested thirty-seven peasant leaders. None of those convicted of Maqlad's murder in May 1968 were closely related to the most influential members of the Fiqqi family. In 1969, a court upheld Muhammad al-Fiqqi's right to evict former tenants who occupied his land. The first desequestrations of land were announced in July 1967. The policy statement of March 30, 1968 was the first official sign of retreat from Arab socialism and the program of authoritarian-populism (Cooper 1982). It allowed so-called "feudalists" who had been investigated by the Higher Committee to Liquidate Feudalism to be elected to the ASU Executive Bureau.

Before its demise, the Higher Committee to Liquidate Feudalism reported 330 cases in Egypt's roughly 5,000 villages where rural notables had abused their power. One such account from the Delta village of Ghazalat ʿAbdun relates that Ahmad Hasan ʿAbdun – a Wafdist parliamentary deputy before 1952 and village headman until 1955 – had violated the land-reform law by failing to report 37 *faddan*s over the limit. The extended ʿAbdun family owned a total of 290 *faddan*s. Ahmad Hasan had no written contracts with his tenants. He had committed eleven discrete acts of beating and torture of specific individuals and general terrorizing of the community, including burning down the warehouse of the agricultural cooperative when the clerk refused to allot him more than his quota of fertilizer. Although these incidents were known in the village, "no one dared accuse him out of fear" (Ansari 1986: 259).

The existence of only 330 reports does not demonstrate that such cases were exceptional. Rather, as Timothy Mitchell argues, the language of the report on Ghazalat ʿAbdun suggests that the peasants were dominated by a culture of fear that is obscured by the centralized conception of power, the focus on individuals to the exclusion of social classes, and the positioning of researchers as objective outsiders in most studies of peasant life (Mitchell 1991a). It is impossible to know how typical the case of Ghazlat ʿAbdun may be because a culture of fear cannot be discerned by studying the behavior and attitudes of individuals and public politics. That the full measure of coercion practiced against peasants cannot be ascertained is precisely an expression of their subaltern status.

The Higher Committee for the Liquidation of Feudalism did not mobilize and empower peasants and thus could not transform their status. Its effect was ultimately to control peasant radicalism by subjecting grievances to a bureaucratic routine whose results were subject to political bargaining. Nonetheless, its documentary record, if critically and sympathetically interrogated, can teach us something about the role of violence in peasant life that is commonly overlooked.

The limits of import-substitution industrialization

Industrial, clerical, and service workers in the greatly expanded public sector typically benefited from state-led development more than peasants because of the urban bias of import-substitution industrialization. They were encouraged to join trade unions and national labor federations linked to ruling parties and states. Union members received job security, higher wages, shorter hours, health care, unemployment insurance, pensions, and access to consumer cooperatives. In exchange, they gave up internal union democracy and the right to make economic and political demands unauthorized by the regimes. The state and labor federation leaders struck a corporatist bargain which might be renegotiated if necessary, but excluded initiatives by rank-and-file workers. As in the agricultural sector, urban middle strata and the privileged sectors of the working-class benefited disproportionately from the expansion of the public sector and increased social spending (Abdel-Fadil 1980; Beinin 1989; Longuenesse 1980: 354–57; Longuenesse 1985; Bianchi 1984: 212–13, 233–37; Batatu 1978: 1095–96, 1127–29; Farouk-Sluglett & Sluglett 1987: 139–40; Alexander 1996a).

Import-substitution industrialization relies on importing machinery and sometimes also raw materials, while its manufactured products are locally marketed. The local market is protected by high tariffs and restrictions on trading in foreign currency. Hence, there is a tendency towards foreign currency shortages. The income-redistribution objectives of authoritarian populism may conflict with the need to increase investment to expand industry. These contradictions led to crises of import-substitution industrialization and state-led development in Tunisia, Egypt, and Turkey in the late 1960s. The regimes responded to these crises by imposing austerity measures and reducing social expenditures. Workers and trade unions then began to challenge the old corporatist bargains and play a more salient political role than they had done since independence. The defeat of these resistance movements was one of the markers of the end of authoritarian-populism and the emergence of anti-popular, bureaucratic-authoritarian regimes.

Tunisia: a brief "socialist experiment"

The Tunisian trade union federation established in 1946, the Union Générale Tunisienne du Travail (UGTT), was the strongest labor federation in the Middle East in the 1950s and 1960s. It collaborated closely with the Neo-Destour Party, which successfully negotiated independence in 1956 and renamed itself the Destourian Socialist Party (PSD) during Tunisia's socialist phase (Alexander 1996a: 76–93).

The leading proponent of socialism, former UGTT secretary general Ahmad Ben Salah, became minister of national economy in 1961. He advocated imposing austerity measures to build socialism. Ben Salah's principal supporters in the UGTT were the unions of white-collar civil servants. They were more willing and able to make such sacrifices than the blue-collar workers who were led by Habib Achour and loyal to President Bourguiba. The white-collar workers' connection to Ben Salah enabled them to win pay raises for teachers and other civil servants in 1968, while the more militant and populist blue-collar unions did not receive wage increases. During the late summer and early fall of 1969 phosphate miners, railway workers, and dockers loyal to Achour launched wildcat strikes protesting against the regime's socialist austerity program (Alexander 1996a: 109–24).

Ben Salah and his policies were dislodged by an alliance of capitalists, especially the large landowners of the Sahel, who feared he would include their lands in an expanded agricultural cooperative program, and lower-paid blue-collar workers who were unwilling to tolerate the erosion of their wages and working conditions to build a form of socialism from which there seemed to be little prospect that they would benefit. After dismissing Ben Salah, Bourguiba engineered the installation of his ally Habib Achour as secretary general of the UGTT in January 1970. The UGTT and the PSD were purged of oppositional elements. A new corporatist agreement between the UGTT and the employers' association including a minimum wage, a small salary increase, and collective contracts was imposed in 1972. To complement these measures, in 1974 Bourguiba had himself declared "president for life" (Alexander 1996a: 151–58).

Egypt: military defeat and labor resurgence

In Egypt, unionized workers at first expressed national solidarity by supporting the austerity measures imposed after the devastating defeat by Israel in the 1967 war. The first protests against wage reductions were a response to exposures of corruption and mismanagement in the public sector in late 1968 (Posusney 1997: 142). The death of Gamal 'Abd al-Nasir in September 1970 and Anwar al-Sadat's consolidation of power by the arrest of leading Nasirists on May 15, 1971 created an opening to articulate economic demands that first emerged during the economic crisis of 1965–66 but were postponed by the 1967 war and the 1969–70 war of attrition over the Suez Canal.

During 1971 and 1972, workers struck at several large public-sector enterprises: the Misr Helwan Spinning and Weaving Company, the Iron and Steel Company, and the port of Alexandria. Cairo taxi drivers, mostly owner-operators, also struck, and thousands of private-sector textile workers in Shubra al-Khayma demonstrated for higher wages. These workers' collective actions, by far the largest since the early 1950s, were not authorized by trade union leaders. They were simultaneously a protest against the limits of the corporatist bargain struck with Nasirist authoritarian populism and a warning to Anwar al-Sadat not to roll back gains achieved under Nasirism. The government responded with a combination of conciliation and repression. The General Federation of Egyptian Trade Unions (GFETU – al-Ittihad al-ʿAmm li-Niqabat ʿUmmal Misr) denounced the August 1971 strike of the Iron and Steel Company workers. Several strike leaders were fired, and many were transferred to other workplaces. The ASU unit in the plant was dissolved, and the local union leaders were isolated. Prime Minister ʿAziz Sidqi personally went to Shubra al-Khayma after the demonstrations there and promised to raise the minimum wage and improve sick-leave policy for private-sector workers (ʿAdli 1993: 267–68; Baklanoff 1988: 215–24).

The strikes and demonstrations of the early 1970s were accompanied by a resurgence of former communists who won leadership positions in several local unions and national federations in the July 1971 elections. One of them, Ahmad al-Rifaʿi, was positioned to become the GFETU president. Instead, he and other like-minded leftists supported President al-Sadat's candidate, Salah Gharib, hoping that avoiding a clash with the regime would encourage al-Sadat to expand trade union freedoms and their room for political action. After briefly collaborating with the leftists who supported his election, in March 1973 Gharib purged them from the GFETU executive committee and canceled both the annual convention and the executive committee elections. The political miscalculation of these leftist labor leaders strengthened Gharib's hand and deprived the rank-and-file upsurge of potential organizational and political support. The GFETU became a reliable element of al-Sadat's ruling coalition. It nominally opposed but did not mobilize resistance to the rollback of Nasirism (Posusney 1997: 95–100).

Turkey: radicalization of the labor movement

The Justice Party (JP), which opposed the orientation of the 1961 constitution, came to power in Turkey in 1965 and tried to reimpose tighter control over labor. Turkish Labor Party supporters and other radicals in the Türk İş federation were isolated. In 1967 they broke away and formed the Confederation of Revolutionary Trade Unions (DİSK – Devrimi İşçi Sendikaları Konfederasyonu). The JP then amended the electoral law to reduce the parliamentary representation of the TLP and enacted a trade union law granting Türk İş a virtually exclusive right of representation and participation in policy making in return for moderation in collective bargaining and exercising the right to strike. In response to these threats to pluralism and democracy in the labor movement, DİSK led the most substantial popular challenge to a corporatist bargain between labor and a regime anywhere in the Middle East.

On June 15–16, 1970, over 100,000 workers blocked the Istanbul–Ankara highway and immobilized the entire Istanbul–Marmara region. They battled the police and army with clubs in what the regime described as "the dress rehearsal for revolution." Student-based new left groups, imagining that this was the case, began to rob banks, attack American institutions, and kidnap American soldiers. These adventurist actions undermined and discredited the workers' social movement, which continued to grow nonetheless. From January 1 to March 12, 1971, more days were lost to strikes than in any full year since 1963 except 1966 (Margulies & Yıldızoğlu 1984; Bianchi 1984: 212; Ahmad 1993: 145–47).

The military coup of March 12, 1971 attempted to control social conflict and political violence by declaring martial law and banning the TLP. The coup broke the student new left. But the workers' movement, after a decline in the mid-1970s, resumed with greater strength at the end of the decade.

The demise of the left–nationalist/Marxist historical paradigm

Popular struggles from the mid-1930s to the 1950s compelled authoritarian-populist Arab regimes, and in somewhat different terms the post-1960 coup Turkish government as well, to acknowledge workers and peasants as central components of the nation. Gamal ʿAbd al-Nasir spoke often of an alliance of the army, workers, peasants, and national capitalists. Variations on this formula were common from the mid-1950s to the early 1970s (Waterbury 1989). These regimes proclaimed that the goal of national economic construction was improving the standard of living of working people, especially peasants, who still comprised as much as 75 percent of the population of Middle Eastern countries in the 1960s. The legitimacy of the regimes and the extent of popular tolerance for authoritarian rule depended on making substantial progress towards this goal.

Even when the limits of import-substitution industrialization were manifested in stagnation or decline in the standard of living of workers and peasants in the late 1960s, the prevailing political discourse required that their existence and interests be acknowledged.

Marxists and other leftists were politically marginalized by authoritarian-populist regimes. Despite their own persecution, all the Egyptian communist groups began to support the Nasirist regime based on its neutralist, anti-imperialist, and Arab nationalist policies: 'Abd al-Nasir's prominent role at the April 1955 Bandung Conference; the purchase of arms from Czechoslovakia in September 1955; the nationalization of the Suez Canal in 1956; and the establishment of the UAR in 1958. The independent political role of Egyptian communism was virtually ended when nearly all the communists were arrested in 1959 because they supported Iraq's refusal to join the UAR, a move that would have weakened or liquidated the CPI. The two communist parties dissolved themselves in 1964. Many former communist intellectuals assumed leading positions in the cultural and educational apparatus of the Arab Socialist Union; working-class former party members were generally not embraced by the regime.

'Abd al-Karim Qasim allied with the Communist Party based on their joint opposition to Iraq's joining the UAR. Ultimately, he was unwilling to share power and turned against the CPI in mid-1959. The Ba'thist regime of February–November 1963 that overthrew Qasim slaughtered hundreds of communists and jailed over 7,000, eliminating the CPI as a viable political force. The collaboration of remnants of the party with the second, post-1968 Ba'th regime had little impact on its character or policies.

The Communist Party of Algeria was crippled by its ties to its French sister party, which supported continued French rule as late as 1956. In July 1956 the CPA dissolved itself. Its members joined the FLN as individuals. The radical impulse of the Algerian revolution was blocked by the overthrow of the first president of independent Algeria, Ahmed Ben Bella, in 1965.

The only role open to communists and other leftists in the Arab authoritarian-populist regimes was to try to push them further to the left without arousing the ire of the ruling circles. Marxist and Marxisant intellectuals were authorized to write about the history and sociology of workers and peasants and their contributions to the nationalist movement (al-Shafi'i 1957; al-Nukhayli 1967; al-Ghazzali 1968; 'Izz al-Din 1967; 'Izz al-Din 1970; 'Izz al-Din 1972; Hanna 1973; Hanna 1975–78; Hanna 1990; Ahmad 1981; Bennoune 1988). Novels and films representing workers and peasants as the most worthy citizens of the nation in a social realist style won official approval and popular acclaim (al-Sharqawi 1954; Idris 1959; Chahine 1958; Chahine 1979; Pontecorvo 1965). In many cases such projects were encouraged by the regimes as a way to domesticate radical intellectuals.

Most Arab Marxists embraced a strategy of stages: first the nationalist, anti-imperialist struggle, then the struggle for social progress and socialism. When it turned out that army officers were more effective than workers and peasants in overthrowing British and French imperialism and their local allies and that the Soviet Union accepted the military regimes as allies despite their refusal to adopt "scientific socialism," the Marxists reluctantly embraced them. The regimes accepted this embrace only if the Marxists abandoned their independent outlook or submerged it far beneath the surface. The strategy of stages provided a rationale for the deferral of class struggle and allowed the Marxists to continue to imagine that they spoke in the name of workers and peasants. In this way they unwittingly collaborated with the authoritarian-populist regimes in simultaneously empowering and disempowering workers and peasants.

6   Post-populist reformation of the working class and peasantry

Since the early 1970s, the working class and the peasantry of the Middle East have been socially reorganized. Simultaneously, their political salience has been discursively reconfigured. These processes are associated with the abandonment of state-led, import-substitution industrialization and other forms of economic nationalism and populist social policies of the previous period. Middle Eastern states fitfully adopted a new orientation towards reintegration into the world economy, encouragement of private enterprise, rollback of agrarian reform, and upward redistribution of national income. The timing, motivation, extent, and consequences of these transitions varied. But the trend across the region, and throughout Asia, Africa, and Latin America, is indisputable.

Tunisia was the first country to turn away from statist development, symbolized by the ouster of Ahmad Ben Salah as minister of national economy in 1969. Egypt began to retreat from Arab socialism in March 1968, even before Gamal ʿAbd al-Nasir's death, although the ideological elaboration of the new orientation did not occur until 1974. The 1980 military coup in Turkey brought to power a regime committed to neo-liberal economic policies. Oil wealth enabled Algeria to avoid facing the contradictions of import-substitution industrialization in the 1970s and to attempt to address them on its own terms at the end of the decade. The specificities of these cases suggest that monocausal or globalist explanations for the demise of state-led development policies – the theory linking these economic changes to the transition from authoritarian-populism to bureaucratic-authoritarianism (O'Donnell 1978), interpretations stressing pressures from the United States and Great Britain during the Reagan–Thatcher era as part of an effort to roll back economic nationalism (Bello 1994), or the all-pervasive power of the International Monetary Fund (IMF) and the World Bank (Abdel-Khalek 1981a; Amin 1995; Niblock 1993) – must be modified by the particularities of each case.

The impact of global economic changes, the consolidation of power by new elites of the authoritarian-populist states, and the rise of new local collaborators with international capital were mediated by regional political developments: rivalries within ruling parties, the balance of social forces, and the collective actions of workers and urban crowds, but increasingly rarely, peasants. The political appeal of state-led development and import-substitution industrialization was dramatically undermined by Israel's massive defeat of the Arabs in June 1967. That debacle demonstrated that Arab socialism and pan-Arab nationalism had failed to effect a revolutionary transformation of Arab societies. They were even weaker relative to Israel than they had been in 1948. The 1967 defeat affected Egypt most immediately and strengthened the hand of those advocating a reconsideration of economic and social policy. The defeat of Nasirism and Ba'thism, suppression of the communists and the new left, and official encouragement of political Islam redrew the political, cultural, and economic contours of the Middle East.

The demise of state-led development was reinforced by the effects of the brief and very permeable Arab oil boycott following the 1973 war. The consequent oil-price spike intersected temporally with the end of the long wave of post-World War II capitalist expansion regulated by the institutions established in the wake of the 1944 Bretton Woods conference: the IMF, the World Bank, and the General Agreement on Tariffs and Trade, precursor of the World Trade Organization. In the industrialized capitalist countries, the Bretton Woods regime consolidated a Fordist regime of capital accumulation: industrial mass production, high fixed-capital investment, labor control through the time–motion discipline of assembly lines, wages high enough to sustain mass consumption, and universal suffrage and parliamentary democracy. After the depression of the 1930s this was modified by various Keynesian adjustments. The Bretton Woods system attempted to regulate the global expansion of Fordism–Keynesianism. Its success was predicated on the preeminence of the US economy, the US dollar and US military power.

In the late 1960s and early 1970s, the Bretton Woods system began to break down. Japan and Europe reemerged as economic powers, while the US economy was overburdened by the simultaneous effort to fund "Great Society" social programs and the Vietnam War. The decline in the relative strength of the US economy was symbolized by the delinking of the dollar from gold in August 1971. The recessions in 1974–75 and 1980–82 were caused primarily by domestic factors in the centers of industrial capitalism: insufficient capital investment exacerbated by Reagan–Thatcher monetarist policies designed to eliminate inflation and break the bargaining power of organized labor. A decade of stagflation (stagnation and inflation) – the longest and deepest recessionary period since the end of World War II – ended the era of Fordism–Keynesianism.

The rise of OPEC in the 1960s also helped to undermine the global position of US capital by shifting the balance of power and revenue flows from (primarily US-based) multinational oil corporations to oil-exporting states. The oil-price spikes following 1973 Arab oil boycott and the Iranian revolution of 1979 were associated with – but not the direct cause – of the protracted recession that brought about the collapse of Fordism–Keynesianism. Nonetheless, the twenty-fold increase in the price of oil, from $2.00 per barrel in 1973 to $40.50 per barrel in 1981, deepened and extended the inflationary element of the stagflation syndrome.

During the oil boom of the 1970s, a deluge of petro-dollars washed over the Middle East, lubricating the transition to a new economic order. Governments of oil-exporting states (especially Saudi Arabia, Kuwait, and the United Arab Emirates, who had large oil reserves and relatively small populations to absorb them) came to control enormous concentrations of petroleum revenues. International lending to Middle Eastern countries increased dramatically, partly motivated by the desire to recirculate petro-dollars. Massive numbers of workers from countries with little or no oil (Egypt, Jordan, Palestine, Syria, Lebanon, Yemen) migrated to oil-exporting states that undertook major programs of construction and development (Saudi Arabia, Kuwait, Libya). Remittances of migrant workers effected a limited redistribution of petroleum revenues, as did Arab development aid to Egypt (until the peace treaty with Israel in 1979) and to the occupied Palestinian territories (until the 1991 Gulf War), and the export of goods and services to Iraq by Turkey and Jordan.

Multinational oil companies enhanced their profits dramatically during the oil boom and regained much of the power they had lost to OPEC and the exporting states when prices collapsed in 1985–86. Declining oil prices curtailed the development plans of oil-exporting countries and diminished their demand for labor, although Iraq's demand for labor power to replace soldiers occupied by the 1980–88 Iran–Iraq War partially compensated for the declining demand for labor in Saudi Arabia, Kuwait, and Libya. The Gulf oil countries, and even more so Algeria, were under pressure to repay international debts contracted with the expectation of high oil revenues.

The emblem of the demise of Middle Eastern state-led development was Egypt's open-door (*infitah*) economic policy announced in Anwar al-Sadat's April 1974 "October Working Paper." Despite this and other grand pronouncements, there was little structural change in the Egyptian economy in the 1970s and early 1980s (Richards 1991). Nonetheless, a new class of importers, financiers, middlemen, and profiteers began to form. Some of its members were self-made; others used the assets and connections available to them as members of the managers of public enterprises; others revived and reconfigured the fortunes of monarchy-era elite families. US aid linked to the peace with Israel, oil exports, tolls from the reopened Suez Canal, renewed international tourism, and remittances from migrant workers masked the depth of the crisis of import-substitution industrialization. These service and rent activities generated sufficient hard currency to avert a crisis and enabled the government to avoid policy choices that would reduce its support from the legions of white- and blue-collar workers employed in public enterprises and the state apparatus.

The end of the oil boom in 1985–86 and the explosion of third-world debt, signaled regionally by the 1978 Turkish foreign-exchange crisis and globally by the 1982 Mexican default, made the Egyptian state more vulnerable to pressure from the new entrepreneurial class and the Bretton Woods institutions, resulting in more intense social conflict and, ultimately, a more decisive transition to the new economic order following the Gulf War. The pressures of international debt contributed to similar processes, with differences in timing due to local circumstances in Turkey, Jordan, Algeria, Tunisia, Morocco, and Israel.

Syria and Iraq do not figure prominently in this story. These regimes proclaimed their desire for economic changes and did cut back the public sector and roll back agrarian reform. State-led associations of workers and peasants were crippled in the process (Springborg 1986; Springborg 1987; Lawson 1992; Lawson 1994; Hinnebusch 1994; Perthes 1994). But the persistence of exceptionally authoritarian and patrimonial regimes preoccupied with the Iran–Iraq war, the civil war in Lebanon, and confrontations with the United States or Israel blocked the possibility of any substantial economic liberalization in Syria and Iraq in the 1980s and 1990s.

The Washington consensus

The IMF and the World Bank began to promote a neo-liberal program of export-led development, private enterprise, and integration into the world capitalist market after the "successful" policy experiment in Chile following the 1973 military coup. The debt crisis of the 1980s allowed the Bretton Woods institutions and the US government to promote this program – the Washington consensus – even more forcefully by attaching conditions to the loans offered to ease the debt crisis (stabilization). Debt-stricken countries were urged to restructure their economies to enable them to continue repaying their debts (structural adjustment).

The typical IMF/World Bank stabilization and structural adjustment program reduced state subsidies on basic consumer goods, thus raising the cost of food and other necessities, cut government spending on social services (education, health, social welfare), and reduced investments in the public sector. Workers, government bureaucrats, and others on fixed incomes bore a disproportionate share of the pain of these austerity measures. Peasant incomes were supposed to rise due to elimination of subsidies, establishment of market-based prices for agricultural goods, and opportunities to market crops freely. But capitalist agribusiness, rather than peasant families, was the main rural beneficiary of the new economic orientation.

Despite *pro forma* rhetoric about promoting economic growth and raising the incomes of the poor, in the 1980s neo-liberal policies were promoted by the Bretton Woods institutions and the US government as an end in themselves. A prominent moderate critic of the Washington consensus notes: "It is roughly accurate to argue that in the early 1980s the international financial and development agencies pressed debtor governments to subordinate virtually all other goals to stabilization and adjustment" (Nelson 1989: 14). Such single-mindedness is not simply a consequence of professional narrowness or policy errors. It is rooted in a reconceptualization of what an economy is and how and for whose benefit it functions. This discursive shift was an integral part of the social reformation of the working class and the peasantry of the Middle East and the fitful integration of the region into the new international capitalist order of post-Fordist flexible accumulation.

Fordism constructed large-scale, mass-production enterprises with a high component of fixed capital, a long time-horizon for amortization, and a strategic perspective (even if imperfectly realized) of transforming local social, cultural, and gender relations through training and employing a stable labor force and producing commodities for the local market. The post-Fordist regime of flexible accumulation entails huge state subsidies to capital, limiting workers' rights, and an enclave strategy of locating facilities in tax-free areas (Port Said in Egypt or the Erez and Karni enterprise zones on the border of the Gaza Strip) or locations with little previously existing social fabric (Jubayl in Saudi Arabia and the new satellite cities of Cairo). Investors pursuing post-Fordist accumulation seek reduced fixed-capital investment, quicker turnaround on investment, less social commitment to the local labor force, and a global export orientation. Fordist-style production necessary for middle-class and elite consumption is increasingly relocated to Asia, Africa, and Latin America. This is no longer the leading edge of the global economy. Aside from providing employment – often less stable and with fewer social benefits than older public sector enterprises – states are less concerned with regulating the social impact of capital on local communities.

The neo-liberal conception of an economy eliminates questions about whose interests it serves. Advocates of the Washington consensus believe that "all things being equal" economies operate according to scientific principles and that markets distribute goods most efficiently. Designating it as "science" enhances the power of this belief. Few advocates of the Washington consensus argue that an economy should privilege the interests of multinational capital and international financial institutions. It just happens to work out that way when neo-liberal policies are dogmatically applied. Those who advocate these policies are well rewarded and are subject to no democratic accountability regardless of the accuracy of their predictions. Those who do not are usually considered "second rate" or worse.

The neo-liberal belief system can never be conclusively confirmed because all things are never equal. Unpredictable political events often affect how economies operate. For example, military coups cleared the way for aggressive implementation of IMF structural adjustment plans in Turkey in 1980 and Tunisia in 1987. Cancelation of nearly half of Egypt's $55 billion foreign debt as a political favor in return for participating in the US-led coalition against Iraq in the 1991 Gulf War opened the way to concluding a successful agreement with the IMF and gave the regime sufficient political credit to begin the long-delayed privatization of public-sector enterprises.

Lest they appear to be "unscientific," even moderate critics commonly adopt the rhetoric of the Washington consensus. Who can oppose "economic stabilization," or "structural adjustment"? These benign terms and others such as "reform," "liberalization," "efficiency," and "rationalization" are nearly universally employed to describe the transformations envisioned by the Washington consensus. "Cutting public investments in housing, health, and education," "upward redistribution of income," "increasing inequality," "diminishing the influence of trade unions and peasant associations," "increasing the power of private capital," and "upward redistribution of agricultural land" are more difficult to defend. Yet these are common effects of neo-liberal programs.

Proponents of the Washington consensus often argue that despite the immediate pain, these policies will promote economic growth and thereby increase the incomes of the poor in the long run. Turkey is widely considered a successful example of reform based primarily on the rapid growth in exports of manufactured goods in the 1980s, when Washington consensus policies prevailed. But economic growth from 1962 to 1977, under a regime of state planning and import substitution, was as good as that of the 1980s. "The verdict would seem to be that expected benefits of reform and liberalization programs have at best materialized unevenly and rather slowly" (Hansen 1991: 391–95).[1] Nonetheless, the contradictions of import-substitution industrialization may have made it impossible to sustain high levels of growth beyond the mid-1970s. No one can know yet the long-term effects of the new policy. But after a decade of structural adjustment programs, the World Bank admitted that there was no "straightforward" way to assess their success and "no conclusive evidence on growth" (World Bank 1991b: 114). Surely if a stronger case could be made for the efficacy of these policies, the World Bank would be making it loudly and forcefully.

Along with a new conception of the economy, the Washington consensus tends to eliminate workers and peasants as social categories altogether, since their very presence recalls the social compact of the era of authoritarian-populism, which the current regimes can not fulfill. One expression of this trend is the widely used textbook *A Political Economy of the Middle East* (Richards & Waterbury 1990). The first edition includes the subtitle, *State, Class, and Economic Development*. This was removed from the second edition, and the conceptual framework of the study was redesigned, replacing "class" with "social actors" (Richards & Waterbury 1996). This might be understood as eliminating a residue of Marxist dogmatism, although the first edition of the text was hardly sympathetic to the interests of workers and peasants and focused primarily on the role of the state in economic development. "Social actors" is an amorphous term not necessarily incompatible with the concept of class. Its main task in this context is to avoid asking: are there structural contradictions in capitalist economies, and in whose interests are such economies most likely to operate?

Urbanization and labor migration

State-led, import-substitution industrialization was overwhelmed by massive urban–rural migration. Industrial development could not provide enough employment opportunities for rapidly growing urban populations. Vast shanty-town districts – *gecekondu*s in Turkey, *bidonvilles* and *gourbivilles* in North Africa, *sarifa*s in Iraq, and the medieval cemeteries on the eastern edge of Cairo – overpowered states' distributive capacities, resulting in declining standards of education, housing, health, and sanitation services in urban peripheries.

Algeria, which had virtually no industry before independence, is the most dramatic example of the general trend. From 1954 to 1984 nonagricultural employment increased from 330,000 to 2,555,500. This impressive growth was inadequate to absorb all the new urban job seekers. Unemployment rates remained very high during the expansionary phase of import-substitution industrialization – 22 percent in 1977 and 18 percent in 1984 – and rose to 24 percent in 1990 when state-led development was in serious crisis (Pfeifer 1996: 30).

In Egypt, the most populous Arab country, the nonagricultural wage-labor force grew from just under 4.5 million in 1973 to just over 7 million in 1986, while nonagricultural union membership increased from about 1.5 to 2.5 million. Despite the high rate of urbanization, the average annual increase of membership in industrial and blue-collar service unions in Egypt from 1971 to 1987 was only 3.2 percent – the lowest rate of growth in all the sections of the General Federation of Egyptian Trade Unions except agriculture (Posusney 1997: 114–15).[2]

A high proportion of new urban dwellers as well as many veterans engaged in services, small manufacturing, and petty commerce – activities often designated as the "informal sector" of the economy. This category, nearly impervious to statistical measure, obscures considerable unemployment, underemployment, unpaid labor of women and children, and irregular financial transactions. Workers in the informal sector rarely joined trade unions. They became part of an urban mass that expressed its disapproval of open-door economic policies by refraining from political participation, collaborating with the black market and other activities that undermined official economic policies, and, *in extremis*, joining in urban riots.

Unemployment, low wages, and lack of access to agricultural land impelled workers and peasants to migrate in search of work. The number of North Africans seeking work in France rose sharply after 1947. Turkish workers began migrating, primarily to Germany, during the European economic expansion of the 1960s (see table 6.1). The recessions of 1974–75 and 1980–82 reduced the demand for Turkish workers. Nonetheless, by 1983 there were over 2.1 million Turks, 4.5 percent of the population, in Europe (European Trade Union Institute 1988: 22). Turkish labor migration to Libya, Saudi Arabia, and other Arab countries in the 1980s partially offset the decline in migration to Europe.

Rapid population growth and inadequate new job opportunities in non-oil-exporting countries intersected with the huge demand for labor in oil-exporting countries embarking on development projects financed by the explosion of petroleum revenues to produce an unprecedented wave of Arab labor migration. Egypt was the largest Arab labor exporter during the peak of oil-induced migration from the mid-1970s to the mid-1980s, sending workers primarily to Saudi Arabia, Libya, and Iraq (see table 6.2). Perhaps as many as 3.5 million Egyptians, about one-third of

Table 6.1 *Turkish workers placed in positions abroad by the Labor Placement Office*

Year	Number	Estimated annual remittances
1965	51,520	
1969	103,975	$169.2 million
1970	129,575	
1973	135,820	$2,000 million
1974	20,211	$1,425 million
1975	4,419	
1976	10,558	$983 million
1980	28,503	
1988	53,023	
1993	63,244	

Sources: Ahmad 1993: 177; Keyder 1987: 184–87; Turkey. State Institute of Statistics 1973–95

Table 6.2 *Arab Labor Migration*

From	To Saudi Arabia 1975	To other Gulf countries 1975	To Saudi Arabia early 80s	To other Gulf countries early 80s	Total early to mid-1990s
Egypt	95,000	58,745	800,000	1,150,000	2,500,000
Yemen(s)	335,400	25,358	390,000	420,000	1,250,000*
Jordan & Palestine	175,000	70,367	140,000	227,850	over 320,000*

Notes:
* Before the 1991 Gulf War
[1] Sudan is next largest labor exporter
[2] Egypt sent as many as 1,250,000 workers to Iraq during the height of the Iran–Iraq War (1980–88)
[3] Libya has imported 250,000–300,000 Egyptian workers annually since the mid-1970s, with some declines due to political crises
Sources: Birks & Sinclair 1980; Owen 1985; Richards & Waterbury 1996; Stevenson 1993; Feiler 1993

the entire labor force, migrated during 1973–85 (Richards & Waterbury 1996: 371). Although the absolute number of migrants was lower, an even higher proportion of Yemenis and Jordanians migrated in search of work. About a quarter of the Jordanian labor force worked abroad, mostly in the Gulf, in the late 1970s; by 1988 the proportion rose to over 37 percent (Layne 1981: 9; Brand 1992: 169). As many as 30 percent of all

Yemeni adult males were abroad at any one time in 1970s and 1980s (Stevenson 1993: 15). In the mid-1980s, when oil-boom-induced labor migration peaked, there were over 5 million migrant Arabs working in the Gulf countries and some 2.5 million North Africans working in Europe (World Bank 1995a: 6). The Tunisian Ministry of Social Affairs estimated that migrants comprised 11.6 percent of the total labor force (Radwan et al. 1991: 23–24).

Remittances of migrant workers contributed substantially to alleviating the foreign-currency shortages associated with import-substitution industrialization. Before the expulsion of some 1 million Yemeni workers from Saudi Arabia in retaliation for their government's failure to support the US-led assault on Iraq in 1991, remittances comprised as much as 20 percent of the GDP in former North Yemen and 50 percent of the GDP in former South Yemen (Stevenson 1993: 16). In Turkey, remittances offset the cost of 15 percent of all imported capital goods and covered the trade deficit in 1972 and 1974 (Ahmad 1993: 177). Declining remittances after 1974 contributed to the 1978 foreign-exchange crisis that was resolved by imposing neo-liberal policies after the 1980 military coup. Egypt's foreign-exchange shortage was alleviated by increasing labor migration in the 1970s and 1980s. By 1988, when at least 20 percent of the Egyptian labor force was employed abroad, annual official transfers of migrant workers were about $3.2 billion; unofficial transfers were estimated at $2–4 billion (Roy 1991: 552, 579). These transfers comprised the single largest source of foreign exchange and contributed about 12 percent to the GDP in the mid-1980s. In Egypt, as elsewhere, labor migration absorbed a substantial amount of potential unemployment and it provided relatively high incomes to landless peasants who might otherwise have been forced into lives of extreme misery as migrant agricultural laborers (Toth 1999).

The macroeconomic balance sheet of labor migration is mixed (Ibrahim 1982: 551–82; Richards & Waterbury 1996). In Egypt it had a small positive impact on alleviating poverty but a negative effect on income distribution (Adams 1986: 9). Whatever its ultimate contribution to economic growth, labor migration was a substantial factor in the social reformation of the working class and peasantry. The number of agricultural workers declined 10 percent in Egypt from 1975 to 1978, 23 percent in Syria from 1975 to 1979, and 40 percent in Iraq from 1973 to 1977 (many were replaced by Egyptian migrants) (Paul 1981: 4–5; Springborg 1987: 16). The combination of rapid urbanization, the declining role of agriculture in national economies, high levels of unemployment and underemployment, and the possibilities of labor migration made organizing workers and peasants as a social and political force extremely difficult.

The continuity and effectiveness of communities and institutions and traditions of collective action that might have facilitated such organization were undermined.

Women in the wage-labor force

Turkey, Egypt, and to a lesser extent other regimes pursuing import-substitution industrialization mobilized women for national economic development by adopting forms of state-sponsored feminism. Inconstant commitment of the regimes and inadequate job opportunities produced only limited successes in drawing women into the wage-labor force. By the late 1970s and mid-1980s female wage-labor-force participation was 3.3 percent in Jordan, 4.4 percent in Algeria, 6.2 percent in Egypt, 13.3 percent in Tunisia, and 21.9 percent in Turkey. The proportion of females in production work was even lower, ranging from 1 percent in Jordan to 17 percent in Tunisia and a high of 23 percent in Morocco. In 1984–85 only 5.8 percent of economically active women in Egypt and 7.6 percent in Turkey worked in manufacturing, compared to 16.8 percent in Mexico and 25.8 percent in South Korea. A very substantial proportion of economically active women worked as unpaid family workers, most commonly in agriculture – 36.3 percent in Egypt and 67.7 percent in Turkey (Moghadam 1993: 40, 44).

In Egypt the Nasirist regime legislated equal education and wages for women and guaranteed jobs to all high school and university graduates; these rights were expanded in the al-Sadat era. Many working-class and lower-middle-class men and women benefited from these policies. The state became the largest employer of women, typically as clerical workers in the state apparatus or public-sector firms (Hoodfar 1991: 108). Though it was economically necessary, many such women were conflicted about the propriety of working outside the home. Some expressed their ambivalence by donning the "new veil," although they did not necessarily become Islamic political activists or more pious than women in similar circumstances who did not veil (Macleod 1991).

Some Islamist groups advocated removing women from the wage-labor force as a solution to male unemployment. Their arguments did not prevent women from seeking employment when jobs and a supportive political environment were available. State intervention and the availability of suitable work were more powerful factors in shaping women's employment opportunities than interpretations of the requirements of Islamic tradition (Hammam 1977; Quataert 1991; Moghadam 1993: 65; Khater 1996: 325–48). However, it is likely that, at least for a certain period, ambivalence about working outside the home inhibited some women's identification with their workplaces and limited their participation in trade unions and work-related collective action.

Sectoral labor shortages created by migration were often filled by women. In Jordan, where the number of women in the wage-labor force was relatively low, 14.4 percent of employees in establishments with five or more employees were women in 1976; only a year later the proportion rose to 18.1 percent. They were concentrated in public administration, communication, education, clerical work, administration, and finance. Most of the very small number of women who worked in manufacturing establishments were employed in the textile sector. Their numbers increased somewhat after the 1994 Jordanian–Israeli peace treaty due to subcontracting by Israeli textile firms (Salfiti 1997). Women commonly worked for piece rates and were subjected to patriarchal and other extra-economic control mechanisms. Only 23 percent of the women in a sample surveyed in 1977 were members of trade unions (Layne 1981: 20–22).

Labor migration brought many peasant women to undertake work formerly done by their husbands or brothers. Studies of two Egyptian villages come to divergent conclusions about the consequences. Fatma Khafagy believes that women were empowered by assuming new responsibilities when their male relatives were absent (Khafagy 1984). Elizabeth Taylor argues that there was no permanent shift in patriarchal family structure because men imposed the previous forms of gender relations, or even more conservative ones they learned in the Gulf, when they returned (Taylor 1984). Research conducted about the same time on a very small sample but based on observed behavior rather than interviews concludes that wives of migrating husbands who lived in nuclear families – but not women living in extended families – did have greater autonomy (Brink 1991: 206).

Male migration and economic necessity brought more women into the wage-labor force in the 1970s and 1980s. But the rate of female wage-labor-force participation remained low compared to Asia and Latin America. Many women were conflicted about working outside the home, and most remained on the margins of the wage-labor force, entering and leaving according to their family circumstances. Wage labor increased women's autonomy in certain circumstances, but was not a liberatory panacea.

Structural adjustment, urban collective action, and state repression

Because national trade union and peasant federations were subordinated to ruling parties and state apparatuses, most political scientists consider workers and peasants to be insignificant in determining economic and social policy (Waterbury 1983). Others argue that labor is a significant social and political force but focus their attention on the bargain between the leaders of national trade union federations and the state (Bianchi 1986; Bianchi 1989; Alexander 1996a; Posusney 1997). This orientation leads most political scientists to ignore the significance of collective actions of local union leaders or ordinary workers.[3] Reliable information about such actions is difficult to obtain because the mass media and political action are subject to various degrees of control. Leaders of wildcat strikes and illegal collective actions are more difficult to locate and more reluctant to speak to researchers about their motives and organizational activities than trade union and government officials. The following three case studies of urban collective action have been selected because Tunisia, Turkey, and even Egypt to a certain extent were considered IMF "success stories," while Egypt is one of the most important long-term sites of remedial Washington consensus policies (Pfeifer 1999). The cases demonstrate the social costs of this success as well as the sustained efforts of national trade union federations, local union officials, rank-and-file workers, and heterogenous urban crowds to resist the imposition of neo-liberal policies and the political order that accompanied them. Such resistance – or often simply regimes' fears of potential resistance – altered the timing and extent to which neo-liberal programs were implemented. This affirms the continuing effect of subaltern presence in the post-Fordist era. Against a global discourse hailing the end of history and proclaiming that "there is no alternative," urban protest was incapable of reversing the trend or articulating a comprehensive new policy.

Tunisia: a new corporatist bargain

Rivalries within the Union Générale Tunisienne du Travail were among the causes of Tunisia's abandonment of its socialist experiment in 1969. The corporatist bargain between the UGTT and employers imposed by the government in 1972 did not stick because it was made by Habib Achour and other UGTT leaders loyal to President Bourguiba. Unions of teachers, bank employees, university professors, engineers, and other educated and higher paid white-collar workers – Ahmad Ben Salah's base of support within the UGTT – began a sustained campaign of resistance to the new economic policies as soon as their economic impact was manifested. Some of the white-collar union activists had been radical students in the 1960s; others had ties to the Communist Party. Achour tried to purge these elements from the national leadership of the UGTT by eliminating the representatives of the teachers and the post, telegraph, and telephone workers' unions (Alexander 1996a: 179).

Table 6.3 *Strikes in Tunisia, 1970–77*

1970:	25
1971:	32
1972:	150
1973:	215
1974:	141
1975:	377
1976:	369
1977:	452
TOTAL:	1,761

Source: Alexander 1996a: 160

The central issue for labor in the 1970s was the rising cost of living. The UGTT estimated that consumer prices increased 36 percent from 1970 to 1977 while the average real wage increased only 18 percent from 1971 to 1975. White-collar workers led many of the wildcat strikes unauthorized by the UGTT central leadership throughout the 1970s (see table 6.3) (Alexander 1996a: 158–62). In 1977 the UGTT and the government concluded a social pact to which neither was fully committed. Wildcat strikes against the pact broke out, and Habib Achour defended the strikers. Rank-and-file unionists pressed the UGTT to declare a general strike against the cost-of-living increases. Achour announced his open opposition to the regime by resigning from the leadership bodies of the ruling Destourian Socialist Party (PSD). A highly successful general strike was held on January 26, 1978, accompanied by rioting of the urban poor. At least one hundred people were killed in clashes with security forces that day. In response, the government jailed Habib Achour and other UGTT leaders and imposed a new executive committee on the union. But the strikes continued (Vandewalle 1988: 607–8).

The government of Muhammad Mzali (1980–86) sought to avoid conflict with the UGTT. But in the fall of 1983 an IMF mission visited and convinced the government to adopt its recommendations to lower the budget deficit by cutting subsidies on consumer products. The cuts were announced on December 29, raising the price of bread, pasta, and semolina by 70 percent. In response, rioting began in Gafsa and other southern cities and then spread to Tunis in early January. More than a hundred people died in clashes with security forces before the price increases were rescinded.

In late 1985 the government began a new campaign of repression against the UGTT. Habib Achour was again placed under house arrest, and the union's offices were occupied by PSD militias. During 1986 most of the UGTT leadership was imprisoned, giving the government more room for maneuver in facing its foreign-exchange crisis. The government resolved the crisis by accepting an IMF standby credit of $180 million in exchange for adopting the standard Washington consensus stabilization policy package: devaluation of the dinar, government budget cuts, liberalization of the trade regime, and a commitment to privatize public-sector enterprises.

The first priority of the new regime established by the coup d'état of Zayn al-ʿAbidin Ben ʿAli on November 7, 1987 was to implement the IMF stabilization plan. In response, there were 2,586 strikes during the next six years, far more than the 1,761 in the seven years preceding the general strike of January 26, 1978. Most were conducted without the approval of the UGTT central committee. Despite the repressive measures of 1985–86 and the active intervention of the Ben ʿAli regime in its internal affairs, UGTT members demonstrated considerable continuing capacity for collective action. The regime faced the choice of breaking the union or enticing it into a new alliance.

The rise of the Islamic Tendency Movement and its successor, al-Nahda, as the strongest opponents of the regime in the mid-1980s tilted the balance towards the option of a renewed corporatist bargain between the regime and the union. Ben ʿAli intervened heavily in the "renewal" of the UGTT to strengthen its secularist elements. The fight against political Islam created pressures for a new state–union alliance in which strikes over wages and working conditions became rare, and there was no longer a contest over fundamental economic policy. The UGTT embarked on a new era of collaborative relations with the government and the federation of employers. In 1992 secretary general Ismaʿil Sahbani, who had been installed at the 1989 national congress consecrating the government-supervised "rehabilitation" of the UGTT, declared: "Our union . . . is trying to adapt to changes in the international economic system, the structural adjustment program, the new world order, and the market economy" (Alexander 1996b: 177).

Egypt: an inconclusive outcome

President Anwar al-Sadat officially introduced Egypt's open-door policy after the crossing of the Suez Canal in the 1973 war legitimized his regime. The first protests against the new course erupted dramatically and unexpectedly with no organized support from trade union or leftist political leaders. On January 1, 1975 workers commuting to the southern Cairo industrial suburb of Helwan occupied the Bab al-Luq railway station while others sat in at the iron and steel mill in Helwan. At the other end of metropolitan Cairo, textile workers in Shubra al-Khayma proclaimed a solidarity strike, and several mills were occupied. In addition to economic demands, workers in these actions raised political slogans, including a call for the prime minister to resign. There were other strikes and collective actions over economic issues during 1975–76 in Cairo, al-Mahalla al-Kubra, Helwan, Alexandria, Tanta, Nagʿ Hammadi, and Port Said (Baklanoff 1988; ʿAdli 1993: 268; Beinin 1994a). The strike and protest movement was concentrated among workers in large public-sector enterprises, who had been major beneficiaries of Nasirist statist development.

Egypt's turn towards the West and continuing foreign-exchange crisis gave the IMF an opening to propose far-reaching economic policy changes. The government adopted the recommendations of a fall 1976 IMF mission to cut subsidies on bread, sugar, tea, and other basic consumer goods, announcing price increases of 25–50 percent. Urban crowds immediately responded with explosive demonstrations and riots on January 18–19, 1977 – the largest and most forceful popular collective actions since the Cairo fire of January 26, 1952. The protests were concentrated in Cairo and Alexandria but spread throughout the country, threatening to topple the regime. Factory workers initiated and played a prominent role in these actions. They were joined by students, the unemployed, and others in urban crowds. Peasants were not prominent in the events.

While President al-Sadat portrayed himself as a great liberal opposed to the undemocratic measures of the Nasirist regime, a chilly and repressive climate descended upon Egypt from the 1977 riots until al-Sadat's assassination by radical Islamists in 1981. The regime claimed that communists and other leftists incited the riots. In fact, the legal and illegal left were surprised by the extent of popular anger and its insurrectionary character (Beinin 1994a). Nonetheless, many suspected communists were put on trial. The intellectual Marxist monthly *al-Taliʿa* (The Vanguard), which dared to explain that though it did not endorse the violence, the anger of the masses was justified, was closed. *Al-Ahali* (The People), the weekly of the legal leftist Tagammuʿ Party, was intermittently proscribed. Law 3 of 1977, a direct response to the riots, allowed the government to punish strikers with imprisonment and hard labor.

Many workers in large public enterprises did have a Nasirist or Marxist-inspired understanding of their situation. Public-sector workers were sometimes quite militant in opposing the open-door policy in the 1970s and 1980s, usually without support from the official trade union leadership. Other elements of the urban crowds in January 1977 were

moved by Islamic sentiment, which was expressed by the trashing of the
casinos on Pyramids Road, long identified by the Muslim Brothers as
symbols of foreign-influenced, moral dissolution. Many skilled and experienced workers, as well as unskilled workers and peasants, migrated to
the oil-exporting countries, thus absenting themselves from the struggle
over the open-door policy. Those in the vast "informal sector" were
largely quiescent and difficult, if not impossible, to organize. Moreover,
years of Nasirist repression of the left, the dissolution of the two communist parties in 1964, subsequent efforts of the leftist intelligentsia to collaborate with the regime, and wishful assessments of the character of the
early al-Sadat regime by these same intellectuals meant there was no
effective oppositional discourse articulating a political program for
workers and their potential allies.

Husni Mubarak began his presidency in 1981 by alleviating the repressive measures of the al-Sadat regime. He ordered the 1,300 political pris-
oners arrested without charges on the eve of al-Sadat's assassination
released. The press and opposition political parties were given more
leeway, and an electoral alliance of the Muslim Brothers and the Wafd
was permitted to participate in the 1984 parliamentary elections. A more
stable and ideologically compatible Muslim Brothers–Labor Party (LP)
electoral alliance was formed in 1987.

After their success in the 1987 national parliamentary elections, the
Brothers–LP alliance participated in national trade union elections for
the first time. The Islamic Current (al-Tayyar al-Islami), as the Muslim
Brothers and their supporters are known, won control of several professional associations (Wickham 1996). But their gains in the trade unions
were modest. Nonetheless, the Islamic Current established itself, along
with the left, as a political tendency opposed to the state and the ruling
party in the labor movement.

The relatively less repressive atmosphere of the early Mubarak era permitted a significant increase in strikes and other workers' collective
action. Some fifty to seventy-five actions a year were reported in the
Egyptian press during 1984–89 (El Shafei 1995:36). Due to censorship
and lack of media interest, this is surely not a comprehensive tally. The
left was an active and sometimes a leading component in struggles involving major confrontations with the state, such as the massive strike and
uprising of textile workers in Kafr al-Dawwar in September–October
1984, the strike at the Misr Spinning and Weaving Company in February
1985, the railway workers strike of July 1986, and the two sit-in strikes at
the Iron and Steel Company in July and August 1989.

Opposition forces made some headway in winning control of enterprise-level trade union committees in the elections of 1991 and 1996. But

they could not break the regime's control of the GFETU at the national level. Nonetheless, both shop-floor and enterprise-level militant actions and the bureaucratic maneuvers of the GFETU leaders were a major factor delaying the full implementation of the neo-liberal economic program. Mubarak irked the IMF, the World Bank, and international financial interests by resisting their calls to further reduce consumer subsidies, unify foreign-exchange rates, and privatize the public sector until after the 1991 Gulf War.

Cancelation of half of Egypt's foreign debt as a reward for participation in the Gulf War prepared the way for a new agreement with the IMF in May 1991. Subsequently, as foreign reserves and other macroeconomic indicators improved, the Mubarak government finally began to privatize state-owned enterprises in earnest. To encourage privatization, in 1995 the regime drafted a new Unified Labor Law that proposed to reorganize the national labor federation, eliminate the job security gained by public-sector workers in the Nasir era, and set stringent conditions for legal strikes. Reorganization of the trade union movement had long been resisted by the GFETU as well as by both the left and the Islamic Current because they feared it would diminish workers' rights and enhance the state's repressive capacity. After much hesitation, the GFETU leadership embraced the proposed labor legislation, hoping that it would reinforce their control over rank-and-file union members who had become alienated as a consequence of the labor federation's weakness in defending their interests. Nonetheless, resistance by rank-and-file workers and lower-level union officials supported by both the left and the Islamic Current blocked enactment of the legislation throughout the 1990s.

Turkey: class struggle and bourgeois victory

Turkish import-substitution industrialization development collapsed after 1973. Increased costs of imported oil, declining remittances from workers in Europe, and reduced foreign lending and aid after the 1974 invasion of Cyprus contributed to escalating social tensions and political violence. The crisis could not be politically resolved as the Justice Party (JP) and the Republican People's Party (RPP) battled to a stalemate.

The foreign exchange crisis of 1977–79 compelled Bulent Ecevit's RPP government formed in January 1978 to negotiate debt-rescheduling arrangements with creditors under IMF supervision. Ecevit imposed austerity measures severe enough to cause his supporters in urban areas to defect. Strike action began to increase in 1978 and reached unprecedented proportions in 1980. As many as 500,000 people participated in

DİSK's May Day demonstrations in Istanbul in 1976, 1977, and 1978. The 1979 demonstration was banned by martial law, a harbinger of the more systematic repression that was to follow (Margulies & Yıldızoğlu 1984: 18).

The RPP defeat in the October 1979 senate elections brought Süleyman Demirel and the JP to power. On January 24, 1980 Demirel's economic advisor, Turgut Özal, announced his IMF-approved austerity plan devaluing the Turkish lira by over 30 percent (on top of the 43 percent devaluation previously imposed by Ecevit) and raising consumer prices by about 70 percent. Özal was aware that political pressures might not allow him to implement his plan. Political violence and strikes provided the pretext for the military coup of September 12, 1980.

The junta banned DİSK and arrested hundreds of trade union leaders. Türk İş was permitted to continue functioning. But strikes were outlawed, and an arbitration board was established to settle wage disputes. The 1983 Labor Code institutionalized labor's subordination to capital. Both the political left and the right were smashed, as the junta strove to depoliticize Turkish society. In January 1981, a European Economic Community committee estimated that there were 30,000 political detainees, many of whom were subjected to torture. With all organized opposition broken, Özal convinced the junta to allow him to implement his economic plan without political interference (Ahmad 1993: 177–83).

Workers paid a heavy price for Turkey's status as a Washington consensus success story in the mid-1980s. As the military regime eased its repression, they moved to recover the losses of the early 1980s. From 1987 to 1991 the average number of strikes per year was higher than the previous peak year of 1980 (see table 6.4). Even the significant wage increases in the collective-bargaining agreements of 1989–91 did not make up for the wage erosion of the previous period (Yeldan 1994: 77, 80–81).

The debt crisis set off by the oil-price spike of 1973–74 and the global recession of the mid-1970s set the international context for Özal's imposition of Washington consensus, neo-liberal economic prescriptions. The intense social conflict of the 1970s was the local impetus for the military coup that consolidated Özal's ascendancy and ultimately his electoral victory as leader of the Motherland Party in 1983. That social conflict is not solely an expression of class struggle. It also involved an adventurist student-based new left, a broad challenge to Kemalist secularism by Islamists, an upsurge of Kurdish ethnic sentiment and the right-wing effort to repress it, sectarian contention between sunnis and Alevis, and other social cleavages, all exacerbated by the personal rivalry between Demirel and Ecevit. Moreover, the working class was not unified.

Table 6.4 *Strikes in Turkey, 1963–94*

Year	Strikes	Strikers	Days lost
1963	8	1,514	19,739
1964	83	6,640	238,161
1965	46	6,593	366,836
1966	42	11,414	430,104
1967	100	9,463	344,112
1968	54	5,179	175,286
1969	86	20,155	323,220
1970	72	21,150	220,189
1971	78	10,916	476,116
1972	48	14,879	659,362
1973	55	12,256	671,135
1974	110	36,628	1,109,401
1975	116	13,708	668,797
1976	58	7,240	325,830
1977	59	15,628	1,397,124
1978	87	9,748	426,127
1979	176	24,920	1,432,078
1980	220	33,832	4,298,413
1987	307	29,734	1,961,940
1988	156	30,057	1,085,057
1989	171	39,435	190,755
1990	458	166,306	1,188,091
1991	398	164,968	1,188,719
1992	98	62,189	158,545
1993	49	6,908	286,789
1994	36	4,782	104,869

Source: Margulies & Yıldızoğlu 1984: 18; Barkey 1990: 102; Turkey. State Institute of Statistics 1973–95

Unionized workers were divided among DISK, which was based mainly in the private sector, Türk İş, based primarily in the public sector, and the much smaller National Action Party-led Confederation of Nationalist Workers' Unions (MİSK) and the Islamist Hak-İş confederations. Only 1.5 million of the 6 million workers covered by social security were unionized in 1980. Other cleavages within the working class included the social adjustment difficulties of migrants returning from Europe in the mid-1970s (Kara 1984). Moreover, the labor movement made little effort to form a political alliance with peasants.

Nonetheless, the increasing politicization of the labor movement, especially private-sector workers organized in DİSK, and the transformation of the RPP into a social democratic party represented a significant threat

to the Turkish business class, much more so than the new left urban guerrilla activity in the early 1970s. Both workers and industrialists benefited
from import-substitution industrialization, but the populist guarantees of
the 1961 constitution allowed organized workers to fight fiercely to maintain and extend their gains during the post-1973 recessionary period.
The mobilization of Turkish workers from the 1960s to the 1980s more
closely resembles the Marxian model of class politics than any other
Middle Eastern case. Turgut Özal's neo-liberal economic policies and
political repression of the labor movement were a clear victory for capital,
although the business class was unwilling to fight for it on its own because
it had benefited from state-led development and had a long history of
political timidity. The consolidation of a bourgeois pole in Turkish politics during the Özal decade was an unanticipated outcome of the collective action of workers and their political allies among the intelligentsia.

The rollback of agrarian reform

The agrarian reform programs enacted from the 1950s to 1970 typically
favored middle and rich peasants. None carried out as radical a redistribution as South Korea or Taiwan, which might have provided land for all
those who wished to farm (Mitchell 1991a). In Egypt, the guarantee of perpetual tenancy at controlled rents had a more radical effect than land redistribution. Peasants in the Fayyum region interviewed in 1989 strongly
supported this aspect of agrarian reform because "before the revolution
you could not speak in front of a person who had money. In the past, the
peasant would rent a piece of land according to the owner's terms. At any
time the owner could kick him out and bring another peasant to farm it . . .
There was no justice." They were deeply attached to Gamal ʿAbd al-Nasir
who "issued the law that said a peasant is not to be thrown out from his
field . . . [and] gave life to the peasant" (Saad 1999: 391–92).

State-administered cooperatives and regulation of agricultural inputs
and outputs distorted crop prices to the disadvantage of peasants.
Technocratic agricultural development policies concentrated on high-
visibility capital-intensive infrastructure projects such as the Aswan High
Dam and land reclamation, neglecting more mundane but critical issues
such as drainage and short-term production growth (Richards 1980;
Pfeifer 1985; Radwan et al. 1991: 30). Import-substitution industrialization tends to disregard agriculture and peasants, and this was exacerbated
during the oil boom. These problems, along with increased social power
of landowners and support of the Washington consensus, generated pressures to roll back agrarian reform and encourage large-scale capitalist
farming.

Large landowners, an important base of support for the PSD, rebelled against the belated inclusion of their farms in the Tunisian cooperative program in 1969. Less than nine months after large holdings were incorporated into the cooperatives, the lands were returned to their former owners. The cooperatives were gradually abandoned and their lands privatized over the next few years after the World Bank and the US government turned against the program (King 1997: 118, 128). Direct investment by the state was replaced by credit and subsidies to individual owners in order to promote capitalist agriculture. These policies increased agricultural production and average agricultural income, though part of this improvement was due to previous public investments. However, the Tunisian government's privatization policies did not create rational, profit-maximizing peasants. Instead, they encouraged the revival of patronage and kinship networks and a moral economy drawing on Islamic norms and practices: a system of social controls tying the poor to the rich and to the state via bureaucratic and traditional welfare mechanisms.

Tunisian small peasants bore a disproportionate share of the costs of agrarian policy from 1970 on. Structural adjustment did not create new rural jobs. It accelerated rural–urban migration and the concentration of poverty in urban migrant zones. Poor farmers producing rain-fed crops did not benefit from the new agricultural price policies. Land holdings became increasingly concentrated. Although medium owners are the most efficient producers, the state consistently favored large landowners. The most intensive examination of peasant responses to the rollback of agrarian reform and the promotion of capitalist agribusiness concludes that "structural adjustment has stabilized the dominance of the agrarian upper class" (King 1997: 136).[4]

The Egyptian case is similar, although on a much larger scale. The al-Sadat regime undermined the power of agricultural cooperatives and pro-tenant agrarian relations dispute committees soon after coming to power. Holdings of large landowners that had not been redistributed were desequestered in 1971. Many expropriated landlords successfully sued to regain their lands. In 1975, agricultural rents, frozen since 1952, were raised and owners were given increased powers to evict tenants. In 1981 the ceiling on private ownership of land was raised to 200 *faddan*s for reclaimed land and was effectively abolished for corporations. A tendency towards reconcentration of agricultural land was apparent by 1982 ('Abd al-Mu'ti & Kishk 1992: 216–17).

The Mubarak regime went even further in dismantling agrarian reform and meeting the demands of landlords. In 1986, price controls were lifted on most crops except cotton and sugarcane. The government encouraged cultivation of cash crops for export rather than food staples. The center-piece of the new pro-landlord orientation was proposed legislation to decontrol agricultural rents and abolish peasants' permanent tenancy rights. Discussions began on the draft law in 1985, though fear of peasant reactions delayed enactment of the measure until 1992. The legislation raised agricultural rents from seven to twenty-two times the land tax until October 1997 and eliminated rent ceilings entirely thereafter. It also gave landlords the right to evict tenants without cause after October 1997 and to sell their lands at market value (Hinnebusch 1993; Saad 1999).

In the summer of 1997 peasants in Bani Suwayf, Minya, Fayyum, Asyut, and Suhag provinces in upper Egypt and the Delta village of al-ʿAttaf, sup-ported by Islamist, Nasirist, and leftist political parties, protested and rioted in anticipation of the removal of rent ceilings and massive evictions of tenants. Agricultural cooperative offices were torched, at least one land-lord was killed, and peasants opened fire on security forces. Fourteen people were killed, dozens wounded, and hundreds arrested (*Al Ahram Weekly* 1997: July 10–16, August 28–September 3, September 25–October 1). Nonetheless, the law was implemented on schedule.

There was a loud debate in the press in the late 1980s over the pro-posed decontrol of agricultural rents. But peasants had no vehicle to voice their opinions. The national press delegitimized peasant tenants, accus-ing them of laziness and overbearing behavior towards landowners. Rather than an expression of democratization, media discussion of the draft law demonstrated the limited channels for substantive political debate and the exclusion of peasants from the political process (Springborg 1991; Saad 1999).

Iraq is probably the most idiosyncratic case of rolling back agrarian reform because the policy cannot be attributed to either pressure from international financial institutions or a domestic class of aspiring capital-ists. Policies dismantling collective farms and cooperatives, encouraging private ownership of land, and directing credit away from agricultural cooperatives were introduced in 1979. Ceilings on agricultural land hold-ings ceased to be strictly enforced. Controls over the cropping patterns of recipients of agrarian reform land were relaxed. In 1987, state agricultu-ral holdings began to be sold. Crops and livestock produced by private owners using large-scale, modern, capital-intensive methods increased significantly. Wealthy urban dwellers enhanced their investment in capi-talist agriculture in irrigated areas near the large cities. Although private agriculture grew rapidly in the 1980s, a new class of capitalist farmers was not consolidated before the Gulf War (Springborg 1986). There was no democratization, no development of civil society, and no marketization of the economy to any extent that the regime could not easily reverse.

Results and prospects

Even before the adoption of open-door policies, states had already sharply limited the autonomy of trade unions and peasant organizations, particularly their radical elements. The imposition of Washington consensus policies was accompanied by significant further repression and a decline in political freedom. In Turkey and Tunisia, the implementation of these policies was preceded by military coups. In Egypt, a limited democratic opening accompanied the new policies. But when the going got rough, the regime cracked down hard. Trade unionists and political leaders who opposed the new policies, whether through enterprise-level actions or national political mobilization, were repressed. Democratic openings, where they occurred, did not include the legalization of communist or Islamist parties (with the partial exception of the Welfare Party and its successor, the Virtue Party, in Turkey). The right to strike was usually limited.

Egypt, Turkey, and Tunisia recovered from the balance-of-payments crises that had prompted the imposition of Washington consensus policies. In Tunisia and Turkey, the combination of state repression, renewed social spending, and the threat of political Islam led to new corporatist bargains between the trade unions and the state, although with workers in a weaker position than in the previous era. Efforts to negotiate such a bargain began in Egypt, but did not come to fruition by the end of the 1990s, perhaps because of the relative weakness of the Egyptian labor movement. The two waves of Egyptian workers' collective action in resistance to open-door policies – 1975–77 and 1984–89 – were much less substantial than the strike waves in Tunisia in the mid-1970s and the mid-1980s or Turkey in the early and late 1970s, late 1980s, and early 1990s. Unlike the Turkish case, the most radical actions in Egypt were concentrated in the public sector, not the growing private sector (El Shafei 1995: 36).

The riots of January 1977 in Egypt and January 1984 in Tunisia exemplify a new form of urban social protest that became common in the era of economic policy shifts inspired by the Washington consensus: "IMF food riots." Other examples include Morocco (1981), Sudan (1985), and Jordan (1989 and 1996). The October 1988 riots in Algeria were not a direct response to an IMF-imposed program, but both the policies they opposed and the social character of the urban revolt were comparable to the new model (Pfeifer 1992). The Tunisian general strike of January 26, 1978 and the September–October 1984 strike and riot at the Kafr al-Dawwar textile mills in Egypt are mixed cases: traditional labor actions commingled with the violence of urban crowds directed broadly against the state and its symbols of authority.

The diffuse and sporadic character of these protests – spontaneous rioting or localized labor strikes rather than a sustained campaign of political and economic action – is partly the result of the structural and ideological heterogeneity of urban workers and the delegitimization of left politics in the open-door era. Collective action of unionized workers, even when well organized, radical, and militant, was only one component of popular protest against the Washington consensus. Workers were not able to organize a counter-hegemonic bloc of forces around themselves. Therefore, their collective actions could delay or modify the implementation of Washington consensus policies, but could not block them or advance an alternative economic course.

Islamist forces attempted to profit by the decline of the left, forming rival trade union federations in Turkey and Algeria and contesting elections in the state-authorized trade union federations in Egypt and Tunisia. But they failed to replace the left as the principal advocates of workers in large-scale modern enterprises (Alexander 1996a: 344, 374–78; Alexander 1996b; Willis 1996: 178; Djabi 1997; Beinin 1998b). Unionized urban workers are one of the social groups least attracted to movements of political Islam that have inspired resistance to capitalist globalization in the Middle East and beyond.

Democracy did not do well in the era of neo-liberal ascendency. Over and above the coup that brought Zayn al-ʿAbidin Ben ʿAli to power in 1987, Tunisia became more authoritarian after the wave of rural economic reorganization began in 1990 (King 1997). The Islamist al-Nahda remained illegal; there were repeated reports of the regime's detention and torture of political opponents; and no real opposition parties participated in the 1994 elections. After July 1992, the Egyptian regime imposed a broad political deliberalization in response to the challenge of armed Islamist groups and opposition to the new economic policies (Kienle 1998). The penal code was revised to replace prison terms with forced labor. Security cases were routinely transferred to military courts with less independence than civil courts. At least 10,000 political detainees were arrested under the state's emergency powers; many were tortured. In May 1995 a new law was enacted sharply restricting freedom of the press. It was abrogated after intense protest by journalists in 1996. Nonetheless, in 1998 two journalists were jailed for writing articles unflattering to a former cabinet minister. The parliamentary elections of 1990 and 1995 were significantly less free than previous elections and resulted in greater majorities for the ruling National Democratic Party than before.

While workers resisted Washington consensus policies to varying degrees, peasants were less engaged. In part this was due to the migration of large numbers of landless peasants to the cities or abroad. Peasant family farms were economically and politically marginalized, further reducing the capacity of peasants for collective action. Rural areas and provincial towns provided important bases for armed Islamic insurgents in Egypt (Fandy 1994). But the activists were typically not peasants. In Tunisia, poor peasants' protest against the inequities of structural adjustment was contained by agrarian relations promoting a revival of a moral economy – a form of state-led Islamization whose unintended consequence was that peasants became more amenable to the discourse of the regime's Islamist opposition. Small peasants were losers from Washington consensus policies in part because they had no voice in their formulation or implementation. Peasants were not part of a ruling coalition undertaking structural adjustment in any Middle Eastern country (Waterbury 1989: 42).

Regardless of the degree of macroeconomic success or failure of Washington consensus policies, one clear consequence was the redistribution of national income away from workers and peasant farmers towards self-employed individuals and corporations. Statistics on such matters are more than usually unreliable, but the overall trend is clear. In the early 1990s real wages in manufacturing in Algeria, Egypt, Syria, Jordan, Morocco, and Tunisia were at or below their 1970 level (World Bank 1995a: 4).

In Tunisia, incomes of self-employed individuals increased 68 percent during 1970–77, after Arab socialist policies were abandoned, while profits increased over 115 percent. Income distribution grew more unequal from 1975 to 1986 as the richest 20 percent of the population increased its share of total consumption from 22 percent to 50 percent while the share of the poorest 20 percent stagnated at 5–6 percent (Alexander 1996a: 162; Pfeifer 1996: 46; Radwan et al. 1991: 49–52, 61–62).

In Egypt, real wages in the private sector rose over 50 percent from 1975 to 1985, while public-sector wages rose by more than a third. By 1990 wages had fallen to their 1972 level, and they continued to decline during the early 1990s (Soliman 1998: 36). Real wages in manufacturing, which rose nearly 50 percent from 1975 to 1982, fell 40 percent from 1985 to 1995 (Hansen 1991: 473; Kienle 1998: 233). Income distribution worsened. From 1981–82 to 1990–91 the Gini coefficient of inequality (for a definition see page 39) rose from 0.32 to 0.38 in the urban sector and 0.29 to 0.32 in rural areas. The biggest losers in this period were the middle 40 percent of households, followed by the lowest 30 percent (Korayem 1995/96: 25–26).

The Turkish statistics seem the most complete and reliable. In the decade following implementation of Washington consensus policies in 1980, real wages in the public sector declined by 39 percent and civil service wages declined 13.5 percent. Real wages in the private sector increased by 16.6 percent. The last figure suggests an apparent success for the new economic policies, but must be judged in the context of increasingly unequal income distribution as expressed by the decline of the popular factor shares in the national income. From 1980 to 1988 the share of agriculture in the national income declined from 26.66 percent to 13.20 percent; wages and salaries, which rose steadily as a percentage of national income from 1963 to 1978, declined from 23.87 percent to 15.8 percent; rents, profits, and interest increased from 49.47 percent to 71 percent (Yeşilada & Fısunoğlu 1992: 199–200; Waterbury 1992: 66). Declining real wages in manufacturing was the main factor that enhanced the competitiveness of Turkey's manufactured exports in the 1980s, the primary basis for neo-liberal claims to success (Hansen 1991: 415–18).

By the mid-1990s, Washington consensus policies were unable to create sufficient jobs anywhere in the Middle East to employ those excluded from the shrinking public sector or displaced from agriculture by mechanization and reconcentration of plots. Unemployment rates were higher than anywhere else in the world: about 10 percent in Turkey (down considerably from 25 percent in 1986); 15 percent in Egypt, Morocco, and Tunisia; 20–25 percent in Algeria, Jordan, and Yemen; and about 20 percent in the West Bank and Gaza Strip, frequently exacerbated by Israel's closure of the territories (World Bank 1995a: 2; Richards & Waterbury 1996: 134).

Although low by international standards, poverty was not generally alleviated by Washington consensus policies. In Egypt the segment of the population under the poverty line ($30 a month) rose 30 percent from 1985 to 1990. During the same period poverty tripled in Jordan (World Bank 1995a: 3–5). Egyptian household income data indicate that in 1990–91 urban poverty was one-and-a-half times the level of 1980–81, while rural poverty more than doubled. Calculations based on household expenditure data yielded an increase of 20 percent in rural poverty and 84 percent in urban poverty over the same period (Korayem 1995/96: 22).

Quite exceptionally, the World Bank believes that in Morocco and Tunisia, poverty levels were reduced by nearly half (World Bank 1995a: 3–5). Samir Radwan disputes the bank's methods for defining the poverty line and argues that in Tunisia between 1975 and 1985 poverty decreased by only one-fifth and 23 percent of all wage earners lived in poverty. Moreover, there was no trickle-down in rural areas where families owned few productive resources. The alleviation of poverty in the face of worsening income distribution in Tunisia was largely due to remittances of migrant workers, not the internal capacity of the economy to generate well-paying jobs. In other words, the structural transformation of the economy was not self-sustaining (Radwan et al. 1991: 52–61, 89).

Washington consensus policies were certainly not the only cause of declining wages, high unemployment, and poverty. The collapse of oil prices and the return of migrant workers in the mid-1980s, the 1991 Gulf War, and the slowdown in the European and Japanese economies all played a role. These conjunctural factors intersected with the stagnation of the public sector and the inability of the private sector to provide a significant number of new high-wage manufacturing jobs.

By 1995 the World Bank had become so concerned about this state of affairs that it issued a special report asking *Will Arab Workers Prosper or be Left out in the Twenty-first Century?* The report made obligatory obeisance to the primacy of markets but also argued that laissez-faire policies were inadequate to set minimum standards for wages, working conditions, and collective bargaining and to reduce income insecurity. The bank called for a "broad vision of a new social contract that is realistic and capable of benefiting most workers" (World Bank 1995a: v). It is too soon to judge the extent to which the World Bank's change of leadership and tone might effect the generally more anti-popular orientation of the IMF and the US government. The World Bank's defection from neo-liberal orthodoxy and, much more significantly, the upsurge of popular struggle against Washington consensus policies at the turn of the twenty-first century suggest that the nearly unchallenged ascendancy of the ideology of unfettered markets and private enterprise is the product of a specific and limited historical conjuncture.

Notes

INTRODUCTION

1 Baer and Porath represent a distinctive Israeli style of Middle East social history. Because Israeli scholars did not have access to any place in the Arab world except Palestine from 1948 to 1979, their social histories tend to be more textualist than others. This unavoidable limitation is exacerbated by the dominance of traditional Orientalism at the Hebrew University of Jerusalem, the institutional home of both Baer and Porath.

2 The comparative value of the work of the Subaltern Studies school was examined in a special issue of *The American Historical Review* with articles by Prakash (1994) on the original India-based project, Mallon (1994) on Latin America, and Cooper (1994) on Africa. The absence of an article on the Middle East reflects both the weakness of subaltern studies approaches in Middle East studies and the view of many American historians (and others) that the Middle East is too unimportant, too exceptional, or too contentious to be of general interest.

3 Some Ottomanists argue that the *çift–hane* system actually prevailed in practice, though this claim has not been empirically demonstrated.

4 McGowan (1981: 47) illustrates specific numbers of retainers and types of equipment.

5 A special issue of the *Journal of Peasant Studies* 18 (nos. 3–4, April/July 1991), entitled "New Approaches to State and Peasant in Ottoman History," is devoted to this effort.

6 Many recent studies do take into account political economy, historical change, and the role of the state. For Egypt see Saad 1988; Saad 1998; El-Karanshawy 1998; Adams 1991; Hopkins 1993; for Jordan and Palestine Mundy 1994; Moors 1995; Tamari & Giacaman 1997; and for Lebanon Gilsenan 1996. Mitchell (forthcoming) contains many detailed and insightful studies of village life in upper Egypt including an updated version of his expose of Richard Critchfield that has broad conceptual value.

7 Two exceptions are Vallet 1911 and al-Khuli 1987–92. The second is discussed extensively in chapter 4.

1 THE WORLD CAPITALIST MARKET, PROVINCIAL REGIMES, AND LOCAL PRODUCERS, 1750–1839

1 Faruk Tabak speculates that the expansion of agricultural production in the second half of the eighteenth century led to intensification of peasant labor

170

due to increased cultivation of summer crops such as tomatoes, potatoes, haricot beans, tobacco, cochineal, and the reintroduction of sugarcane around Sidon and Beirut (Tabak 1991: 145–46). But he does not make a strong case for this claim, and even if it is true to some extent, rising peasant incomes would have partially compensated for working longer hours.

2 Basing himself on Cuno's first published article, Gerber maintains that "from the beginning of the seventeenth century the status of the peasant declined rapidly" (Cuno 1980; Gerber 1987: 65). Cuno subsequently clarified his argument and does not accept Gerber's claim (Cuno 1992: 10–11).

3 A prominent example of the use of the concept of feudalism in the service of modernization theory and Lebanese Christian exceptionalism is Harik 1968. Harik's designation of Lebanon as feudal is criticized by Chevallier (1971: 84–85) on grounds that are somewhat formalist. Khalaf (1987) also tends towards an exceptionalist modernization theory understanding of Lebanon. Schölch (1986) and Havemann (1991) use the term "feudalism" without these associations.

4 Following Doumani and Tamari (1982: 188), I use the term "patron–client relations" descriptively, not in the sense of an extended system as suggested in Gellner 1977. For a critique of patron–client relations as a system or a framework for the analysis of political economy and social order see Gilsenan 1977.

5 Marsot uses the term "mercantilism" rather than "industrial revolution," but her argument is otherwise similar to Fahmy's. Clark (1974) suggests a similar argument for Anatolia, which is dismissed by Pamuk (1987: 250–51 n. 62).

2 OTTOMAN REFORM AND EUROPEAN IMPERIALISM, 1839–1907

1 My formulation develops those of Roger Owen and E. J. Hobsbawm (Owen 1972; Owen 1989; Hobsbawm 1989). In the 1950s and 1960s the school of British imperial and commonwealth historians and others pursuing an intellectual agenda shaped by the cold war denied any structural relationship between the depression of 1873–96, intensified competition of European powers for control of markets, raw materials, and investment opportunities in Asia and Africa, and European military conquest and rule in those territories (Robinson & Gallagher 1961; Louis 1976). A central project of the materialist approaches to history that reemerged in the subsequent generation was to establish that imperialism was a valid category of historical analysis and that the scramble for Africa and other European incursions into the non-European world in the late nineteenth and early twentieth centuries were related to changes in the character of capitalism which intensified military and political competition among European powers (Owen & Sutcliffe 1972; Brewer 1990; Kennedy 1996; Wolfe 1997).

2 Maoz (1968) argues the standard Orientalist position with some qualifications. On the conflict of civilizations see Huntington 1996.

3 This figure is based on Schilcher (1985: 91). She carefully surveys the figures of casualty estimates, which range from 600 to 10,000.

4 Several pages distant from an orthodox Marxist declaration supported by a quote from Lenin, I. M. Smilianskaya offers a more nuanced formulation, roughly compatible with Gilsenan's approach, that changes in the agrarian regime resulted in a "complex combination of feudal exploitation and capitalistic elements" (Smilianskaya 1966: 239).

5 Meijer (1985: 25–38) offers an exposition and al-Disuqi (1981) a critique of these views.

6 Owen (1981a: 164) has a less positive evaluation of the movement's success.

4 FIKRI AL-KHULI'S JOURNEY TO AL-MAHALLA AL-KUBRA

1 Bayram al-Tunisi and others did speak to and about workers and peasants, but in ways very different from *al-Rihla*. See Beinin 1994a.

2 In addition to Sawsan El-Messiri, as far as I know, the only others who have written about *al-Rihla* are Ellis Goldberg (1994) and Amina Rachid (1991). Goldberg uses *al-Rihla* as evidence for his argument that workers were more rational than capitalists. I agree that workers were neither irrational or childish in the manner imagined by most of the *effendiyya* and the elites. But it is not clear that the behavior of workers at Misr Spinning and Weaving was rational in post-Enlightenment terms. Rachid assimilates *al-Rihla* to the progressivist, nationalist modernity of the *effendiyya* by characterizing it as "an expression of the consciousness of a proletarian class that is still embryonic, still close to its peasant origin" (p. 364).

3 This formulation rejects Spivak's argument in her widely discussed essay (1988) that subalterns cannot speak in favor of the one advanced by Gail Hershatter:

> If we replace "The subaltern cannot speak" (or, what I take to be closer to Spivak's actual argument, "The subaltern cannot represent herself in discourse") with "Many subalterns making cacophonous noise, some hogging the mike, many speaking intermittently and not exactly as they please, and all aware to some degree of the political uses of their own representation in that historical moment," we probably have a closer approximation of the situation confronting historians. If we are lucky, we also have a way out of the "disappearing subaltern" impasse in which any subaltern who speaks loses the right to that status. Finally, we have a chance to complicate the picture of one overarching discourse, in which subalterns appear only as positioned by their elite spokespersons. This picture might be fruitfully replaced not with a conception of "competing discourses" (with its overtones of free market bonanza and may the best discourse win) but with a recognition that some discourses can be seen only *in relation* to each other. (Hershatter 1997: 26)

4 "Turn, Motor!" Lyrics by Bayram al-Tunisi, as sung by Layla Murad in *Sayyidat al-Qitar*.

> Turn, motor, turn!

> Play your role, the greatest role.
> Turn as you like, and wind your thread.
> Don't mind the supervisor and the counter.
> Turn, motor, turn!

Free Egypt would rather go naked
Than dress in imported fabric:
Neither pink silk nor calico.
Turn, motor, turn!

Take this from our hands, our brother:
Something beautiful,
Of really strong manufacture, indeed strong.
Go to hell London and Bristol!
Turn, motor, turn!

We are the spindle.
We are the loom.
We are the finisher.
We are the exporters to Marseille and Darfur [Sudan].
Turn, motor, turn!

The age of industry is the age of victory.
Wear the crown of glory, Egypt!
Build your skyscrapers seventy stories high.
Turn, motor, turn!

Translated by Nancy Reynolds, with input from Ahmed Abdalla and Joel Beinin

5 For an argument that workers were able to do so, see Goldberg 1994.

5 POPULIST NATIONALISM, STATE-LED DEVELOPMENT, AND AUTHORITARIAN REGIMES, 1939–1973

1 Information in this section is drawn from Lockman 1996 and Beinin 1990.
2 Information in this section is drawn from Beinin & Lockman 1987 and Beinin 1990.
3 Information in this section is drawn from Batatu 1978: 470–75, 545–66, 616–24, 666–70, 749–57 and Farouk-Sluglett & Sluglett 1983.

6 POST-POPULIST REFORMATION OF THE WORKING CLASS AND PEASANTRY

1 For another frank admission of the limits of Washington consensus policies by a zealous advocate, see Clawson 1992.
2 Posusney translates the name of the labor federation as Egyptian Trade Union Federation (ETUF).
3 Important exceptions are Goldberg 1986 and Posusney 1997.
4 For Tunisia, King's argument is supported by Radwan et al. 1991.

References

ʿAbbas, K., et al (1994) *al-Haraka al-ʿummaliyya fi maʿrakat al-tahawwul: dirasat fi al-intikhabat al-niqabiyya 1991*. Cairo: Markaz al-Buhuth al-ʿArabiyya.

ʿAbd al-Muʿti, ʿA. & Kishk, H. (1992) Ahamm al-taghayyurat al-ijtimaʿiyya fi al-qarya al-misriyya dhat al-sila bi-masaʾil al-sukkan. In *al-Masʾala al-fallahiyya waʾl-ziraʿiyya fi misr: abhath wa-munaqqashat al-nadwa allati ʿuqidat bi-al-qahira*, ed. Markaz al-Buhuth al-ʿArabiyya, pp. 201–29. Cairo: Markaz al-Buhuth al-ʿArabiyya.

Abdel-Fadil, M. (1975) *Development, Income Distribution, and Social Change in Rural Egypt (1952–1970): A Study in the Political Economy of Agrarian Transition*. Cambridge: Cambridge University Press.

(1980) *The Political Economy of Nasserism: A Study in Employment and Income Distribution Policies in Urban Egypt, 1952–1972*. Cambridge: Cambridge University Press.

Abdel-Khalek, G. (1981a) Looking Outside or Turning NW? On the Meaning and External Dimension of Egypt's Infitah, 1971–1980. *Social Problems*, 28 (4, April), 394–409.

(1981b) The Open Door Economic Policy in Egypt: Its Contribution to Investment and Equity Implications. In *Rich States and Poor States in the Middle East: Egypt and the New Arab Order*, ed. M. H. Kerr & E. S. Yassin, pp. 259–83. Boulder: Westview Press.

Abdel-Malek, A. (1969) *Idéologie et renaissance nationale*. Paris: Editions Anthropos.

Abrahamian, E. (1982) *Iran Between Two Revolutions*. Princeton: Princeton University Press.

Abun-Nasr, J. (1975) *A History of the Maghrib*, 2nd ed. Cambridge: Cambridge University Press.

Adams Jr., Richard H. (1986) *Development and Social Change in Rural Egypt*. Syracuse: Syracuse University Press.

(1991) *The Effects of International Remittances on Poverty, Inequality, and Development in Rural Egypt*. Washington, DC: International Food Policy Research Institute.

ʿAdli, H. (1993) *al-ʿUmmal waʾl-siyyasa: al-dawr al-siyyasi liʾl-haraka al-ʿummaliyya fi misr min 1952–1981*. Cairo: al-Ahali.

ʿAfifi, H. (1938) *ʿAla hamish al-siyasa: baʿd masaʾilina al-qawmiyya*. Cairo: Matbaʿat Dar al-Kutub al-Misriyya.

Ahmad, F. (1980) Vanguard of a Nascent Bourgeoisie: The Social and Economic Policy of the Young Turks, 1908–1918. In *Social and Economic History of*

Turkey (1071–1920), ed. O. Okyar & H. İnalcık, pp. 329–50. Ankara: Meteksan Ltd.

(1981) Military Intervention and the Crisis in Turkey. *Merip Reports* (93, January), 5–24.

(1983) The Agrarian Policy of the Young Turks, 1908–1918. In *Economie et société dans l'Empire Ottoman (fin du XVIIIe– début du XXe siècle)*, ed. J. Bacqué-Grammont & P. Dumont, pp. 275–88. Paris: Editions du Centre de la Recherche Scientifique.

(1993) *The Making of Modern Turkey*. London: Routledge.

(1995) The Development of Class-Consciousness in Republican Turkey, 1923–45. In *Workers and the Working Class in the Ottoman Empire and the Turkish Republic*, ed. D. Quataert & E. J. Zürcher, pp. 75–94. London: I. B. Tauris.

Ahmad, K. M. (1981) *al-Tabaqa al-ʿamila al-ʿiraqiyya: al-takawwun wa-bidayat al-taharruk*. Baghdad: Dar al-Rashid.

Al Ahram Weekly (1997) July 10–16, August 28–September 3, September 25–October 1.

al-Ahsan, S. ʿA. (1984) Economic Policy and Class Structure in Syria: 1958–1980. *International Journal of Middle East Studies*, 16 (3, August), 301–23.

Akarli, E. D. (1985–86) *Gedik*: Implements, Mastership, Shop Usufruct, and Monopoly among Istanbul Artisans, 1750–1850. *Wissenschaftskolleg Jahrbuch*, 1985/86, 223–32.

(1998) Law and Order in the Marketplace: Istanbul Artisans and Shopkeepers, 1730–1840. Eighth Annual Biennial Conference on the Ottoman Empire and the World-Economy: Law and Legitimation in the Ottoman Empire. Unpublished, November 13–14, 1998.

Alexander, M. C. (1996a) Between Accommodation and Confrontation: State, Labor, and Development in Algeria and Tunisia. Ph.D. thesis, Duke University.

(1996b) State, Labor and the New Global Economy in Tunisia. In *North Africa: Development and Reform in a Changing Global Economy*, ed. D. Vandewalle, pp. 177–202. New York: St. Martin's Press.

Alleaume, G. (1999) An Industrial Revolution in Agriculture? Some Observations on the Evolution of Rural Egypt in the Nineteenth Century. In *Agriculture in Egypt from Pharaonic to Modern Times*, ed. A. K. Bowman & E. Rogan, pp. 331–45. Oxford: Oxford University Press for the British Academy.

ʿAllush, N. (1978) *al-Haraka al-wataniyya al-filastiniyya: amam al-yahud wa'l-sahyuniyya, 1882–1948*. Beirut: Dar al-Taliʿa li'l-Tibaʿa wa'l-Nashr.

al-ʿAmara, M. H. (1975/76) Min mudhakkirat niqabi qadim. *al-Thaqafa al-ʿummaliyya*, October 1975–May 1976.

Amin, G. A. (1995) *Egypt's Economic Predicament: A Study in the Interaction of External Pressure, Political Folly and Social Tension in Egypt, 1960–1990*. Leiden: E. J. Brill.

Amin, S. & van der Linden, M. (1997) *"Peripheral" Labour? Studies in the History of Partial Proletarianization: International Review of Social History Supplement 4*. Cambridge: Cambridge University Press.

Andréa, G. C. (1937) *La Révolte druze et l'insurrection de Damas, 1925–1926.* Paris: Payot.

Ansari, H. (1986) *Egypt: The Stalled Society.* Albany: State University of New York Press.

al-ʿAqiqi, A. (1959) *Lebanon in the Last Years of Feudalism, 1848–1868,* Malcolm Kerr, trans. and ed. Beirut: American University of Beirut Press.

Arai, M. (1992) *Turkish Nationalism in the Young Turk Era.* Leiden: E. J. Brill.

Aricanli, T. (1986) Agrarian Relations in Turkey: A Historical Sketch. In *Food, States, and Peasants: Analyses of the Agrarian Question in the Middle East,* ed. A. Richards, pp. 23–67. Boulder: Westview Press.

Arnon-Ohanna, Y. (1982) *Falahim be-mered ha-ʿaravi be-eretz yisraʾel, 1936–1939.* Tel Aviv: Papyrus.

Asad, T. (1987) Are there Histories of Peoples without Europe? A Review Article. *Comparative Studies in Society and History,* 29 (3, July), 594–607.

al-ʿAskari, M. (1995) *Safahat min tarikh al-tabaqa al-ʿamila.* Hilwan: Dar al-Khadamat al-Niqabiyya.

ʿAtiyya, ʿA. I. (1926) *Mudhakkirat ʿamil.* Cairo: Matbaʿat Wadi [al-Nil].

Ayrout, H. H. (1963) *The Egyptian Peasant.* Boston: Beacon Press.

Baer, G. (1964) *Egyptian Guilds in Modern Times.* Jerusalem: Israel Oriental Society.

(1969a) The Development of Private Ownership of Land. In *Studies in the Social History of Modern Egypt,* ed. Gabriel Baer, pp. 62–78. Chicago: University of Chicago Press.

(1969b) Submissiveness and Revolt of the Fellah. In *Studies in the Social History of Modern Egypt,* ed. Gabriel Baer, pp. 93–108. Chicago: University of Chicago Press.

(1969c) Slavery and its Abolition. In *Studies in the Social History of Modern Egypt,* ed. Gabriel Baer, pp. 161–89. Chicago: University of Chicago Press.

(1980) Ottoman Guilds: A Reassessment. In *Social and Economic History of Turkey (1071–1920),* ed. O. Okyar & H. İnalcık, pp. 95–102. Ankara: Meteksan Ltd.

(1982) *Fellah and Townsman in the Middle East: Studies in Social History.* London: Frank Cass.

Baklanoff, A. (1988) *al-Tabaqa al-ʿamila fi misr al-muʿasira.* Damascus: Markaz al-Abhath waʾl-Dirasat al-Ishtirakiyya fi al-ʿAlam al-ʿArabi.

Barbir, K. K. (1996) Memory, Heritage and History: The Ottoman Legacy in the Arab World. In *Imperial Legacy: The Ottoman Imprint on the Balkans and the Middle East,* ed. L. Carl Brown, pp. 100–14. New York: Columbia University Press.

Barkey, H. J. (1990) *The State and the Industrialization Crisis in Turkey.* Boulder: Westview Press.

Batatu, H. (1978) *The Old Social Classes and the Revolutionary Movements of Iraq: A Study of Iraq's Old Landed and Commercial Classes and of its Communists, Baʾthists, and Free Officers.* Princeton: Princeton University Press.

(1999) *Syria's Peasantry, the Descendants of its Lesser Rural Notables, and their Politics.* Princeton: Princeton University Press.

Bauer, Y. (1966) The Arab Revolt of 1936. *New Outlook,* 9 (6 and 7, June and July), 49–57; 21–28.

Beinin, J. (1989) Labor, Capital and the State in Nasserist Egypt, 1952–1961. *International Journal of Middle East Studies*, 21 (1, February), 71–90.

(1990) *Was the Red Flag Flying There? Marxist Politics and the Arab–Israeli Conflict in Egypt and Israel, 1948–1965.* Berkeley: University of California Press.

(1994a) Will the Real Egyptian Working Class Please Stand Up? In *Workers and Working Classes in the Middle East: Struggles, Histories, Historiographies*, ed. Z. Lockman, pp. 247–70. Albany: State University of New York Press.

(1994b) Writing Class: Workers and Modern Egyptian Colloquial Poetry (Zagal). *Poetics Today*, 15 (2, Summer), 191–215.

(1998a) Egypt: Economy and Society, 1923–1952. In *The Cambridge History of Egypt*, vol. II, ed. M. Daly, pp. 309–33. Cambridge: Cambridge University Press.

(1998b) The Islamic Current in the Egyptian Trade Union Movement: A Historical Comparison and Some Questions to Consider. Conference on Globalization, Political Islam, and Urban Social Movements. University of California, Berkeley, unpublished, March 6–8, 1998.

(1998c) *The Dispersion of Egyptian Jewry: Culture, Politics, and the Formation of a Modern Diaspora.* Berkeley: University of California Press.

Beinin, J. & Lockman, Z. (1987) *Workers on the Nile: Nationalism, Communism, Islam, and the Egyptian Working Class, 1882–1954.* Princeton: Princeton University Press.

Bello, W., with Cunningham, S. and Rau, B. (1994) *Dark Victory: The United States, Structural Adjustment, and Global Poverty.* London: Pluto Press.

Bennoune, M. (1988) *The Making of Contemporary Algeria, 1830–1987.* Cambridge: Cambridge University Press.

Berkes, N. (1964) *The Development of Secularism in Turkey.* Montreal: McGill University Press.

Berktay, H. (1987) The Feudalism Debate: The Turkish End – is "Tax-vs.-Rent" Necessarily the Product and Sign of a Modal Difference? *Journal of Peasant Studies*, 14 (3, April), 291–333.

Berktay, H. & Faroqhi, S., eds. (1991) *New Approaches to State and Peasant in Ottoman History. Journal of Peasant Studies*, 18 (3–4, April/July).

Bernal, V. (1994) Peasants, Capitalism, and (Ir)Rationality. *American Ethnologist*, 21 (4), 792–810.

Bernstein, D. S. (1996) Expanding the Split Labor Market Theory: Between and Within Sectors of the Split Labor Market of Mandatory Palestine. *Comparative Studies in Society and History*, 38, 243–66.

Bianchi, R. (1984) *Interest Groups and Political Development in Turkey.* Princeton: Princeton University Press.

(1986) The Corporatization of the Egyptian Labor Movement. *Middle East Journal*, 40 (3, summer), 429–44.

(1989) *Unruly Corporatism: Associational Life in Twentieth-Century Egypt.* New York: Oxford University Press.

Bint al-Shati‘ (‘A’isha ‘Abd al-Rahman) (1936) *al-Rif al-misri.* Cairo: Maktabat wa-Matba‘at al-Wafd.

[1938 or later] *Qadiyyat al-fallah.* Cairo: Maktabat al-Nahda al-Misriyya.

Birks, J. & Sinclair, C. (1980) *International Migration and Development in the Arab Region.* Geneva: International Labour Office.

Blair, T. L. (1970) *The Land to Those who Work it: Algeria's Experiment in Workers' Management.* Garden City, NY: Doubleday & Company.

Bodman, J. & Herbert, L. (1963) *Political Factions in Aleppo, 1760–1826.* Chapel Hill: University of North Carolina Press.

Bokova, L. (1990) *La Confrontation franco-syrienne à l'époque du mandat, 1925–1927.* Paris: L'Harmattan.

Booth, M. (1990) *Bayram al-Tunisi's Egypt: Social Criticism and Narrative Strategies.* Exeter: Ithaca Press.

Brand, L. (1992) Economic and Political Liberalization in a Rentier Economy: The Case of the Hashemite Kingdom of Jordan. In *Privatization and Liberalization in the Middle East,* ed. I. Harik & D. J. Sullivan, pp. 167—88. Bloomington: Indiana University Press.

Brewer, A. (1990) *Marxist Theories of Imperialism: A Critical Survey.* New York: Routledge.

Brink, J. H. (1991) The Effect of Emigration of Husbands on the Status of their Wives: An Egyptian Case. *International Journal of Middle East Studies,* 23 (2, May), 201–11.

Brown, N. (1990) *Peasant Politics in Modern Egypt: The Struggle against the State.* New Haven: Yale University Press.

Buheiry, M. (1984) The Peasant Revolt of 1858 in Mount Lebanon: Rising Expectations, Economic Malaise, and the Incentive to Arm. In *Land Tenure and Social Transformation in the Middle East,* ed. T. Khalidi, pp. 291–301. Beirut: American University of Beirut.

Burke III, E. (1986) Understanding Arab Protest Movements. *Arab Studies Quarterly,* 8 (4, Fall), 333–45.

(1988) Rural Collective Action and the Emergence of Modern Lebanon: A Comparative Historical Perspective. In *Lebanon: A History of Conflict and Consensus,* ed. N. Shehadi & D. H. Mills, pp. 14–30. London: Centre for Lebanese Studies and I. B. Tauris.

(1991) Changing Patterns of Peasant Protest, 1750–1950. In *Peasants and Politics in the Modern Middle East,* ed. F. Kazemi & J. Waterbury, pp. 24–37. Miami: Florida International University Press.

Canclini, N. G. (1995) *Hybrid Cultures: Strategies for Entering and Leaving Modernity.* Minneapolis: University of Minnesota Press.

Carson, W. M. (1953) *The Mehalla Report.* Badr es-Sheyn: n.p.

Ceyhum, F. (1989) Development of Capitalism and Class Struggles in Turkey. In *Power and Stability in the Middle East,* ed. Berch Berberoğlu, pp. 55–69. London: Zed Books.

Chahine, Y. (1952) *Sayyidat al-qitar.* 100 min., b&w.

(1958) *Bab al-hadid.* 74 min., b&w.

(1979) *al-Ard.* 130 min., color.

Chakrabarty, D. (1989) *Rethinking Working-Class History: Bengal, 1890–1940.* Princeton: Princeton University Press.

(1992) The Death of History? Historical Consciousness and the Culture of Late Capitalism. *Public Culture,* 4 (2, Spring), 47–65.

Chevallier, D. (1968) Western Development and Eastern Crisis in the Mid-Nineteenth Century: Syria Confronted with the European Economy. In *Beginnings of Modernization in the Middle East: The Nineteenth Century,* ed. W.

R. Polk & R. L. Chambers, pp. 205–22. Chicago: University of Chicago Press.

(1971) *La Société du Mont Liban a l'époque de la révolution industrielle en Europe.* Paris: Librairie Orientaliste P. Geunther.

Cizre-Sakallıoğlu, Ü. (1992) Labour and the State in Turkey: 1960–80. *Middle Eastern Studies*, 28 (4, October), 712–28.

Clark, E. C. (1974) The Ottoman Industrial Revolution. *International Journal of Middle East Studies*, 5 (1, February), 65–76.

Clawson, P. (1992) What's so Good about Stability? In *The Politics of Economic Reform in the Middle East*, ed. Henri J. Barkey, pp. 213–36. New York: St. Martin's Press.

Clegg, I. (1971) *Workers' Self-Management in Algeria.* New York: Monthly Review.

Cole, J. R. I. (1993) *Colonialism and Revolution in the Middle East: Social and Cultural Origins of Egypt's 'Urabi Revolt.* Princeton: Princeton University Press.

Commander, S. (1987) *The State and Agricultural Development in Egypt since 1975.* London: Ithaca Press.

Cooper, F. (1994) Conflict and Connection: Rethinking Colonial African History. *American Historical Review*, 99 (5, December), 1516–45.

Cooper, F. et al. (1993) *Confronting Historical Paradigms: Peasants, Labor and the Capitalist World System in Africa and Latin America.* Madison: University of Wisconsin Press.

Cooper, M. N. (1982) *The Transformation of Egypt.* Baltimore: Johns Hopkins University Press.

Critchfield, R. (1978) *Shahhat: An Egyptian.* Syracuse: Syracuse University Press.

(1991) A Response to "The Invention and Reinvention of the Egyptian Peasant." *International Journal of Middle East Studies*, 23 (2, May), 277–79.

Cuno, K. (1980) The Origins of Private Ownership of Land in Egypt: A Reappraisal. *International Journal of Middle East Studies* 12 (3, November), 245–75.

(1984) Egypt's Wealthy Peasantry, 1740–1820: A Study of the Region of al-Mansura. In *Land Tenure and Social Transformation in the Middle East*, ed. T. Khalidi, pp. 303–32. Beirut: American University of Beirut Press.

(1988a) Commercial Relations between Towns and Villages in Eighteenth and Early Nineteenth Century Egypt. *Annales Islamologiques*, 24, 111–35.

(1988b) Review of Judith Tucker, *Women in Nineteenth Century Egypt. Jusur: The UCLA Journal of Middle Eastern Studies*, 4, 77–85.

(1992) *The Pasha's Peasants: Land, Society, and Economy in Lower Egypt, 1740–1858.* Cambridge: Cambridge University Press.

(1999) A Tale of Two Villages: Family, Property, and Economic Activity in Rural Egypt in the 1840s. In *Agriculture in Egypt from Pharaonic to Modern Times*, ed. A. K. Bowman & E. Rogan, pp. 301–29. Oxford: Oxford University Press for the British Academy.

Dahir, M. (1988) *al-Intifadat al-lubnaniyya didda al-nizam al-muqata'ajiyya.* Beirut: Dar al-Farabi.

Dallal, A. (2000) Appropriating the Past: Twentieth Century Reconstruction of Pre-Modern Islamic Thought. *Islamic Law and Society*, 7 (1, Autumn), 1–34.

Davis, E. (1983) *Challenging Colonialism: Bank Misr and Egyptian Industrialization, 1920–1941*. Princeton: Princeton University Press.

Davison, R. (1963) *Reform in the Ottoman Empire*. Princeton: Princeton University Press.

al-Disuqi, ʿA. (1975) *Kibar mullak al-aradi al-ziraʿiyya wa-dawruhum fi al-mujtamaʿ al-misri, 1914–1952*. Cairo: Dar al-Thaqafa al-Jadida.

(1981) *Nahwa fahm misr al-iqtisadi al-ijtimaʿi*. Cairo: Dar al-Kitab al-Jamiʿi.

Djabi, A. (1997) The Islamist Workers Movement and the UGTA. Conference on After Socialism: Islam and the Market in Algeria. University of California, Berkeley, unpublished, May 23, 1997.

Doumani, B. (1995) *Discovering Palestine: Merchants and Peasants in Jabal Nablus, 1700–1900*. Berkeley: University of California Press.

Dubar, C. & Nasr, S. (1976) *Les Classes sociales au Liban*. Paris: Presses de la Fondation Nationale des Sciences Politiques.

Dumont, P. (1980) Sources inédites pour l'histoire du mouvement ouvrier et des courants socialistes dans l'Empire Ottoman au début du XXe siècle. In *Social and Economic History of Turkey (1071–1920)*, ed. O. Okyar & H. İnalcık, pp. 383–96. Ankara: Meteksan Ltd.

Egypt. Census Department (1909) *The Census of Egypt Taken in 1907*. Cairo: National Printing Department.

Eickelman, D. F. (1998) *The Middle East and Central Asia: An Anthropological Approach*, 3rd ed. Upper Saddle River, NJ: Prentice Hall.

El-Karanshawy, S. (1998) Class, Family, and Power in an Egyptian Village. *Cairo Papers in Social Science*, 20 (1, Spring), iv–75.

El-Messiri, S. (1980) Class and Community in an Egyptian Textile Town. Ph.D. thesis, Hull University.

El Shafei, O. (1995) Workers, Trade Unions, and the State in Egypt: 1984–1989. *Cairo Papers in Social Science*, 18 (2, Summer), 5–43.

Elpeleg, T. (1978) The 1936–39 Disturbances: Riot or Rebellion. *Wiener Library Bulletin*, 29, 40–51.

Eman, A. (1943) *L'Industrie du coton en Egypte: Etude d'économie politique*. Cairo: Institut Français d'Archeologie Orientale.

Establet, C. & Pascual, J. (1994) *Familles et fortunes à Damas: 450 foyers damascains en 1700*. Damascus: Institut Français de Damas.

European Trade Union Institute (1988) *The Trade Union Movement in Turkey*. Brussels: European Trade Union Institute.

Fahmy, K. (1997) *All the Pasha's Men: Mehmed Ali, his Army and the Making of Modern Egypt*. Cambridge: Cambridge University Press.

(1998) The Era of Muhammad ʿAli Pasha. In *The Cambridge History of Egypt*, vol. II, ed. M. Daly, pp. 139–79. Cambridge: Cambridge University Press.

Fahmy, M. (1954) *La Révolution de l'industrie en Egypte et ses conséquences sociales au 19e siècle (1800–1850)*. Leiden: E. J. Brill.

Fandy, M. (1994) Egypt's Islamic Group: Regional Revenge? *Middle East Journal*, 48 (4, Autumn), 607–25.

Farah, B. (1991) *Min tarikh al-kifah al-filastini al-musallah: idrab wa-thawrat 1936–1939*. Haifa: Jamʿiyyat al-Tatawwur al-Ijtimaʿi.

Farjani, N. (1983) *al-Hijra ila al-naft*. Lebanon: Markaz Dirasat al-Wahda al-ʿArabiyya.

Faroqhi, S. (1994) Crisis and Change, 1590–1699. In *An Economic and Social History of the Ottoman Empire, Volume 2, 1600–1914*, ed. H. İnalcık and D. Quataert, pp. 411–636. Cambridge: Cambridge University Press.

Farouk-Sluglett, M. & Sluglett, P. (1983) Labor and National Liberation: The Trade Union Movement in Iraq, 1920–1958. *Arab Studies Quarterly*, 5 (2, Spring), 139–154.

(1984) The Application of the 1858 Land Code in Greater Syria: Some Preliminary Observations. In *Land Tenure and Social Transformation in the Middle East*, ed. T. Khalidi, pp. 409–21. Beirut: American University of Beirut Press.

(1987) *Iraq since 1958: From Revolution to Dictatorship*. London: KPI.

Fattah, H. (1997) *The Politics of Regional Trade in Iraq, Arabia, and the Gulf, 1745–1900*. Albany: State University of New York Press.

Fawaz, L. (1994) *An Occasion for War. Civil Conflict in Lebanon and Damascus in 1860*. Berkeley: University of California Press.

Feiler, G. (1993) *Labour Migration in the Middle East following the Iraqi Invasion of Kuwait*. Jerusalem: Israel/Palestine Center for Research and Information.

Firestone, Y. (1975a) Crop-Sharing Economics in Mandatory Palestine. *Middle East Studies*, 11 (1 and 2, January and May), 3–23, 175–94.

(1975b) Production and Trade in an Islamic Context: Sharika Contracts in the Transitional Economy of Northern Samaria, 1853–1943 (II). *International Journal of Middle East Studies*, 6, 185–209, 308–25.

Firro, K. (1990) Silk and Agrarian Changes in Lebanon, 1860–1914. *International Journal of Middle East Studies*, 22 (2, May), 151–69.

Frangakis-Syrett, E. (1991) The Trade of Cotton and Cloth in Izmir: From the Second Half of the Eighteenth Century to the Early Nineteenth Century. In *Landholding and Commercial Agriculture in the Middle East*, ed. Ç. Keyder & F. Tabak, pp. 97–117. Albany: State University of New York Press.

Franklin, R. (1985) Migrant Labor and the Politics of Development in Bahrain. *Merip Reports* (132, May), 7–13.

Gabbay, R. (1978) *Communism and Agrarian Reform in Iraq*. London: Croom Helm.

Gellner, E. (1977) Patrons and Clients. In *Patrons and Clients in Mediterranean Societies*, ed. E. Gellner & Waterbury, pp. 1–6. London: Duckworth.

Gelvin, J. L. (1998) *Divided Loyalties: Nationalism and Mass Politics in Syria at the Close of Empire*. Berkeley: University of California Press.

Gerber, H. (1987) *The Social Origins of the Modern Middle East*. Boulder: Lynne Rienner.

Ghali, M. (1938) *Siyasat al-ghad: barnamij siyasi wa-iqtisadi wa-ijtimaʿi*. Cairo: Matbaʿat al-Risala.

(1945) *al-Islah al-ziraʿi: al-milkiyya, al-ijar, al-ʿamal*. Cairo: Jamaʿat al-Nahda al-Qawmiyya.

Ghazaleh, P. (1995) The Guilds: Between Tradition and Modernity. In *The State and its Servants: Administration in Egypt from Ottoman Times to the Present*, ed. N. Hanna, pp. 60–74. Cairo: American University in Cairo Press.

(1999) Masters of the Trade: Crafts and Craftspeople in Cairo, 1750–1850. *Cairo Papers in Social Science*, 22 (3, Fall), 1–151.

al-Ghazzali, ʿA. (1968) *Tarikh al-haraka al-niqabiyya al-misriyya, 1899–1952*. Cairo: Dar al-Thaqafa al-Jadida.

Gibb, H. & Bowen, H. (1950) *Islamic Society and the West: A Study of the Impact of Western Civilization on Moslem Culture in the Near East*, 2 vols. Oxford: Oxford University Press.

Gilsenan, M. (1977) Against Patron–Client Relations. In *Patrons and Clients in Mediterranean Societies*, ed. E. Gellner & J. Waterbury, pp. 167–83. London: Duckworth.

(1984) A Modern Feudality? Land and Labour in North Lebanon, 1858–1950. In *Land Tenure and Social Transformation in the Middle East*, ed. T. Khalidi, pp. 449–63. Beirut: American University of Beirut Press.

(1996) *Lords of the Lebanese Marches: Violence and Narrative in an Arab Society*. London: I. B. Tauris.

Glavanis, K. & Glavanis, P., eds. (1990) *The Rural Middle East: Peasant Lives and Modes of Production*. London: Zed Books.

Goitein, S. (1967–93) *A Mediterranean Society: The Jewish Communities of the Arab World as Portrayed in the Documents of the Cairo Geniza*, 6 vols. Berkeley: University of California Press.

Goldberg, E. (1986) *Tinker, Tailor, and Textile Worker: Class and Politics in Egypt, 1930–1954*. Berkeley: University of California Press.

(1992a) The Foundations of State–Labor Relations in Contemporary Egypt. *Comparative Politics*, 24 (2, January), 147–61.

(1992b) Peasants in Revolt: Egypt 1919. *International Journal of Middle East Studies*, 24 (2, May), 265–80.

(1994) Worker's Voice and Labor Productivity in Egypt. In *Workers and Working Classes in the Middle East: Struggles, Histories, Historiographies*, ed. Z. Lockman, pp. 111–31. Albany: State University of New York Press.

(1996) Reading from Left to Right: The Social History of Egyptian Labor. In *The Social History of Labor in the Middle East*, ed. E. J. Goldberg, pp. 163–92. Boulder: Westview Press.

Gramsci, A. (1971) *Selections from the Prison Notebooks of Antonio Gramsci; Edited and Translated by Quintin Hoare and Geoffrey Nowell Smith*. London: Lawrence & Wishart.

Gran, P. (1978) *Islamic Roots of Capitalism: Egypt, 1760–1840*. Austin: University of Texas Press.

Gupta, A. (1997) *Postcolonial Developments: Agriculture in the Making of Modern India*. Durham, NC: Duke University Press.

Güzel, M. Ş. (1995) Capital and Labor during World War II. In *Workers and the Working Class in the Ottoman Empire and the Turkish Republic*, ed. D. Quataert & E. J. Zürcher, pp. 127–45. London: I. B. Tauris.

Haj, S. (1997) *The Making of Iraq, 1900–1963: Capital, Power, and Ideology*. Albany: State University of New York Press.

al-Hakim, T. (1933) *'Awdat al-ruh*. Cairo: Maktabat al-Adab.

(1990) *Return of the Spirit*. Washington, DC: Three Continents Press.

(1938) *Yawmiyyat na'ib fi al-aryaf*. Cairo: Maktabat al-Adab.

(1989) *Maze of Justice*. Austin: University of Texas Press.

Halliday, F. (1984) Labor Migration in the Arab World. *Merip Reports* (123, May), 3–10.

Hammam, M. (1977) Women Workers and the Practice of Freedom as Education: The Egyptian Experience. Ph.D. thesis, University of Kansas.

Handoussa, H. & Potter, G., eds. (1991) *Employment and Structural Adjustment: Egypt in the 1990s.* Cairo: American University in Cairo Press.

Hanna, ʿA. (1973) *al-Haraka al-ʿummaliyya fi suriyya wa-lubnan, 1900–1945.* Damascus: Dar Dimashq.

(1975–78) *al-Qadiyya al-ziraʿiyya waʾl-harakat al-fallahiyya fi suriyya wa-lubnan, 1820–1945*, 2 vols. Beirut: Dar al-Farabi.

(1990) *al-ʿAmmiyya waʾl-intifadat al-fallahiyya fi jabal hawran, 1850–1918.* Damascus: Dar al-Ahali liʾl-Tibaʿa waʾl-Nashr waʾl-Tawziʿ.

Hanna, N. (1998) *Making Big Money in 1600: The Life and Times of Ismaʿil Abu Taqiyya, Egyptian Merchant.* Syracuse: Syracuse University Press.

Hannoyer, J. (1980) Le Monde rural avant les réformes. In *La Syrie d'aujourd'hui*, ed. A. Raymond, pp. 273–95. Paris: Editions du Centre de la Recherche Scientifique.

Hansen, B. (1991) *The Political Economy of Poverty, Equity, and Growth: Egypt and Turkey.* Oxford: Oxford University Press.

Haqqi, M. T. (1906) *ʿAdhraʾ dinshaway.* Cairo: n.p.

(1986) *The Maiden of Dinshway.* In *Three Pioneering Egyptian Novels*, S. El-Gabalawy, trans. and ed., pp. 17–48. Fredericton, NB: York Press.

Harb, T. (1939) *Majmuʿat khutab*, vol. III. Cairo: Matbaʿat Misr.

Harik, I. F. (1968) *Politics and Change in a Traditional Society, Lebanon 1711–1845.* Princeton: Princeton University Press.

Harris, G. S. (1967) *The Origins of Communism in Turkey.* Stanford: Hoover Institution.

Havemann, A. (1991) The Impact of Peasant Resistance on Nineteenth-Century Mount Lebanon. In *Peasants and Politics in the Modern Middle East*, ed. F. Kazemi & J. Waterbury, pp. 85–100. Miami: Florida International University Press.

Haykal, M. H. (1963) *Zaynab: manazir wa-akhlaq rifiyya.* Cairo: Maktabat al-Nahda al-Misriyya.

(1989) *Zainab: The First Egyptian Novel.* London: Darf Publishers.

Hershatter, G. (1997) *Dangerous Pleasures: Prostitution and Modernity in Twentieth Century Shanghai.* Berkeley: University of California Press.

Heydemann, S. (1992) The Political Logic of Economic Rationality: Selective Stabilization in Syria. In *The Politics of Economic Reform in the Middle East*, ed. Henri J. Barkey, pp. 11–39. New York: St. Martin's Press.

Hiltermann, J. (1992) *Behind the Intifada: Labor and Women's Movements in the Occupied Territories.* Princeton: Princeton University Press.

Hinnebusch, R. A. (1985) *Egyptian Politics under Sadat: The Post-Populist Development of an Authoritarian–Modernizing State.* Cambridge: Cambridge University Press.

(1989) *Peasant and Bureaucracy in Baʿthist Syria: The Political Economy of Rural Development.* Boulder: Westview Press.

(1990) *Authoritarian Power and State Formation in Baʿthist Syria: Army, Party, and Peasant.* Boulder: Westview Press.

(1993) Class, State, and the Reversal of Egypt's Agrarian Reform. *Middle East Report* (184, September–October), 20–23.

(1994) Liberalization in Syria: The Struggle of Economic and Political Rationality. In *Contemporary Syria: Liberalization between Cold War and Cold Peace*, ed. Eberhard Kienle, pp. 97–113. London: British Academic Press.

Hobsbawm, E. (1989) *The Age of Empire, 1875–1914.* New York: Vintage Books.

Hoexter, M. (1984) Egyptian Involvement in the Politics of Notables in Palestine: Ibrahim Pasha in Jabal Nablus. In *Egypt and Palestine: A Millennium of Association (868–1948)*, ed. A. Cohen & G. Baer, pp. 190–213. Jerusalem: Ben Zvi Institute for the Study of Jewish Communities in the East and Yad Izhak Ben Zvi Institute for the Study of Eretz Israel.

Holt, P. & Lewis, B., eds. (1962) *Historians of the Middle East.* London: Oxford University Press.

Hoodfar, H. (1991) Return to the Veil: Personal Strategy and Public Participation in Egypt. In *Working Women: International Perspectives on Labour and Gender Ideology*, ed. N. Redclift & T. M. Sinclair, pp. 104–24. London: Routledge.

Hopkins, N. S. (1988) Class and State in Rural Arab Communities. In *Beyond Coercion: The Durability of the Arab State*, ed. A. Dawisha & I. W. Zartman. London: Croom Helm.

(1993) Small Farmer Households and Agricultural Sustainability in Egypt. In *Sustainable Agriculture in Egypt*, ed. M. A. Faris & M. H. Khan, pp. 185–95. Boulder: Lynne Rienner.

Hopkins, N. S. & Westergaard, K., eds. (1999) *Directions of Change in Rural Egypt.* New York: Columbia University Press.

Hourani, A. (1962) *Arabic Thought in the Liberal Age, 1789–1939.* Oxford: Oxford University Press.

(1968) Ottoman Reform and the Politics of Notables. In *Beginnings of Modernization in the Middle East in the Nineteenth Century*, ed. W. R. Polk & R. L. Chambers, pp. 41–68. Chicago: University of Chicago Press.

Huntington, S. P. (1996) *The Clash of Civilizations and the Remaking of World Order.* New York: Simon & Schuster.

Hurewitz, J. C. (1975) *The Middle East and North Africa in World Politics: A Documentary Record*, 2 vols., 2nd ed., revised and enlarged. New Haven: Yale University Press.

al-Hut, B. N. (1981) *al-Qiyadat wa'l-mu'assasat al-siyyasiyya fi filastin, 1917–1948.* Beirut: Institute for Palestine Studies.

Ibrahim, S. E. (1982) *The New Arab Social Order: A Study of the Social Impact of Oil Wealth.* Boulder: Westview Press.

Idris, Y. (1959) *al-Haram.* Cairo: al-Kitab al-Fiddi.

(1984) *The Sinners.* Washington, DC: Three Continents Press.

İnalcık, H. (1991) The Emergence of Big Farms, Çiftliks: State, Landlords, and Tenants. In *Landholding and Commercial Agriculture in the Middle East*, ed. Ç. Keyder & F. Tabak, pp. 17–34. Albany: State University of New York Press.

İnalcık, H. & Quataert, D. eds. (1994) *An Economic and Social History of the Ottoman Empire, 1300–1914.* Cambridge: Cambridge University Press.

'Isawi, 'A. (1969) Safha matwiyya min tarikh niqabat 'ummal al-nasij. *al-Thaqafa al-'ummaliyya* (May 1, 1969), 12.

Islamoğlu, H. & Keyder, Ç. (1987) Agenda for Ottoman History. In *The Ottoman Empire and the World-Economy*, ed. H. Islamoğlu-Inan, pp. 42–62. Cambridge: Cambridge University Press.

Islamoğlu-Inan, H. (1987) Introduction: "Oriental Despotism" in World-System Perspective. In *The Ottoman Empire and the World-Economy*, ed. H. Islamoğlu-Inan, pp. 1–24. Cambridge: Cambridge University Press.

Issawi, C. (1980) *The Economic History of Turkey, 1800–1914*. Chicago: University of Chicago Press.

(1982) *An Economic History of the Middle East and North Africa*. New York: Columbia University Press.

(1988) *The Fertile Crescent, 1800–1914: A Documentary Economic History*. New York: Oxford University Press.

Işıklı, A. (1987) Wage Labor and Unionization. In *Turkey in Transition: New Perspectives*, ed. I. C. Schick & E. A. Tonak, pp. 309–32. New York: Oxford University Press.

'Izz al-Din, A. (1967) *Tarikh al-tabaqa al-ʿamila al-misriyya mundhu nashʾatiha hatta thawrat 1919*. Cairo: Dar al-Kitab al-ʿArabi.

(1970) *Tarikh al-tabaqa al-ʿamila al-misriyya, 1919–1929*. Cairo: Dar al-Shaʿb.

(1972) *Tarikh al-tabaqa al-ʿamila al-misriyya, 1929–1939*. Cairo: Dar al-Shaʿb.

(1987) *Tarikh al-tabaqa al-ʿamila al-misriyya mundhu nushuʾiha hatta sanat 1970*. Cairo: Dar al-Ghad al-ʿArabi.

Jelavich, B. (1983) *History of the Balkans*, 2 vols. Cambridge: Cambridge University Press.

Kamil, F. (1985) *Maʿa al-haraka al-niqabiyya fi nisf qarn: safahat min dhikrayat*. Cairo: Dar al-Ghad al-ʿArabi.

Kanafani, G. (1972) Thawrat 1936–1939 fi filastin: khalfiyya, tafasil wa-tahlil. *Shuʾun filastiniyya*, 6 (1, January), 45–77.

Kara, M. (1984) The Workers as a Class Were Defeated. *Merip Reports* (121, February), 21–27.

Karakışla, S. Y. (1992) The 1908 Strike Wave in the Ottoman Empire. *Turkish Studies Association Bulletin*, 16 (2, September), 153–77.

Karpat, K. H. (1968) The Land Regime, Social Structure, and Modernization in the Ottoman Empire. In *Beginnings of Modernization in the Middle East: The Nineteenth Century*, ed. W. R. Polk & R. L. Chambers, pp. 69–90. Chicago: University of Chicago Press.

(1976) *The Gecekondu: Rural Migration and Urbanization*. Cambridge: Cambridge University Press.

Kasaba, R. (1988) *The Ottoman Empire and the World Economy: The Nineteenth Century*. Albany: State University of New York Press.

(1991) Migrant Labor in Western Anatolia, 1750–1850. In *Landholding and Commercial Agriculture in the Middle East*, ed. Ç. Keyder & F. Tabak, pp. 113–21. Albany: State University of New York Press.

Kayyali, A. (1978) *Palestine: A Modern History*. London: Croom Helm.

Kazemi, F. & Waterbury, J., eds. (1991) *Peasants and Politics in the Modern Middle East*. Miami: Florida International University Press.

Kennedy, D. (1996) Imperial History and Postcolonial Theory. *Journal of Imperial and Commonwealth History*, 24 (3, September), 345–63.

Keyder, Ç. (1983) Paths of Rural Transformation in Turkey. In *Sociology of "Developing Societies": The Middle East*, ed. T. Asad & R. Owen, pp. 163–77. New York: Monthly Review Press.

(1987) *State and Class in Turkey: A Study in Capitalist Development*. London: Verso.

(1991) Introduction: Large-Scale Commercial Agriculture in the Ottoman Empire? In *Landholding and Commercial Agriculture in the Middle East*, ed. Ç. Keyder & F. Tabak, pp. 1–13. Albany: State University of New York Press.

Keyder, Ç. & Tabak, F., eds. (1991) *Landholding and Commercial Agriculture in the Middle East*. Albany: State University of New York Press.

Khafagy, F. (1984) Women and Labor Migration: One Village in Egypt. *Merip Reports* (124, June), 17–21.

Khalaf, S. (1987) *Lebanon's Predicament*. New York: Columbia University Press.

Khalidi, R. (1987) Review of Kenneth Stein, *The Land Question in Palestine, 1917–1939* and Ylana N. Miller, *Government and Society in Rural Palestine, 1920–1948*. *Journal of Palestine Studies*, 17 (1, Fall), 146–49.

(1997) *Palestinian Identity: The Construction of Modern National Consciousness*. New York: Columbia University Press.

Khater, A. F. (1996) "House" to "Mistress of the House": Gender, Class and Silk in 19th Century Mt. Lebanon. *International Journal of Middle East Studies*, 28 (3, August), 325–48.

Khoury, D. R. (1991) The Introduction of Commercial Agriculture in the Province of Mosul and its Effects on the Peasantry, 1750–1850. In *Landholding and Commercial Agriculture in the Middle East*, ed. Ç. Keyder & F. Tabak, pp. 155–71. Albany: State University of New York Press.

(1997) *State and Provincial Society in the Early Modern Ottoman Empire: Mosul, 1540–1834*. Cambridge: Cambridge University Press.

Khoury, P. (1987) *Syria and the French Mandate: The Politics of Arab Nationalism, 1920–1945*. Princeton: Princeton University Press.

al-Khuli, F. (1987–92) *al-Rihla*, 3 vols. Cairo: Dar al-Ghad.

Kienle, E. (1994) *Contemporary Syria: Liberalization between Cold War and Peace*. London: I. B. Tauris.

(1998) More than a Response to Islamism: The Political Deliberalization of Egypt in the 1990s. *Middle East Journal*, 52 (2, Spring), 219–35.

Kimmerling, B. & Migdal, J. S. (1993) *Palestinians: The Making of a People*. New York: The Free Press.

King, S. J. (1997) The Politics of Market Reform in Rural Tunisia. Ph. D. thesis, Princeton: Princeton University.

Koptiuch, K. (1994) Other Workers: A Critical Reading of Representations of Egyptian Petty Commodity Production at the Turn of the Twentieth Century. In *Workers and Working Classes in the Middle East: Struggles, Histories, Historiographies*, ed. Z. Lockman, pp. 41–70. Albany: State University of New York Press.

Korayem, K. (1995/96) Structural Adjustment, Stabilization Policies, and the Poor in Egypt. *Cairo Papers in Social Science*, 18 (4, Winter), 1–111.

Kurmuş, O. (1981) Some Aspects of Handicraft and Industrial Production in Ottoman Anatolia, 1800–1915. *Asian and African Studies*, 15 (1, March), 85–101.

Kushner, D. (1977) *The Rise of Turkish Nationalism*. London: Frank Cass.

Labaki, B. (1983) La Filature de la soie dans le sandjak du Mont-Liban: Une expérience de croissance industrielle dépendante (1810–1914). In *Economie et société dans l'Empire Ottoman (fin du XVIIIe–début du XXe siècle)*, ed. J. Bacqué-Grammont & P. Dumont, pp. 433–39. Paris: Editions du Centre de la Recherche Scientifique.

Lachman, S. (1982) Arab Rebellion and Terrorism in Palestine, 1929–39: The Case of Sheikh Izz al-Din al-Qassam and his Movement. In *Zionism and Arabism in Palestine and Israel*, ed. E. Kedourie & Sylvia G. Haim, pp. 52–99. London: Frank Cass.

LaTowsky, R. J. (1984) Egyptian Labor Abroad, Mass Participation and Modest Returns. *Merip Reports* (123, May), 11–18.

Lawson, F. (1981) Rural Revolt and Provincial Society in Egypt, 1820–24. *International Journal of Middle East Studies*, 13 (2, May), 131–53.

(1992) Divergent Modes of Economic Liberalization in Syria and Iraq. In *Privatization and Liberalization in the Middle East*, ed. I. Harik & D. J. Sullivan, pp. 123–44. Bloomington: Indiana University Press.

(1994) Domestic Pressures and the Peace Process: Fillip or Hindrance. In *Contemporary Syria: Liberalization between Cold War and Cold Peace*, ed. E. Kienle, pp. 139–54. London: British Academic Press.

Layne, L. (1981) Women in Jordan's Workforce. *Merip Reports* (95, March/April 1981), 19–23.

Lerner, D. (1958) *The Passing of Traditional Society: Modernizing the Middle East*. Glencoe, IL: Free Press.

Lesch, A. M. (1990) Egyptian Labor Migration. In *The Political Economy of Contemporary Egypt*, ed. I. M. Oweiss, pp. 90–108. Washington, DC: Center for contemporary Arab Studies, Georgetown University.

Levtzion, N. & Voll, J. O., eds. (1987) *Eighteenth-Century Renewal and Reform in Islam*. Syracuse: Syracuse University Press.

Lewis, B. (1937) The Islamic Guilds. *Economic History Review*, 8 (1, November), 20–37.

(1961) *The Emergence of Modern Turkey*. London: Oxford University Press.

Lloyd, G. (1933–34) *Egypt since Cromer*, 2 vols. London: Macmillan & Co.

Lockman, Z. (1994a) Imagining the Working Class: Culture, Nationalism and Class Formation in Egypt, 1899–1914. *Poetics Today*, 15 (2, Summer), 157–90.

(1994b) Introduction. In *Workers and Working Classes in the Middle East, Struggles, Histories, Historiographies*, ed. Z. Lockman, pp. xi–xxix. Albany: State University of New York Press.

(1994c) "Worker" and "Working Class" in pre-1914 Egypt. In *Workers and Working Classes in the Middle East, Struggles, Histories, Historiographies*, ed. Z. Lockman, pp. 71–109. Albany: State University of New York Press.

(1996) *Comrades and Enemies: Arab and Jewish Workers in Palestine, 1906–1948*. Berkeley: University of California Press.

Longuenesse, E. (1978) La Classe ouvrière au Proche Orient: La Syrie. *La Pensée* (197, January–February), 120–32.

(1980) L'Industrialisation et sa signification sociale. In *La Syrie d'aujourd'hui*, ed. A. Raymond, pp. 327–58. Paris: Editions du Centre National de la Recherche Scientifique.

(1985) The Syrian Working Class Today. *Merip Reports* (134, July–August), 17–24.

Louis, W. R., ed. (1976) *Imperialism: The Robinson and Gallagher Controversy.* New York: Viewpoints.

Lustick, I. (1993) *Unsettled States, Disputed Lands: Britain and Ireland, France and Algeria, Israel and the West Bank–Gaza.* Ithaca: Cornell University Press.

Macleod, A. E. (1991) *Accommodating Protest: Working Women, the New Veiling, and Change in Cairo.* New York: Columbia University Press.

Mallon, F. (1994) The Promise and Dilemma of Subaltern Studies: Perspectives from Latin American History. *American Historical Review,* 99 (5, December), 1491–1515.

Mandel, N. J. (1976) *The Arabs and Zionism before World War I.* Berkeley: University of California Press.

Maoz, M. (1968) *Ottoman Reform in Syria and Palestine, 1840–1861.* Oxford: Oxford University Press.

(1980) Intercommunal Relations in Ottoman Syria during the Tanzimat Era: Social and Economic Factors. In *Social and Economic History of Turkey (1071–1920),* ed. O. Okyar & H. İnalcık, pp. 205–10. Ankara: Meteksan Ltd.

Marcus, A. (1989) *The Middle East on the Eve of Modernity: Aleppo in the Eighteenth Century.* New York: Columbia University Press.

Margulies, R. & Yıldızoğlu, E. (1984) Trade Unions and Turkey's Working Class. *Merip Reports* (121, February), 15–20, 31.

(1987) Agrarian Change, 1923–1970. In *Turkey in Transition: New Perspectives,* ed. I. Schick & E. A. Tonak, pp. 269–92. New York: Oxford University Press.

(1988) Austerity Packages and Beyond: Turkey since 1980. *Capital and Class* (36, Winter), 141–62.

Marsot, A. L. al-S. (1984) *Egypt in the Reign of Muhammad Ali.* Cambridge: Cambridge University Press.

Masters, B. (1990) The 1850 Events in Aleppo: An Aftershock of Syria's Incorporation into the Capitalist World System. *International Journal of Middle East Studies,* 22 (1, February), 3–20.

Mattar, P. (1988) *al-Hajj Amin al-Husayni and the Palestinian National Movement.* New York: Columbia University Press.

McGowan, B. (1981) *Economic Life in Ottoman Europe: Taxation, Trade and the Struggle for Land, 1600–1800.* Cambridge: Cambridge University Press.

(1994) The Age of the Ayans, 1699–1812. In *An Economic and Social History of the Ottoman Empire, 1300–914,* ed. H. İnalcık & D. Quataert, pp. 637–758. Cambridge: Cambridge University Press.

McPherson, J. W. (1985) *The Man who Loved Egypt: Bimbashi McPherson, Edited by Barry Carman and John McPherson.* London: British Broadcasting Corporation.

Mehanna, S., Hopkins, N. S., and Abdelmaksoud, B. (1994) Farmers and Merchants: Background to Structural Adjustment in Egypt. *Cairo Papers in Social Science,* 17 (2, Summer), v–148.

Meijer, R. (1985) *al-Dirasat al-tarikhiyya al-misriyya al-muʿasira ʿan fatrat 1936–1952: bahth fi al-tabiʿ al-ʿilmi w'al-siyyasi lil-minhaj.* Cairo: Dar Shuhdi lil-Nashr.

Meswari-Gualt, M. (1991) The Palestinian Peasant Revolt in the 1930s. MA thesis, University of California, Santa Cruz.

Miller, J. L. (1977) The Syrian Revolt of 1925. *International Journal of Middle East Studies*, 8 (4, October), 543–63.

Mitchell, T. (1990a) The Invention and Reinvention of the Egyptian Peasant. *International Journal of Middle East Studies*, 22 (2, May), 129–50.

(1990b) Everyday Metaphors of Power. *Theory and Society*, 19 (5, October), 545–77.

(1991a) The Representation of Rural Violence in Writings on Political Development in Nasserist Egypt. In *Peasants and Politics in the Modern Middle East*, ed. F. Kazemi & J. Waterbury, pp. 222–51. Miami: Florida International University Press.

(1991b) Response to Richard Critchfield. *International Journal of Middle East Studies*, 23 (2, May), 279–80.

(forthcoming) *Out of Egypt*. Berkeley: University of California Press.

Moghadam, V. M. (1993) *Modernizing Women: Gender and Social Change in the Middle East*. Boulder: Lynne Rienner.

Moors, A. (1990) Gender Hierarchy in a Palestinian Village: The Case of al-Balad. In *The Rural Middle East: Peasant Lives and Modes of Production*, ed. K. Glavanis & P. Glavanis, pp. 195–209. London: Zed Books and Birzeit University.

(1995) *Women, Property and Islam: Palestinian Experiences*. Cambridge: Cambridge University Press.

al-Mudarrik, M. Y. (1967–69) Safha min harakat al-ʿummal qabla al-thawra. *al-Thaqafa al-ʿummaliyya*, August 15, 1967–September 1, 1969.

Mundy, M. (1994) Village Land and Individual Title: Mushaʿ and Ottoman Land Registration in the ʿAjlun District. In *Village, Steppe and State: The Social Origins of Modern Jordan*, ed. E. L. Rogan & T. Tell, pp. 58–79. London: British Academic Press.

Murshid, ʿA. ʿA. (1981) *Nushuʾ wa-tatwwur al-haraka al-niqabiyya waʾl-ʿummaliyya fi al-yaman*. Aden: Wizarat al-Thaqafa.

Musa, A. I. (1985) *al-Tabaqa al-ʿamila al-misriyya, 1943–1971: ruʾya mawduʿiyya min khilali tajriba shakhsiyya*. Cairo: Dar al-Mustaqbal al-ʿArabi.

Myntti, C. (1984) Yemeni Workers Abroad: The Impact on Women. *Merip Reports* (124, June), 11–16.

Najm, Z. (1987) *Bur saʿid: tarikhuha wa-tatawwuruha mundhu nashʾatiha, 1859 hatta ʿamm 1882*. Cairo: al-Hayʾa al-Misriyya al-ʿamma lil-Kitab.

Nelson, J. M. (1989) Overview: The Politics of Long-Haul Reform. In *Fragile Coalitions: The Politics of Economic Adjustment*, ed. J. M. Nelson, pp. 3–26. Washington, DC: Overseas Development Corporation.

Niblock, T. (1993) International and Domestic Factors in the Economic Liberalization Process in Arab Countries. In *Economic and Political Liberalization in the Middle East*, ed. T. Niblock & E. Murphy, pp. 55–87. London: British Academic Press.

Nieuwenhuis, T. (1982) *Politics and Society in Early Modern Iraq: Mamluk Pashas, Tribal Shaykhs and Local Rule between 1802 and 1831*. The Hague: Martinus Nijhoff.

al-Nukhayli, S. M. (1967) *al-Haraka al-ʿummaliyya fi misr wa-mawqif al-sahafa wa'l-sultat minha min sanat 1882 ila sanat 1952*. Cairo: al-Ittihad al-ʿAmm li'l-ʿUmmal.

O'Donnell, G. (1978) Reflections on the Patterns of Change in the Bureaucratic-Authoritarian State. *Latin American Research Review*, 12 (1), 3–38.

Okonjo-Iweala, N. & Fuleihan, Y. (1993) Structural Adjustment and Egyptian Agriculture: Some Preliminary Indications of the Impact of Economic Reforms. In *Sustainable Agriculture in Egypt*, ed. M. A. Faris & M. H. Khan, pp. 127–39. Boulder: Lynne Rienner.

Olson, R. (1974) The Esnaf and the Patrona Halil Rebellion of 1730: A Realignment in Ottoman Politics? *Journal of the Economic and Social History of the Orient*, 17 (3, September), 329–44.

Owen, R. (1969) *Cotton and the Egyptian Economy, 1820–1914: A Study in Trade and Development*. Oxford: Oxford University Press.

  (1972) Egypt and Europe: From French Expedition to British Occupation. In *Studies in the Theory of Imperialism*, ed. R. Owen & B. Sutcliffe, pp. 195–209. London: Longman.

  (1981a) *The Middle East and the World Economy, 1800–1914*. London: Methuen.

  (1981b) The Development of Agricultural Production in Nineteenth Century Egypt: Capitalism of What Type? In *The Islamic Middle East, 700–1900: Studies in Economic and Social History*, ed. A. Udovitch, pp. 521–46. Princeton: The Darwin Press.

  (1985) *Migrant Workers in the Gulf, Report No. 68*. London: The Minority Rights Group.

  (1987) The Silk-Reeling Industry of Mount Lebanon, 1840–1914: A Study of the Possibilities and Limitations of Factory Production in the Periphery. In *The Ottoman Empire and the World-Economy*, ed. H. Islamoğlu-Inan, pp. 271–83. Cambridge: Cambridge University Press.

  (1989) The Movement of Labor in and out of the Middle East Over the Last Two Centuries: Peasants, Patterns, and Policies. In *The Modern Economic and Social History of the Middle East in its World Context*, ed. G. Sabagh, pp. 29–43. Cambridge: Cambridge University Press.

  (1992) *State, Power and Politics in the Making of the Modern Middle East*. London: Routledge.

Owen, R. & Pamuk, Ş. (1999) *A History of the Middle East Economies in the Twentieth Century*. Cambridge, MA: Harvard University Press.

Owen, R. & Sutcliffe, B., eds. (1972) *Studies in the Theory of Imperialism*. London: Longman.

Özbudun, E. (1976) *Social Change and Political Participation in Turkey*. Princeton: Princeton University Press.

Paige, J. M. (1975) *Agrarian Revolution: Social Movements and Export Agriculture in the Underdeveloped World*. New York: Free Press.

Pamuk, Ş. (1984) The Ottoman Empire in the "Great Depression" of 1873–1896. *Journal of Economic History*, 44 (1, March), 107–18.

  (1987) *The Ottoman Empire and European Capitalism, 1820–1913*. Cambridge: Cambridge University Press.

Paul, J. (1981a) Perspective on the Land Crisis. *Merip Reports* (99, September), 3–5.

  (1981b) Riots in Morocco. *Merip Reports* (99, September), 30–31.

(1984) States of Emergency: The Riots in Tunisia and Morocco. *Merip Reports* (127, October), 3–6.

Perthes, V. (1994) Stages of Economic and Political Liberalization. In *Contemporary Syria: Liberalization between Cold War and Cold Peace*, ed. Eberhard Kienle, pp. 44–71. London: British Academic Press.

(1995) *The Political Economy of Syria under Asad*. New York: I. B. Tauris.

Pfeifer, K. (1985) *Agrarian Reform under State Capitalism in Algeria*. Boulder: Westview Press.

(1992) Algeria's Implicit Stabilization Program. In *The Politics of Economic Reform in the Middle East*, ed. H. J. Barkey, pp. 153–81. New York: St. Martin's Press.

(1996) Between Rocks and Hard Choices: International Finance and Economic Adjustment in North Africa. In *North Africa: Development and Reform in a Changing Global Economy*, ed. D. Vandewalle, pp. 25–63. New York: St. Martin's Press.

(1999) How Tunisia, Morocco, Jordan and even Egypt Became IMF "Success Stories" in the 1990s. *Middle East Report* (210), 23–27.

Polk, W. R. (1963) *The Opening of South Lebanon: A Study of the Impact of the West on the Middle East, 1788–1840*. Cambridge, MA: Harvard University Press.

Polk, W. R. & Chambers, R. L., eds. (1968) *Beginnings of Modernization in the Middle East in the Nineteenth Century*. Chicago: University of Chicago Press.

Pontecorvo, G. (1965) *The Battle of Algiers*. 123 min., b&w.

Popkin, S. L. (1979) *The Rational Peasant: The Political Economy of Rural Society in Vietnam*. Berkeley: University of California Press.

Porath, Y. (1966) The Peasant Revolt of 1858–61 in Kisrawan. *Asian and African Studies*, 2, 77–157.

(1977) *The Palestinian Arab National Movement: From Riots to Rebellion, Volume 2, 1929–1939*. London: Frank Cass.

Posusney, M. P. (1992) Labor as an Obstacle to Privatization: The Case of Egypt. In *Privatization and Liberalization in the Middle East*, ed. Iliya Harik and Denis J. Sullivan, pp. 81–105. Bloomington: Indiana University Press.

(1993) Irrational Workers: The Moral Economy of Labor Protest in Egypt. *World Politics*, 46 (1, October), 83–120.

(1997) *Labor and the State in Egypt: Workers, Unions, and Economic Restructuring, 1952–1996*. New York: Columbia University Press.

Posusney, M. P. & Pfeifer, K. (1997) Islam, Islamists and Labor Law. *International Journal of Comparative Public Policy*, 9, 195–223.

Prakash, G. (1994) Subaltern Studies as Postcolonial Criticism. *American Historical Review*, 99 (5, December), 1475–90.

Quataert, D. (1979) The Economic Climate of the "Young Turk Revolution" in 1908. *Journal of Modern History*, 51 (3, September), D1147–61.

(1981) Agricultural Trends and Government Policy in Ottoman Anatolia, 1800–1914. *Asian and African Studies*, 15 (1, March), 69–84.

(1983) *Social Disintegration and Popular Resistance in the Ottoman Empire, 1881–1908: Reactions to European Economic Penetration*. New York: New York University Press.

(1991a) Ottoman Women, Households and Textile Manufacturing, 1800–1914. In *Women in Middle East History*, ed. N. Keddie & B. Baron, pp. 161–76. New Haven: Yale University Press.

(1991b) Rural Unrest in the Ottoman Empire, 1830–1914. In *Peasants and Politics in the Modern Middle East*, ed. F. Kazemi & J. Waterbury, pp. 38–49. Miami: Florida International University Press.

(1994a) The Age of Reforms, 1812–1914. In *An Economic and Social History of the Ottoman Empire, 1300–914*, ed. H. İnalcık & D. Quataert, pp. 759–943. Cambridge: Cambridge University Press.

(1994b) *Manufacturing in the Ottoman Empire and Turkey, 1500–1950*. Albany: State University of New York Press.

(1995) The Workers of Salonica, 1850–1912. In *Workers and the Working Class in the Ottoman Empire and the Turkish Republic*, ed. D. Quataert & E. J. Zürcher, pp. 59–74. London: I. B. Tauris.

Rabbath, E. (1982) L'Insurrection syrienne de 1925–1927. *Revue Historique* (542, April–June), 405–47.

Rachid, A. (1991) Popular Voice in the Novel: A Comparative Study of Fikry El-Kholy's Al-Rihla (The Journey), Jack London's Martin Eden, and Jules Valle's Trilogy. In *Images of Egypt in Twentieth Century Literature: Proceedings of the International Symposium on Comparative Literature, 18th–20th December 1989*, ed. H. Gindi, pp. 355–66. Cairo: Department of English Language and Literature, University of Cairo.

Radwan, S., Jamal, V., and Ghose, A. (1991) *Tunisia: Rural Labour and Structural Transformation*. London: Routledge.

Radwan, S. & Lee, E. (1986) *Agrarian Change in Egypt: An Anatomy of Rural Poverty*. London: Croom Helm.

Rafeq, A. (1966) *The Province of Damascus, 1723–1783*. Beirut: Khayat's.

(1976) The Law-Court Registers of Damascus with Special Reference to Craft-Corporations during the First Half of the Eighteenth Century. In *Les Arabes par leurs archives (XVIe–XXe siècles)*, ed. J. Berque & D. Chevallier, pp. 141–59. Paris: Editions du Centre National de la Recherche Scientifique.

(1983) The Impact of Europe on a Traditional Economy: The Case of Damascus, 1840–1870. In *Economie et société dans l'Empire Ottoman (fin du XVIIIe–début du XXe siècle)*, ed. J. Bacqué-Grammont & P. Dumont, pp. 419–32. Paris: Editions du Centre de la Recherche Scientifique.

(1984) Land Tenure Problems and their Social Impact in Syria around the Middle of the Nineteenth Century. In *Land Tenure and Social Transformation in the Middle East*, ed. T. Khalidi, pp. 371–96. Beirut: American University of Beirut Press.

(1991) Craft Organization, Work Ethics, and the Strains of Change in Ottoman Syria. *Journal of the American Oriental Society*, 111 (3, July–September), 495–511.

Raffinot, M. & Jacquemot, P. (1977) *Le Capitalisme d'état algérien*. Paris: F. Maspero.

al-Rafi'i, 'A. (1961) *Muhammad farid: ramz al-ikhlas wa'l-tadhiyya, tarikh misr al-qawmi min sanat 1908 ila sanat 1919*. Cairo: Maktabat al-Nahda al-Misriyya.

Rapley, J. (1996) *Understanding Development: Theory and Practice in the Third World*. Boulder: Lynne Rienner.

Raymond, A. (1973–74) *Artisans et commerçants au Caire au XVIIIe siècle.* Damascus: Institut Français de Damas.

(1975) Deux leaders populaires au Caire à la fin du XVIIIe et au début du XIXe siècle. *La Nouvelle revue du Caire,* 1, 281–98.

(1981) The Economic Crisis of Egypt in the Eighteenth Century. In *The Islamic Middle East, 700–1900,* ed. A. Udovitch, pp. 687–707. Princeton: Darwin Press.

(1995) The Role of the Communities in the Administration of Cairo. In *The State and its Servants: Administration in Egypt from Ottoman Times to the Present,* ed. N. Hanna, pp. 32–43. Cairo: American University in Cairo Press.

Richards, A. (1980) Egypt's Agriculture in Trouble. *Merip Reports* (84, January), 3–13.

(1982) *Egypt's Agricultural Development, 1800–1980: Technical and Social Change.* Boulder: Westview Press.

(1987) Primitive Accumulation in Egypt, 1798–1882. In *The Ottoman Empire and the World-Economy,* ed. H. Islamoğlu-Inan, pp. 203–43. Cambridge: Cambridge University Press.

(1991) The Political Economy of Dilatory Reform: Egypt in the 1980s. *World Development,* 19 (12, December), 17–21.

Richards, A. & Waterbury, J. (1990) *A Political Economy of the Middle East: State, Class, and Economic Development,* 1st ed. Boulder: Westview Press.

(1996) *A Political Economy of the Middle East,* 2nd ed. Boulder: Westview Press.

Rivlin, H. (1961) *The Agricultural Policies of Muhammad 'Ali in Egypt.* Cambridge, MA: Harvard University Press.

Robinson, G. E. (1997) *Building a Palestinian State: The Incomplete Revolution.* Bloomington: Indiana University Press.

Robinson, R. & Gallagher, J. with Alice Denny (1961) *Africa and the Victorians: The Climax of Imperialism in the Dark Continent.* New York: St. Martin's Press.

Rodinson, M. (1978) *Islam and Capitalism.* Austin: University of Texas Press.

Rogan, E. L. (1995) Reconstructing Water Mills in Late Ottoman Transjordan. *Studies in the History and Archaeology of Jordan,* 5, 753–56.

(1999) *Frontiers of State in the Late Ottoman Empire: Transjordan, 1850–1921.* Cambridge: Cambridge University Press.

Roy, D. A. (1991) Egyptian Emigrant Labor: Domestic Consequences. *Middle Eastern Studies,* 22 (4, October), 551–82.

Roy, S. (1995) *The Gaza Strip: The Political Economy of De-development.* Washington, DC: Institute for Palestine Studies.

Ruedy, J. (1992) *Modern Algeria: The Origins and Development of a Nation.* Bloomington: Indiana University Press.

Rushdie, S. (1991) *Imaginary Homelands: Essays and Criticism, 1981–1991.* London: Granta.

Rustum, A. (1938) *The Royal Archives of Egypt and the Disturbances in Palestine, 1834.* Beirut: The American Press.

Saad, R. (1988) Social History of an Agrarian Reform Community in Egypt. *Cairo Papers in Social Science,* 11 (4, Winter), v–115.

(1999) State, Landlord, Parliament and Peasant: The Story of the 1992 Tenancy Law in Egypt. In *Agriculture in Egypt: From Pharaonic to Modern*

Times, ed. A. K. Bowman & E. Rogan, pp. 387–404. Oxford: Oxford University Press for the British Academy.

Saʿd, S. (1945) *Mushkilat al-fallah*. Cairo: Dar al-Qarn al-ʿIshrin lil-Nashr.

Safran, N. (1961) *Egypt in Search of Political Community: An Analysis of the Intellectual and Political Evolution of Egypt, 1804–1902*. Cambridge, MA: Harvard University Press.

Salah, M. (1984) The Turkish Working Class and Socialist Movement in Perspective. *Khamsin* (11), 86–116.

Said, E. (1978) *Orientalism*. New York: Pantheon.

Salfiti, F. (1997) *Israel's "Peace Dividend": The Jordanian Case*. Nablus: Center for Palestine Research and Studies.

Salibi, K. (1988) *A House of Many Mansions: The History of Lebanon Reconsidered*. Berkeley: University of California Press.

Satloff, R. (1992) Jordan's Greatest Gamble: Economic Crisis and Political Reform. In *The Politics of Economic Reform in the Middle East*, ed. Henri J. Barkey, pp. 129–52. New York: St. Martin's Press.

Schilcher, L. (1985) *Families in Politics: Damascene Factions and Estates of the eighteenth and nineteenth Centuries*. Stuttgart: Franz Steiner Verlag.

(1991a) The Grain Economy of Late Ottoman Syria and the Issue of Large-Scale Commercialization. In *Landholding and Commercial Agriculture in the Middle East*, ed. Ç. Keyder & F. Tabak, pp. 173–95. Albany: State University of New York Press.

(1991b) Violence in Rural Syria in the 1880s and 1890s: State Centralization, Rural Integration, and the World Market. In *Peasants and Politics in the Modern Middle East*, ed. F. Kazemi & J. Waterbury, pp. 50–84. Miami: Florida International University Press.

Schölch, A. (1982) European Penetration and the Economic Development of Palestine, 1856–1882. In *Studies in the Economic and Social History of Palestine in the Nineteenth and Twentieth Centuries*, ed. R. Owen, pp. 10–87. Carbondale, IL: Southern Illionois University Press.

(1986) Was there a Feudal System in Ottoman Lebanon and Palestine? In *Palestine in the Late Ottoman Period: Political, Social and Economic Transformation*, ed. D. Kushner, pp. 130–45. Jerusalem: Yad Izhak Ben-Zvi.

(1993) *Palestine in Transformation, 1856–1882: Studies in Economic, Social and Political Development*. Washington, DC: Institute for Palestine Studies.

Schulze, R. C. (1991) Colonization and Resistance: The Egyptian Peasant Rebellion, 1919. In *Peasants and Politics in the Modern Middle East*, ed. F. Kazemi & J. Waterbury, pp. 171–202. Miami: Florida International University Press.

Scott, J. C. (1979) *The Moral Economy of the Peasant: Rebellion and Subsistence in Southeast Asia*. New Haven: Yale University Press.

(1985) *Weapons of the Weak: Everyday Forms of Peasant Resistance*. New Haven: Yale University Press.

(1992) *Domination and the Arts of Resistance: Hidden Transcripts*. New Haven: Yale University Press.

Scott, J. W. (1988) *Gender and the Politics of History*. New York: Columbia University Press.

Seddon, D. (1984) Winter of Discontent: Economic Crisis in Tunisia and Morocco. *Merip Reports* (127, October), 7–16.

(1989) Riot and Rebellion in North Africa: Political Responses to Economic Crisis in Tunisia, Morocco and Sudan. In *Power and Stability in the Middle East*, ed. B. Berberoğlu, pp. 114–35. London: Zed Books.

al-Shafiʿi, S. ʿA. (1957) *Tatawwur al-haraka al-wataniyya al-misriyya*. Cairo: Dar al-Misriyya.

Shafir, G. (1989) *Land, Labor, and the Origins of the Israeli–Palestinian Conflict, 1882–1914*. Cambridge: Cambridge University Press.

Shamir, S. (1984) Egyptian Rule (1832–1840) and the Beginning of the Modern Period in the History of Palestine. In *Egypt and Palestine: A Millennium of Association (868–1948)*, ed. A. Cohen & G. Baer, pp. 214–31. Jerusalem: Ben Zvi Institute for the Study of Jewish Communities in the East and Yad Izhak Ben Zvi Institute for the Study of Eretz Israel.

al-Shantanawi, H. (1935) Min ajl al-ʿamal waʾl-ʿummal. *Majallat Kulliyyat al-Huquq* (January 15, 1935), 1–3.

al-Sharqawi, ʿA. (1954) *al-Ard*. Cairo: Nadi al-Qissa.

(1990) *Egyptian Earth*. Austin: University of Texas Press.

Shaw, S. J. (1971) *Between Old and New: The Ottoman Empire under Sultan Selim III, 1789–1807*. Cambridge, MA: Harvard University Press.

Shaw, S. J. & Shaw, E. K. (1976–77) *History of the Ottoman Empire and Modern Turkey*, 2 vols. Cambridge: Cambridge University Press.

Shechter, R. I. (1999) The Egyptian Cigarette: A Study of the Interaction between Consumption, Production, and Marketing in Egypt, 1850–1956. Ph.D. thesis, Harvard University.

Shields, S. D. (1991) Regional Trade and Nineteenth-Century Mosul: Revising the Role of Europe in the Middle East Economy. *International Journal of Middle East Studies*, 23 (1, February), 19–37.

Siniora, R. G. (1989) Palestinian Labor in a Dependent Economy: Women Workers in the West Bank Clothing Industry. *Cairo Papers in Social Science*, 12 (3, Fall), 1–82.

Slama, B. (1967) *L'Insurrection de 1864 en Tunisie*. Paris: Maison Tunisienne d'Edition.

Smilianskaya, I. (1966) The Disintegration of Feudal Relations in Syria and Lebanon in the Middle of the Nineteenth Century. In *The Economic History of the Middle East, 1800–1914: A Book of Readings*, ed. C. Issawi, pp. 227–47. Chicago: University of Chicago Press.

(1988) Peasant Uprisings in Lebanon, 1840s–1850s. In *The Fertile Crescent, 1800–1914: A Documentary Economic History*, ed. C. Issawi, pp. 48–51. Oxford: Oxford University Press.

Soliman, S. (1998) State and Industrial Capitalism in Egypt. *Cairo Papers in Social Science*, 21 (2, Summer), vii–104.

Spivak, G. C. (1987) *In Other Worlds: Essays in Cultural Politics*. New York: Methuen.

(1988) Can the Subaltern Speak? In *Marxism and the Interpretation of Culture*, ed. C. Nelson & L. Grossberg, pp. 271–313. Urbana: University of Illinois Press.

Springborg, R. (1986) Iraqi Infitah: Agrarian Transformation and Growth of the Private Sector. *Middle East Journal*, 40 (1, Winter), 33–52.

(1987) Iraq's Agrarian Infitah. *Middle East Report* (145, March–April), 16–21.

(1990) Rolling Back Egypt's Agrarian Reform. *Middle East Report* (166, September–October), 28–30.

(1991) State–Society Relations in Egypt: The Debate over Owner–Tenant Relations. *Middle East Journal*, 45 (2, Spring), 232–49.

Stavrianos, L. (1958) *The Balkans since 1453*. New York: Rinehart & Company.

Stein, K. W. (1984) *The Land Question in Palestine, 1917–1939*. Chapel Hill: University of North Carolina Press.

Stevenson, T. B. (1993) Yemeni Workers Come Home: Reabsorbing One Million Migrants. *Middle East Report* (181, March–April), 15–20.

Swedenburg. T. (1995) *Memories of Revolt: The 1936–1939 Rebellion and the Palestinian National Past*. Minneapolis: University of Minnesota Press.

Tabak, F. (1991) Agrarian Fluctuations and Modes of Labor Control in the Western Arc of the Fertile Crescent, c. 1700–1850. In *Landholding and Commercial Agriculture in the Middle East*, ed. Ç. Keyder & F. Tabak, pp. 135–54. Albany: State University of New York Press.

Tamari, S. (1982) Factionalism and Class Formation in Recent Palestinian History. In *Studies in the Economic and Social History of Palestine in the Nineteenth and Twentieth Centuries*, ed. R. Owen, pp. 177–202. Carbondale: Southern Illinois University Press.

Tamari, S. & Giacaman, R. (1997) *Zbeidat: The Social Impact of Agricultural Technology on the Life of a Peasant Community in the Jordan Valley*. Birzeit: Birzeit University Publications.

Taylan, T. (1984) Capital and the State in Contemporary Turkey. *Khamsin* (11), 5–46.

Taylor, E. (1984) Egyptian Migration and Peasant Wives. *Merip Reports* (124, June), 3–10.

Thieck, J. (1992) Décentralisaton ottomane et affirmation urbaine à Alep à la fin du XVIIIe siècle. In *Passion d'Orient*, ed. G. Kepel, pp. 113–76. Paris: Karthala.

Thompson, E. (1963) *The Making of the English Working Class*. New York: Vintage Books.

Todorova, M. (1996) The Ottoman Legacy in the Balkans. In *Imperial Legacy: The Ottoman Imprint on the Balkans and the Middle East*, ed. L. C. Brown, pp. 45–77. New York: Columbia University Press.

Toledano, E. R. (1990) *State and Society in Mid-Nineteenth-Century Egypt*. Cambridge: Cambridge University Press.

Toth, J. (1991) Pride, Purdah or Paychecks: What Maintains the Gender Division of Labor in Rural Egypt. *International Journal of Middle East Studies*, 23 (2, May), 213–36.

(1999) *Rural Labor Movements in Egypt and their Impact on the State, 1961–1992*. Gainesville, FL: University Press of Florida.

Touma, T. (1972) *Paysans et institutions féodales chez les Druses et les Maronites du Liban du XVIIe siècle a 1914*, 2 vols. Beirut: Publications de L'Université Libanaise.

Tucker, J. E. (1985) *Women in Nineteenth Century Egypt*. Cambridge: Cambridge University Press.

Turkey. State Institute of Statistics (1973–95) *Turkiye Istatistik Yıllığı*. Istanbul: Prime Ministry, Republic of Turkey.

al-Usta Hanafi (Abu Mahmud) [1923] *Mudhakkirat ʿarabagi*. Cairo: Matbaʿat al-Maktaba al-tijariyya.

ʿUthman, T. S. (1982–94) *Mudhakkirat wa-wathaʾiq min tarikh ʿummal misr,* 4 vols. Cairo: n.p.

Vallet, J. (1911) *Contribution a l'étude de la condition des ouvriers de la grande industrie au Caire*. Valence: Impr. Valentinoise.

Vandewalle, D. (1988) From the New State to the New Era: Toward a Second Republic in Tunisia. *Middle East Journal,* 42 (4, Autumn), 602–20.

(1992) Ben Ali's New Era: Pluralism and Economic Privatization in Tunisia. In *The Politics of Economic Reform in the Middle East,* ed. Henri J. Barkey, pp. 105–26. New York: St. Martin's Press.

Van Leeuwen, R. (1991) Monastic Estates and Agricultural Transformation in Mount Lebanon in the Eighteenth Century. *International Journal of Middle East Studies,* 23 (4, November), 601–17.

Vatikiotis, P. (1969) *The History of Egypt*. Baltimore: Johns Hopkins University Press.

Vatter, S. (1993) Journeymen Textile Weavers in Nineteenth-Century Damascus: A Collective Biography. In *Struggle and Survival in the Middle East,* ed. E. Burke III, pp. 75–90. Berkeley: University of California Press.

(1994) Militant Journeymen in Nineteenth-Century Damascus: Implications for the Middle Eastern Labor History Agenda. In *Workers and Working Classes in the Middle East: Struggles, Histories, Historiographies,* ed. Z. Lockman, pp. 1–20. Albany: State University of New York Press.

(1995) Militant Textile Weavers in Damascus: Waged Artisans and the Ottoman Labor Movement, 1850–1914. In *Workers and the Working Class in the Ottoman Empire and the Turkish Republic,* ed. D. Quataert & E. J. Zürcher, pp. 35–57. London: I. B. Tauris.

Veinstein, G. (1976) Ayan de la region d'Izmir et commerce du Levant: deuxième moitié du XVIIIe siècle. *Etudes Balkaniques,* 12 (3), 71–83.

Velikov, S. (1964) Sur le mouvement ouvrier et socialiste en Turquie après la révolution jeune-turque de 1908. *Etudes Balkaniques,* 1 (1), 29–48.

Voll, J. O. (1982) *Islam: Continuity and Change in the Modern World*. Boulder: Westview Press.

Wallerstein, I. (1979) The Ottoman Empire and the Capitalist World-Economy: Some Questions for Research. *Review,* 2 (3, Winter), 389–98.

Wallerstein, I. & Kasaba, R. (1983) Incorporation into the World Economy: Change in the Structure of the Ottoman Empire. In *Economie et sociétés dans l'Empire Ottoman (fin du XVIIIe–début du XXe siècle),* ed. J. Bacqué-Grammont & P. Dumont, pp. 335–54. Paris: Editions du Dentre de la Recherche Scientifique.

Warburg, G. (1978) *Islam, Nationalism and Communism in a Traditional Society: The Case of the Sudan*. London: Frank Cass.

Warriner, D. (1948) *Land and Poverty in the Middle East*. London: Royal Institute for International Affairs.

Waterbury, J. (1983) *The Egypt of Nasser and Sadat: The Political Economy of Two Regimes*. Princeton: Princeton University Press.

(1989) The Political Management of Economic Adjustment and Reform. In *Fragile Coalitions: The Politics of Economic Adjustment,* ed. Joan M. Nelson, pp. 39–56. Washington, DC: Overseas Development Corporation.

(1992) Export-Led Growth and the Center-Right Coalition in Turkey. In *Economics and Politics of Turkish Liberalization*, ed. T. F. Nas & M. Odekon, pp. 44–72. Bethlehem: Lehigh University Press.

Weiss, F. (1970) *Doctrine et action syndicales en Algérie*. Paris: Editions Cujas.

White, J. B. (1994) *Money Makes us Relatives: Women's Labor in Urban Turkey*. Austin: University of Texas Press.

Wickham, C. R. (1996) Islamic Mobilization and Political Change: The Islamist Trend in Egypt's Professional Associations. In *Political Islam: Essays from Middle East Report*, ed. J. Beinin & J. Stork, pp. 120–35. Berkeley: University of California Press.

Wickham, C. (1985) The Uniqueness of the East. *Journal of Peasant Studies*, 12 (2–3, January/April), 166–96.

Willis, M. (1996) *The Islamist Challenge in Algeria: A Political History*. New York: New York University Press.

Wolf, E. R. (1968) *Peasant Wars of the Twentieth Century*. New York: Harper & Row.

Wolfe, P. (1997) History and Imperialism: A Century of Theory from Marx to Postcolonialism. *American Historical Review*, 102 (2, April), 388–420.

World Bank (1991a) *Egypt: Alleviating Poverty during Structural Adjustment*. Washington, DC: World Bank.

(1991b) *World Development Report 1991: The Challenge of Development*. Washington, DC: World Bank.

(1995a) *Will Arab Workers Prosper or Be Left Out in the Twenty-First Century*. Regional Perspectives on World Development Report 1995. Washington, DC: World Bank.

(1995b) *World Development Report 1995: Workers in an Integrating World*. Oxford: Oxford University Press.

Yavuz, E. (1995) The State of the Industrial Workforce, 1923–40. In *Workers and the Working Class in the Ottoman Empire and the Turkish Republic*, ed. D. Quataert & E. J. Zürcher, pp. 95–125. London: I. B. Tauris.

Yeldan, A. E. (1994) The Economic Structure of Power under Turkish Structural Adjustment: Prices, Growth and Accumulation. In *Recent Industrialization Experience of Turkey in a Global Context*, ed. F. Şenses, pp. 75–89. Westport, CN: Greenwood Press.

Yeşilada, B. A. & Fısunoğlu, M. (1992) Assessing the January 24, 1980 Economic Stabilization Program in Turkey. In *The Politics of Economic Reform in the Middle East*, ed. Henri J. Barkey, pp. 183–210. New York: St. Martin's Press.

Younis, M. (2000) *Liberation and Democratization: The South African and Palestinian National Movements*. Minneapolis: University of Minnesota Press.

Yusuf, H. (1920) *Mudhakkirat futuwwa*. Cairo: al-Matba'a al-'Arabiyya.

Zeman, Z. & Scharlau, W. (1965) *The Merchant of Revolution: The Life of Alexander Israel Helphand (Parvus), 1867–1924*. London: Oxford University Press.

Index